Growing Minds

Also by Stephanie Thornton

Children Solving Problems

Growing Minds

An Introduction to Cognitive Development

Stephanie Thornton

First published 2002 by
PALGRAVE MACMILLAN
Houndmills, Basingstoke, Hampshire RG21 6XS and
175 Fifth Avenue, New York, N.Y. 10010
Companies and representatives throughout the world

PALGRAVE MACMILLAN is the global academic imprint of the Palgrave
Macmillan division of St. Martin's Press, LLC and of Palgrave Macmillan Ltd.
Macmillan® is a registered trademark in the United States, United Kingdom
and other countries. Palgrave is a registered trademark in the European
Union and other countries.

ISBN 0–333–77741–7 hardback
ISBN 0–333–77742–5 paperback

This book is printed on paper suitable for recycling and
made from fully managed and sustained forest sources.

A catalogue record for this book is available
from the British Library.

A catalogue record of this book is available
from the Library of Congress.

10 9 8 7 6 5 4 3 2 1
11 10 09 08 07 06 05 04 03 02

Printed and bound in Great Britain by
Creative, Print & Design, Ebbw Vale (Wales)

Contents

List of Figures

List of Tables

Acknowledgements

It would be impossible to thank everyone who has helped or influenced me in the preparation of this book. Among many colleagues, I owe most to the ideas of Annette Karmiloff-Smith, Robert Siegler and Julie Rutkowska. The enthusiasm and robust comment of my students and young friends on the readability (or otherwise!) of the early drafts of the text has been enormously useful. And I should never have begun or finished the project without the support, encouragement and patience of Frances Arnold.

The author and publisher would like to thank the following for permission to reproduce copyright material:

Figure 2.2: Reproduced from W. Maxwell Cowan, 'The development of the brain', *Scientific American 241*; © 1979. Reproduced with permission from Nelson H. Prentiss.

Figure 2.5: Reproduced from A. Slater, 'Visual organization in early infancy', in *Infant Development: Recent Advances*, ed. G. Bremner, A. Slater and G. Butterworth; © 1997. Reproduced with permission from Psychology Press, Erlbaum, UK.

Figure 2.6: Reproduced from M. Johnson, S. Dziurawiec, H. Ellis and J. Morton, 'Newborn's preferential tracking of face-like stimuli and its subsequent decline', *Cognition 40*, pp. 1–19; © 1991. Reproduced with permission from Elsevier Science.

Figure 2.7: Reproduced from A. N. Meltzoff, 'Imitation, intermodal coordination and representation', in G. E. Butterworth, *Infancy and Epistemology: An Evaluation of Piaget's Theory*; © 1981. Reproduced with permission of Harvester Wheatsheaf.

Figure 2.8: Reproduced from A. Slater, 'Visual organization in early infancy', in *Infant Development: Recent Advances*, ed. G. Bremner, A. Slater and G. Butterworth; © 1997. Reproduced with permission from Psychology Press, Erlbaum, UK.

Figure 3.1: Reproduced from J. Berko, 'The child's learning of English morphology', *Word 14*, pp. 150–77; © 1958. Reproduced with permission from the International Linguistics Association.

Figure 5.2: Reproduced from R. Siegler, 'Three aspects of cognitive development', *Cognitive Psychology* 8, pp. 481–520. Reproduced with permission from Academic Press, London.

Figure 6.3: Reproduced from R. Siegler, 'The rebirth of children's learning', *Child Development* 71, pp. 26–36; © 2000. Reproduced with permission from the Society for Research in Child Development.

Figure 6.4: Reproduced from A. Karmiloff-Smith, 'Macro- and Micro-developmental changes in language acquisition and problem solving', *Cognitive Science* 3, pp. 81–118; © 1979. Reproduced with permission from the Cognitive Science Society and the author.

Figure 6.5: Reproduced from A. Karmiloff-Smith, *Beyond Modularity: A Developmental Perspective on Cognitive Science*; © 1992. Reproduced with permission from the MIT Press.

Figure 6.6: Reproduced from Stephanie Thornton, *Children Solving Problems*, Cambridge, MA: Harvard University Press; copyright © 1995. Reproduced with permission from the President and Fellows of Harvard College.

Figure 8.2: Reproduced from G. Patterson, J. Reid and T. Dishion, *Antisocial Boys*; © 1992. Reproduced with the permission of Scot Patterson and Castilia Publishing.

Figure 8.5: Reproduced from L. Selfe, *Normal and Anomalous Representational Abilities in Children*; © 1977. Reproduced with permission of Academic Press.

Table 5.1: Reproduced from G. Holyoak, E. Junn and D. Billman, 'Development of analogical problem solving skills', *Child Development* 55, pp. 2042–55; © 1984. Reproduced with permission from the Society for Research in Child Development.

Table 6.1: Reproduced from Stephanie Thornton, 'Creating the conditions for cognitive change: the interaction between task structures and specific strategies', *Child Development* 70, pp. 588–603; © 1999. Reproduced with permission from the Society for Research in Child Development.

This book is dedicated to

Elizabeth, Kate, Lizzie, Lois, Marcelle

and above all to Andrew and Simon

Studying How Minds Grow

At the very beginning of our lives, you and I were each a single cell, a fertilised ovum, no more able to think or reason than an amoeba. But bit by bit those simple cells changed and grew, until today, here I am writing this book, and there you are, reading it. How is that possible? How can all the complexities of adult human intelligence and understanding grow from such a very simple start? What exactly happens along the way from that simple fertilised cell to the development of an adult mind? What factors in our biological makeup, or in the world, or in the people who nurtured us, taught us, played with us, influence how our minds develop? Do we simply learn more about the world, or does the very way our minds work change in some fundamental way as we grow?

Questions such as these form the basic puzzles which psychologists who study cognitive development try to solve. And that is what this book is about.

The Problem of Development

In a very real sense, watching a newborn baby grow into a thinking, reasoning adult is one of the wonders of the world. Step by step the baby progresses from an individual with little ability to engage the world, dominated by immediate wants and needs into a person capable of understanding complex ideas, planning a convoluted social life, reflecting on the meaning of existence, solving problems and a thousand other things. The change from infant to adult is so gradual that we scarcely notice it from day to day. Nonetheless, the transformation is amazing.

As you read this book, take every chance you can get to watch children playing or working. Compare children of different ages with one another. Listen carefully to what they say, watch what they do. Of course, every child is an individual, with their own peculiarities and talents. But psychologists have discovered that there are also patterns in how children of different ages behave, patterns which are typical for all children. Most five-year-olds, for example, will have a lot in common with other five-year-olds, just as most ten-year-olds have a lot in common with one another. It is these regular patterns of change through childhood which concern the developmental psychologist, and will concern us in this book. How can we characterise these patterns? What do they mean? What causes them?

Let's look at one little example of how children of different ages think, and the puzzles it raises for psychology: nine-year-old Mary and her four-year-old neighbour, Simon, are playing in Simon's home with his new puppy, Honey. Honey is a great dane, and will one day be a very large dog indeed. Already she stands over 80 centimetres high, although she is only a few months old. She's strong: she can pull both the children around the room on a plastic sled. Mary's mother calls by to take Mary home for tea. With her is Daisy, Mary's dog. Daisy is old and grey. She's a chihauhua, a tiny, fragile animal.

Now, both these children have known Daisy all their lives. Both know that Honey is a new puppy. But both become intrigued and mystified by the difference in the two dogs' sizes. Simon is particularly puzzled. How can Honey be *younger*, when she is so much *bigger*? He becomes unshakeably convinced that really, Honey must be older than Daisy. He can't see any other explanation of their sizes. For four-year-old Simon, babies are small and adults are bigger, and that is that. He is simply bemused by all efforts to persuade him otherwise.

Mary has a more subtle grasp of the situation. Although she agrees with Simon's general observation about size and age, Mary knows that babies aren't actually defined that way: a baby elephant is always going to be bigger than an elderly mouse. She understands the principle that babies are defined as being the young of the species, rather than by their size, as Simon thinks. But she is still puzzled. We aren't comparing a mouse and an elephant here. Both these animals are *dogs*. So how can young Honey be so much bigger than old Daisy? To an adult mind, the answer is obvious, but it involves ideas about selective breeding and genetics which are too complicated for Mary to understand. Like Simon, Mary finds the situation bemusing, though her confusion comes from a quite different problem, and is at a different level. Where Simon holds fast to a theory which contradicts the facts, Mary is confused by two conflicting theories.

This little domestic episode is not unique. Far from it: in fact, it provides a classic illustration of the puzzle of how children's minds grow. As we shall explore further later in this book (in Chapter 5), each of the two children in my example shows a way of thinking about size, age and species which is very typical of their own age group, and different in kind from one another, and from an adult way of thinking. The puzzle for us is: why do they hold such very different views? Where did Simon's strange theory come from? Why are they both so mystified by something adults take for granted, and what compels them to try to understand this mystery? Why can't Mary convince Simon that small size is not the key thing about being a baby, not even with her mouse and elephant example? Of course, his understanding will gradually develop over time (just as hers has already done). But how does that happen? What is it that stretches and shapes the mind as children move away from childish ways of thinking to more mature perspectives?

So far, no one can fully explain how the human mind develops. Each answer we find opens up new puzzles. As we shall see, the answers we do have are more surprising, and more intriguing than one might suppose. And those answers are harder to discover than we imagined. And yet, the need to know is powerful. The way we think, the way our thinking grows and changes is critical to everything which makes us human. Our minds make us the individuals that we are. They shape the cultures that we live in. So understanding how minds grow is a central part of understanding the very nature of what it is to be human. It's one of the great challenges for psychology, and one of the great intellectual adventures for science as a whole.

But there are other, more practical reasons for studying how minds grow, too. Not all children develop equally. By understanding normal development, we can better see what has gone wrong for those who fail to develop as they should, and maybe find ways to help them. And then, our species is less rational than we would like to think. For example, we struggle reluctantly with some useful ideas, such as mathematics, the manual for a new computer and the like. But we leap to embrace other less constructive things such as the stereotypes and fears which fuel racism. Understanding how minds grow has a bearing on many practical, social and political issues far beyond what one might expect at first sight.

Methods for Research

Let's pause for a minute and give more thought to a very basic problem: how on earth can we study what someone is thinking, or how or why their thinking changes over time? How can we find out, for example, how Mary discovered that being little is not the critical thing about being young, or why Simon can't take the point about elderly mice and baby elephants? How can we work out why the dogs' sizes and ages came to seem so fascinating to these children?

Of course, we could simply guess what the answers to such questions might be. Educated guessing, or theorising, is an important element in improving our understanding of anything. But as scientists, psychologists want to go beyond this, to test their theories and get evidence, data which will refine and improve those theories. This is where the problem lies: how can we get good data about such intangible things as thoughts?

The mental processes which make up the human mind are invisible. We can't directly see them or touch them. The best we can do is to *draw inferences* about what is in another person's mind, whether that be a child or an adult, on the basis of the clues we *can* see or hear, what the individual says or does, for example. This point is a very important one. For there is a natural human tendency to believe that we can tell what another person is thinking, why they think that and how they came to that conclusion. Sometimes we may be right, but often we are wrong. Any given behaviour or comment might be produced for a number of different reasons, and by many different processes. As scientists, our job is to be cautious, to find ways of checking our theories about another person's thoughts.

Luckily, there are quite a number of ways of drawing inferences about mental processes from what we see, and of checking how good those inferences are. For example, we can listen to what children themselves tell us, or what they say about the world, as in the example of Simon and Mary puzzling over their dogs. We can note the detail of what children do as they play, or as they try to work out problems or make plans, and we can analyse what their words and actions imply about their understanding of the world, or the way they think. We can identify the things which young children find difficult, and trace the gradual changes in what they can do successfully. We can use all the little clues from their mistakes to their sudden triumphs to build up theories of what the child's mind is like at different ages, and how it changes. And then we can test those theories by looking to see if they can predict how children will behave in some new situation, or perhaps by testing out whether computer programmes written to simulate the way we believe that children think will come to the same answers and make the same mistakes as a real child does.

About this Book

The aim of this book is to give you a thorough, up-to-date review of what we know so far, and what we have yet to find out about how children's minds grow. Each successive chapter will review a key area of cognitive development, from early infancy to late adolescence. Each chapter will outline the key questions which researchers have studied in that field, comparing different theories and reviewing the evidence for and against these, and ending up with a summary of what the current conclusions and outstanding puzzles in that field are, and some suggestions of what you could read if you wanted to explore the research further.

In one way each chapter in the book builds on the ones before it. For example, the chapter on infancy, which looks at what the baby's mind is like, comes before the chapter on how children learn to speak, which is the great achievement of the toddler. But it is not essential to read the book from cover to cover: each chapter can be read on its own. Where the content of one chapter might be directly interesting or useful in understanding another, there is a cross reference.

One important theme running right through the book, surfacing again and again in different chapters, is the issue of how we can study particular aspects of the way the mind works, what methods we can use, and what the strengths and weaknesses of those methods are. How good are the data we have, and how reliable are our interpretations of those data, or the theories we build on them? In studying psychology, your task is not just to learn what others have discovered, but to learn how to judge for yourself whether a given theory really fits the data or not. Many questions have as yet no definitive answer, no conclusion that all psychologists can agree on. How can we decide which theory best fits the data? And how can we devise better studies to extend our knowledge still further, or to resolve controversies? At the end of each of the main chapters of this book, you will find questions and exercises to help you think about these 'methodological' questions.

A second key theme in the book is the puzzle which began this chapter: how is human intelligence possible at all? How does it develop, time after time, in what starts out as such an apparently simple one-cell organism? How does our biology relate to the growth of our human intelligence? How big a role does it play? This question is first addressed in Chapter 2, in looking at the origins of intelligence in infant minds from birth to toddlerhood.

Chapters 3 to 6 each take a particular aspect of human intelligence and explore its nature and development through childhood. Chapter 3 looks at language, which is a uniquely human achievement. How does our genetic legacy predispose us to learn a language, even to invent new codes and secret languages? What role do other people play in making us talkers? Chapters 4 and 5 look at the basic nature of human reasoning and the structure of the mind. How does memory develop? Are we logical creatures, as philosophers long supposed, or are our minds organised in some other way, as more recent research is suggesting? Chapter 6 looks at some key functions of the mind: planning and solving problems. How and why do these things change as we grow and develop? Chapter 7 picks up some of the themes first raised in looking at how infant intelligence begins, asking the question: what is it that drives all this development? What mechanisms in the mind or experiences in the world foster the immense changes in our intelligence as it develops? This chapter raises another key issue: is there an end to development? For example, as you embark on new studies now, are you at the end of a process of developing your mind, or only at a new beginning? Certainly you will go on learning new facts, developing new skills and new insights. But will your mind go on restructuring itself, changing in quality as well as in the amount it knows, as happened in your infancy and childhood? Are there limits to the kinds of thing we can understand?

Although this book is about normal processes of development, the regular patterns we see in all children, no study of the development of intelligence should overlook the stark fact that not all children develop so quickly or so successfully as the average child, and some develop startlingly faster and further than their peers. Why is this so? How far does it reflect factors inherited at birth, or the specific experiences and opportunities the child has, or the surrounding culture? Are such individual differences inevitable, or could we soften them, reduce them? These issues are explored in Chapter 8.

If you read through the whole book, you will notice parallels in the research between one topic and another, themes that recur in our discoveries about how the mind grows. These threads are pulled together in Chapter 9 to present an overview of what we presently understand about development of mind, and what puzzles are left unsolved.

As I wrote earlier in this first chapter: understanding how minds grow is perhaps the greatest challenge for psychology, and is one of the great intellectual adventures for science as a whole. I hope that this book will also persuade you that it is a fascinating and rewarding area of research.

Infant Minds

Puppies, kittens, foals, calves, the young of most mammals, in fact, are able to move about in a fairly independent and coordinated way very soon after their births, often within hours. By contrast, the human baby looks weak and helpless, its limbs uncoordinated, its eyes unfocused. Newborn children can't support their own heads, still less roll over, sit or stand up. They cry, sleep, feed, defecate, show a few rather limited reflexes and seemingly little else.

And yet, within a very short time, these helpless infants will be interacting with others, even imperiously controlling their behaviour! They will understand and anticipate a great deal of what goes on around them, and will soon be behaving and reasoning in a way far ahead of anything the young of other species will ever achieve: using tools, engaging the artefacts of human culture and trying to control objects in their physical worlds (Figure 2.1). What accounts for this extraordinary progress? What is it about newborn human babies that allows them to grow and change so very fast, to become so complex and so clever?

The Physiology of Intelligence

Quite clearly, a great deal of what makes a human being is genetically given. The DNA that defines each of us from our conception carries within it the blueprint we need to develop a specifically human body. This genetic code directs the dividing cells of the fertilised egg to specialise and thus to create all our organs and limbs, in ways which we cannot yet fully explain. Most intriguing of all is the development of the brain, the prerequisite for our intelligence and reasoning.

Figure 2.1 Starting to engage in adult activities

Prenatal development of the brain

Before birth, the growth of the human brain is very similar to that of other primate brains. Intriguingly, human intelligence is not the product of special new structures in the brain which other primates do not have. In fact, all the main structures of our brains are present, not only in other primates, but in almost all other mammal species too (Johnson, 1998). The key difference between us and a chimpanzee, say, or any other primate is in the sheer amount of cerebral cortex we have.

The cortex is a strange, thin layer of brain that bunches up, creating convoluted patterns, like a piece of cloth laid out on a table and then squished together into a far smaller space throwing up rucks, mountains and valleys across its surface. No-one really understands how it works nor how or why the human cortex differs so much from that of other species in its size and functioning. Unravelling this mystery will call for a collaboration between two relatively new sub-disciplines within psychology: cognitive neuroscience and evolutionary psychology. What exactly does a standard mammal cortex do? How is what the human cortex does different from that? What twist in our evolutionary history selected for that difference? Answering these questions will be one of the challenges for psychology in the coming decades.

A short while after conception, just six or seven weeks, the fetus has a rudimentary brain, a spinal cord, the basis for eyes and ears, all the essentials for a whole nervous system (Figure 2.2). Already it has the basic equipment to allow it to be startled by loud noises heard through the mother's body and through its own amniotic fluid (Joseph, 2000). Even at this early stage, ultrasound scans can detect spontaneous movements of developing limbs. Tiny as the fetus is, there can be few mothers, few fathers confronted by ultrasound pictures of this strange, small, mobile creature who do not respond profoundly to its nascent humanity. And rightly so. To be startled, one must have at least a minimal expectation of what is normal: without that, how could one detect the unusual? Rocks and stones have no expectations. Even the most trivial expectations imply a

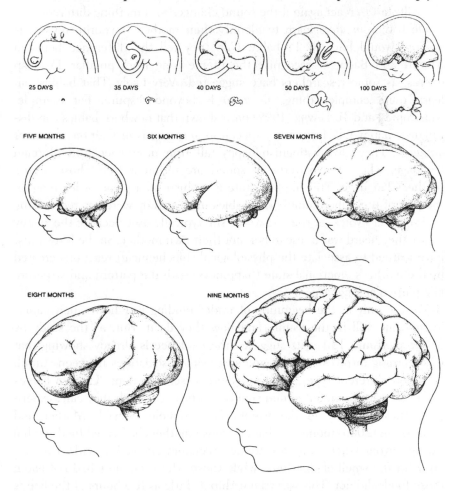

Figure 2.2 Fetal development of the human brain
Source: Cowan (1979), pp. 106–17.

living creature, some form of sentience, the very beginnings of feeling and intelligence.

Exactly what a human fetus responds to *in utero* changes as pregnancy advances (Joseph, 2000). The younger the fetus, the cruder and larger the stimulus needed for any sort of response. But by late pregnancy, the fetus responds to an impressive range of sounds, making fairly fine discriminations between one sound and another.

What kind of response does a fetus make to the noises heard in the womb? Some responses seem to be more or less reflexive. But there is also evidence that the fetus is already capable of learning (Joseph, 2000). For example, about 30 weeks after conception an unborn baby can learn to recognise a repeated sound as familiar and stop reacting to it, though he or she will start to react again if the sound changes to something different.

Do babies *in utero* learn to identify their mother's favourite music, as folklore would have it? Probably. Can they tell the difference between Mozart and Bach, or recognise the theme tune from popular TV soap operas, as some researchers have suggested? Very likely. That babies can learn quite complex things *in utero* is beyond dispute. For example, Mastropieri and Turkewitz (1999) have shown that newborn babies can distinguish 'happy talk' from other speech *so long as it is in their own mother's language*. They can't distinguish 'happy' talk from other speech in a foreign language, where the patterns of sound are different from those of the mother's language. This implies quite a sophisticated piece of learning on the part of the unborn child. The babies in this study were not recognising their mother's voice, or specific words she typically uses because the 'happy talker' they heard was a researcher, not their own mother. So the fetus must have learned to associate the physiological (biochemical) reactions created by the mother's emotional state (happiness) with the pattern and structure of a particular language.

We are only at the beginning of understanding just how much babies learn while still in the womb, and how they do it. But, as the study by Mastropieri and Turkewitz suggests, the evidence is already showing that this learning involves complex and surprising associations between stimuli of widely different types, and very subtle discriminations. Unborn babies can even learn to prefer certain smells and tastes, though they can't experience these directly in the womb. For example, Schaal, Marlier and Soussignan (2000) found that babies whose mothers had eated foods with a strong flavour (such as anise) during pregnancy showed a marked preference for the smell of that food, while those whose mothers had not eaten those foods did not. This was true within as little as five hours of the baby's birth, though the babies had had no previous opportunity to experience those smells since birth.

Postnatal development of the brain

But despite this impressive growth before birth, the newborn baby's brain is still very different from that of an adult (Johnson, 1998). Most obviously, it is less than a quarter of the weight of an adult brain. This does not reflect differences in the basic structure of adult and baby brains, nor in the number of neurons. Eighteen weeks after conception the fetus has virtually all the neurons he or she will ever have, about a million million (Rakic, 1995). Seven months after conception, the main structures of the brain are all present, with some groups of neurons specialised to perform certain functions: control breathing, say, or operate specific limbs. The newborn human baby has all the basic physiological equipment for intelligence. But whereas in an adult brain individual neurons or groups of neurons may be connected to thousands of other neurons in complex patterns, the baby's brain has relatively few such connections. In effect, many of the cells in the baby's brain are not yet committed to a particular job or function and so have not yet made the connections and patterns between cells that will one day serve those functions. So the newborn baby's brain is rather like a computer which hasn't yet been fully programmed, isn't yet fully 'configured'. It is the growth of the nerves and fibres which connect one neuron to another as the infant brain becomes properly 'wired up' which accounts for the dramatic growth of the brain after birth, and for the differences between human and other primate brains.

How do baby brains get properly 'wired up'? This issue is still quite controversial. There are a number of physiological changes in the brain after birth, which may reflect pre-programmed processes of maturation. For example, the myelin sheath which surrounds and protects the nerves is not fully developed in a baby's brain, so that messages pass less quickly and less reliably in infant brains than in adult ones (Johnson, 1998). This myelin sheath goes on developing for many years after birth. It develops at different rates in different areas of the brain, developing first in areas which process more basic functions, and last in areas such as the cortex. This development continues even into the second decade of life for some areas of the brain. Do such maturational changes influence what the infant can learn, what neural connections he or she can make? This idea received a lot of attention at one time. But even partly myelinated nerves can pass information fairly effectively (Johnson, 1998), which makes it seem less likely that learning is constrained by the maturation of the myelin sheath in any very profound way. It is even possible that partial myelination somehow supports the flexibility of the infant brain as it learns, rather than limiting it.

The idea that the physical immaturity of the newborn nervous system might be an advantage in learning rather than a disadvantage is interesting, though controversial. There are quite a number of ways in which the nervous system is immature at birth (Johnson, 1998; Kellman and Banks, 1998). For instance, even the visual system is not fully formed, so that a newborn baby has a much shorter range of focus than an adult and much less clear visual acuity. Some researchers have argued that the immaturity of such systems puts a brake on cognitive development, and that many important developmental steps (such as the wide range of changes in the infant's behaviour and understanding which we see at about nine months after birth) are only made possible by the maturing of various elements of the nervous system. The opposite view is that certain neurological immaturities are critically helpful to the newborn baby in starting to make sense of the world: for example, the immaturity of the visual system means that the newborn baby is forced to focus on just that range of stimuli in the immediate world which he or she needs to understand first: human faces for example. If newborn babies had the same visual powers as adults, they would be so swamped with information that it would be difficult to make sense of anything at all (Bjorklund and Pellegrini, 2000).

How far specific developmental changes reflect the maturing of the neurological system, and how far the neurological system matures in response to the child's developmental progress and the demands placed on it by that development remains to be explored. Very probably there is a complex pattern of interaction between these factors. Indeed, most researchers would now accept that the development of the brain is the product of interactions between a great many factors (Johnson, 1998).

One point to emphasise is that various key structures of the brain are surprisingly flexible. For example, the particular area of the cortex which will deal with any given activity is not predetermined, not fixed. In fact, the way the cortex develops, and the specific areas of cortex which will deal with a given type of processing (visual information, say) is determined by our individual experience of the world and our interactions with it (Johnson, 1998). For example, in a baby born blind the areas of the brain that in a sighted child would develop to process visual input do not develop in that way. Instead, the blind baby's brain may use those areas for other processes: processing sounds, say. Thus even the 'hardware' of our brains is shaped by learning and experience.

Of course, the individual human neural system is not infinitely flexible. For example, it has the potential to develop complex visual processes. Even though realising that potential requires appropriate experience of the world, there are physiological limits on the kinds of experience to which we can respond. We can't see the infra-red, for example, and so cannot develop neural processes to respond to it. The way our brains develop can never be *purely* the result of physiology, nor *purely* the result of experience: the two must always co-exist and interact.

There is a certain amount of flexibility in all newborn mammal brains. For example, even in a rat, a piece of cortex transplanted from an area of the brain typically associated with one function (motor control, say) to an area typically associated with another function (vision, say) will grow the patterns of neural connection typical of its new location rather than the old. But one of the secrets of human intelligence is that our brains are a great deal more flexible, a great deal less 'pre-specified' than those of other species. For instance, in some species of birds, blueprints for crucial activities such as nest building, chick rearing, courtship displays, etc., seem to be innately given so that the chick will grow up to behave in ways typical of its species without ever having had the opportunity to observe or learn from others. There is clear evidence of such innate specification of key adult behaviours in many mammal species too. But few important adult human activities seem to be pre-programmed in that way. We don't arrive pre-programmed to drive a car or read newspapers or (alas!) understand statistics, for example, though we may be born with the raw materials from which such skills can be created. Human brains are more *plastic*, that is to say, more flexible and more adaptable than those of other species, which gives us our crucial advantage: we are freer than any other species to explore new patterns of neural connection, and so to master new things.

The process through which infant brains make new patterns of connection between neurons and so become efficiently 'wired up' is only just beginning to be explored. Infant brains may be less efficient in passing messages between neurons, because of the immaturity of the myelin sheath around nerves, as we have seen. But infant brains function at a far higher metabolic rate than is typical of the adult brain (Chugani, Phelps and Mazziotta, 1987), peaking at around 150 per cent of the adult rate at about four or five years of age. And the activity of neurotransmitters seems to be far greater in the early stages of development than it will be in adult life (Benes, 1994). These high levels of brain activity relate to the rapid learning which occurs at this time.

The key to brain development in infancy and childhood is the creation of the complex patterns of connection between neurons which serve understanding and behaviour. Such connections reflect the infant's learning and experience. Intriguingly, infant brains start out by creating very many more such neural connections than are found in the adult brain (Huttenlocher, 1994; Johnson, 1998). In a real sense, a great deal of brain development involves pruning this overly complex system of neural connections, deleting the excess connections until adult structures have been built. At first, this seems a very strange way for development to proceed. Why should infants make so many redundant neural connections? But in fact, the more neural connections the infant develops, the greater the number of possible patterns the child can try out. The first pattern created may well not be the best, nor even very efficient, just as the first thing you do in trying to solve a new problem may not work very well. Trying out different things is the best way of finding a good solution. The more different possibilities for patterns of neural connection that the child explores, the greater the chance of finding the very best one for the job in hand. This optimal neural pattern can then be chosen, and the less successful patterns deleted (Johnson, 1998). So although producing too many neural connections may look inefficient, it is in fact the very best way to be flexible in creating the structures for intelligence.

Through the growth of research on neurological development we are beginning to have a very much better picture of the human brain than ever before. But whatever the role of neurological factors in development, it is clear that we cannot understand the emergence of intelligence through such factors alone. The physiology of the brain cannot tell us what the newborn mind is like.

Are Babies 'Blank Slates'?

One traditional theory about what a newborn baby is like is that he or she starts out, in effect, with a functional but empty brain: a 'blank slate' which experience and learning must fill in. This theory was first associated with philosophers, such as John Locke in the seventeenth century, although different versions of the idea have been proposed by many theorists since.

In a way, the blank slate (*tabula rasa*) theory seems to fit the facts. As we have noted, a very great deal of what makes an adult mind has to be acquired by interacting with the world, rather than being 'given' at birth. But the theorists who had the biggest impact on early studies of infant minds meant much more than this: they saw the newborn as lacking not only the general skills and knowledge of the adult, but as lacking even the very basic tools for interpreting the physical world around them. Hebb (1949) was one such theorist, who believed that newborns cannot even see simple shapes like triangles or squares, but must learn to recognise such things through repeated experience of their key components. The most influential theorist of all, Jean Piaget, described the young infant's visual world as being devoid of meaning: 'a world of pictures, lacking in depth or constancy, permanence or identity which disappear or reappear capriciously' (Piaget, 1954). A very blank slate indeed! Modern research into infancy has been very much shaped by our efforts to understand whether this theory is right. It is quite obvious that the infant mind can't be *completely* empty, nor passive. If it were, how could it ever learn anything? Let's look at that last question a bit more closely. Imagine yourself swept up in a spacecraft, confronted by aliens. They make sounds, perhaps they're speaking to you. But the sounds are completely new, like nothing you've ever heard. Would you understand them? No. There would be nothing in your experience, nothing in your mind which could help you decipher the meaning of such alien sounds. But what if they not only spoke, but also made gestures indicating what they meant? What if the incomprehensible sounds were accompanied by, say, offering you food? You might not be quite sure exactly what each burst of noise meant, but you'd get the general drift, because you could use your past knowledge and your existing understanding to interpret what the new sounds mean. (The Natural History Museum in London has a vivid illustration of just this effect.) And it is worth emphasising that it would be *your* effort to make sense of the situation which would be critical to you learning anything: if you were merely passive, 'brain disengaged', you wouldn't notice the connections between sounds and gestures, so you wouldn't learn what they mean.

The key point here is that we can only make sense of events, learn things, if we have at least *something* to build on, some basis for drawing inferences. If a newborn baby's brain were truly completely empty, truly passive, there would be no basis for learning or development. So what does the baby have, at birth, as a basis for learning?

Piaget's theory

The most influential theory about how the infant mind develops from very little was put forward by a Swiss researcher, Jean Piaget. It was he who first emphasised the fact that, even if they cannot interpret objects, infants have to have something to start from or they could never develop a mind (e.g. Piaget, 1968). He pointed out that, in fact, the infant comes into the world with a number of reflexes, and suggested that certain of these provide the basis for all new learning.

A reflex is an automatic, involuntary response to some stimulus, such as when you shut your eye if something comes towards it, or jerk your knee when a doctor strikes a certain spot. Babies have those reflexes too, and they also have some others, which disappear quite early on. For example, newborn babies 'root': they turn automatically toward the breast and seek out the nipple. Simply stroking the baby's cheek will evoke this reflex, the infant turning toward the stroking. Babies reflexively suck anything placed in their mouths: a breast or bottle, a finger or an object. Newborn babies will also reflexively grasp anything put in their hands, and grip onto it. They can cling on strongly enough to support their own weight in that way. Newborns also have a reflex to make stepping movements, so that if you hold the baby up with his or her feet touching some surface, the child will appear to 'walk'. More exotically, newborns have reflexes against drowning: the tract to the lungs closes automatically when they are submerged, and the baby makes swimming motions.

Such simple reflexes mean that newborn babies have at least a bare minimum of ways of acting on the world around them, and of responding to it. It isn't hard to imagine how useful these things were in our evolutionary history. But how could such simple responses be the basis for building up all the complexities of the adult human mind? Piaget's answer is subtle and ingenious.

Piaget points out that every living organism must *adapt* to its environment if it is to survive. That is to say, every organism has to modify or *accommodate* its behaviour to fit in with the environment, and also has to find a way of subduing or *assimilating* that environment to make it serve its needs. Piaget believed that this process of *adaptation* is the basis not only of survival, but of the growth of intelligence, of the mind. Some reflexes are rigidly fixed, such as the knee jerk or blinking reflexes. Such reflexes don't change or develop, they always remain outside our voluntary control. But human babies have other, special reflexes which are more modifiable, such as looking, listening, sucking, grasping. These reflexes *can* develop and change, and can come under voluntary control. Piaget argues that these special reflexes are never passive. Details of the situation will always affect the baby's response. For example, the breast is not always in exactly the same place, and its shape will vary depending on how full of milk it is. Babies rooting for the breast must respond to these facts, and must shape their search for the nipple and how hard they suck accordingly. So even when responding reflexively, babies do not just *react* to things, they also *take action* (and indeed, accommodation and assimilation always occur together). Acting on the world in this way is the key to all mental development, according to Piaget. Through the process of adaptation, each experience with a given special reflex teaches the baby something new, so that the reflex gradually becomes more flexible, easier to generalise to new situations, and eventually less automatic and more under voluntary or intentional control. In effect, then, these special reflexes gradually evolve from fairly rigid and limited responses like a knee jerk to more plastic *schemas* for action. And so this gradual extension and transformation of a few of the primitive reflexes present at birth provides the child with new awareness of the world, and new ways of thinking about it.

For example Piaget argued that babies at first have no understanding of themselves as entities, or of the distinction between the self and the physical world. It is as if the infant mind 'believed' that the world were simply an extension of itself, existing only to serve its needs, merely the other half of its basic reflexes. In effect, the newborn infant (according to Piaget) is profoundly unaware, uncomprehending, without any self awareness. But through adapting basic reflexes to events, recognising the need to accommodate to events as well as assimilating them to their needs, infants gradually come to recognise that they *are* separate from the rest of the world, and that objects in the world do not simply behave as one wants them to. Through assimilation and accommodation babies gradually realise that objects have properties quite independent of one's own wishes or actions: objects continue to exist whether one wants them to or not, whether one can see them or not. They gradually discover that objects retain their identities even though they may look very different this way up or that way, or when they are near or far away. They aren't 'created' by one's own actions.

Piaget described the very first stage of intelligence in the young infant as being *egocentric,* not in the sense of being selfish, or self-obsessed (because those things require a sense of self, which the infant does not have): simply, profoundly unconscious of anything but a basic set of needs and actions. Piaget called this type of intelligence the 'sensori-motor' stage of development, that is intelligence revolving around sensory impressions and motor actions.

Piaget's theory is fascinating and radical. It was the first theory to offer any sort of explanation of how a simple, relatively rigid biological mechanism (such as a reflex driven organism) could begin to develop the flexible, intentional intelligence characteristic of our species. And the theory suggests that infant minds are at first dramatically different from a more mature mind, not just in the amount of experience or of facts stored away, but also in the very way the child represents and thinks about things. The discovery that the world exists separately from oneself (which takes most of the first two years of life, according to Piaget) is a revolutionary breakthrough for the infant. Before that discovery the infant mind is utterly alien to our adult minds: it is *qualitatively* different from the adult mind.

Piaget devised various tests of his theory. For example, he argued that, if it is true that young infants have no notion that objects exist separately from themselves, then if you suddenly make an object disappear (by hiding it under a cloth, say, or behind something else), a baby will behave as if it has ceased to exist. And in fact, that is just what babies do, up to the age of about nine months. Young babies will make no effort to find an object which is suddenly hidden from them, just as if its disappearance meant that it no longer existed. This phenomenon is very easy to demonstrate, with any young child. But does it really mean that the infant has no notion of *object permanence,* as Piaget calls it? That question has been one of the major challenges for research into baby minds for many years, as we shall see later in this chapter, because not all theorists think Piaget is right.

Gibson's theory

One theorist with a very different view of infant minds is James Gibson. Where Piaget focused on the origins of intelligence as a whole, Gibson tried to understand specifically how perceptual systems work, and how they support action: how looking at a rattle, say, supports reaching for it. Where Piaget concluded that every infant must individually *construct* an understanding of the world, and even of simple objects in the visual world, by interacting with it, Gibson concluded that this is not so. Gibson's theory is that human infants are born with a visual system which is *already* innately 'wired up' to take information from the world and to use this to support action. Thus according to Gibson, there is no need for the baby to interact with the world to discover the fundamental nature of objects, as Piaget and other 'blank slate' theorists propose.

Gibson (1979) pointed out that the environment around us is very rich in information. For example, all objects have a texture. His theory is that the human visual system is wired up from birth to use the information provided by textures to guide action. For example, textures change as we move nearer or further away from an object: the leaves on a tree may be a single blur of colour from a distance, but become separate, individual, distinct as we move closer. Gibson's theory is that right from birth, the visual system can use this type of information to guide action, so that babies will try to grasp nearby objects but not ones which are too far away. The texture of the object is directly conveying information about its distance to the infant, without the infant having to discover about the visual effects of distance as Piaget thought.

According to Gibson, the visual system is innately attuned to many other types of information in the visual environment, too. For instance, if we see a block getting larger in our visual field, we see it as *looming* towards us rather than staying where it was and expanding. If only one part of the visual field gets larger we see *it* as moving towards *us*. If everything in the visual field gets larger, we see *ourselves* as moving towards *it*. These biases are built into our visual systems, and even adults can't get away from them.

Gibson's most famous experiment is the 'visual cliff'. Here, an infant is placed on one side of a glass surface, opposite the mother (Figure 2.3). Beneath the glass surface is a chequered pattern, so designed that at each side of the surface, the squares of the pattern are large. But in the centre they become small *just as they would, if all the squares were really the same size, but the ones in the centre were further away,* at the bottom of a drop, say. In effect, manipulating the size of the squares underneath the glass surface creates a visual illusion of a cliff edge. Gibson found that babies would not crawl over this cliff edge, and argued that this meant that they were using the visual information about depth from the chequerboard to direct their actions. The edge of the 'cliff' did not look to the babies as if it *afforded* safe crawling.

This concept that visual appearances 'afford' actions is crucial to Gibson's theory. For example, certain surfaces simply *look* too frail or inadequate to sit or stand on. A reasonably solid, rigid, flat surface at the right height directly looks like a chair and so affords sitting, whereas a watery or very flimsy surface does not. Such *direct perceptions* are not universal. Rather, they reflect the properties of the individual or species. A surface which affords a safe perch for a starling does not afford sitting for a man! And equally, a surface which affords safe crawling for a baby may not afford support to a much heavier adult, or to an infant who does not yet crawl. Nonetheless, Gibson does not believe that infants need to develop the very explicit understanding of the world which Piaget argues for, in order to respond to affordances. Rather, babies are born with visual systems already attuned to make these perceptions. All experience does is fine-tune the innate system.

Figure 2.3 The visual cliff

Gibson's theory is, in its way, as radical as Piaget's. It suggests that the human infant is very much more sophisticated at birth than Piaget thought. It suggests that the way we view the world and structure our actions in it is innate, a part of our biological specification, to a far greater extent than any of the 'blank slate' theorists supposed. And it proposes that the connection between our perceptions and our actions is far less *cognitive*, far less a process of explicit understanding and reasoning than Piaget's theory implies.

These two theories about the infant mind offer starkly contrasting views of the origins of intelligence. Piaget's theory is a *constructivist* theory, in that it argues that the infant is born with very few abilities and must construct his or her mind in interaction with the world. Gibson's theory is a *nativist* theory, in that it argues that the infant has many innate abilities. How can we judge between these two very different theories? How can we tell which is more nearly right, or indeed, if either one right at all?

Studying Baby Minds

Let's go back to a question we raised in Chapter 1: how can we know *how* another person thinks, or *what* they are thinking, or even what they see? This problem is particularly acute with babies. They can't speak to us to tell us what they are thinking. And their range of behaviour is so very limited that we haven't got much to go on in drawing inferences from what they do. So how could we test a theory like Piaget's or Gibson's, or find out more about how a baby views the world?

As is often the case in psychology, new methods for research have led to some giant strides in understanding what the human baby is born with, and what basic skills and knowledge he or she brings to the immense task of learning about the world and learning to think. Three key techniques have been critical in this work: observation studies, habituation studies and methods for studying the activity of the living brain.

Observation studies

One way to study baby minds is through carefully observing what the child does. We can look in very fine detail at patterns in the baby's behaviour. For example, how and when do babies move their hands when reaching towards an object? Do they anticipate how big the object is, and open their fingers to an appropriate stretch? Are there coordinated sequences of movements in the baby's behaviour which seem to be driven by some specific intention? For instance, does the infant swipe at the crib rattle deliberately,

to make it sound? Does the baby look round for an object which has disap-
peared from sight?

Techniques like these can give us a lot of information about how the
baby sees the world. But they are more effective with older infants, who
have already learned quite a bit about controlling their bodies. Observation
techniques are of relatively little use in telling us much about the very start
of intelligence in the newborn baby.

Habituation studies

The most powerful tool for research on the very youngest baby's mind is
what is called the *habituation* paradigm. Most organisms will 'habituate'
(that is, get used to) some stimulus after it has been around for a period of
time, and stop responding to it. An example would be that one can fall
asleep in a lecture, despite the continuing voice of the lecturer. But let
some *new* stimulus come along (such as when the sound gets quicker or
louder as the lecturer winds down or asks a question) and we are alert
again: we wake up, pay attention. So it is with babies. By discovering what
changes they can notice, we can work out what they do and what they do
not perceive or understand.

For example, can a newborn baby tell the difference between a triangle
and a square? A study to find out might create a display, in front of the
baby, on which there was a square, say. Even newborn babies can look at
such displays, though they are more short-sighted than older infants. One
can measure how interesting the display is to babies by measuring how long
they look at it before losing interest. Now suppose we change the original
display, showing a new square, and go on changing it at intervals for other
squares. The babies will gradually habituate to squares, losing interest,
becoming a little bored, look less and less at the display, even though it is
changing to show new squares all the time. But what if we now display a
triangle instead? If they see no difference between a triangle and a square,
babies will go on being bored by the 'same old display'. But if infants suddenly show a new interest when the triangle appears, look longer at the
display, we can conclude that they can tell the difference between squares
and triangles. The babies have recognised that they are seeing something
new to them. A variant on this type of task is the 'visual preference' task,
where the infant is shown two stimuli, one familiar and the other new. If
the baby looks longer at the new stimulus, we can infer that he or she has
recognised something new, or something surprising.

This sort of habituation study can be done even with newborn babies. It
can be used to ask a wide range of questions: is the baby born able to tell
one shape from another, or one colour from another? Is the ability to distin-

guish between big and little objects part of the newborn baby's equipment? Does the newborn already know that things close up seem bigger than things a distance away? Can they discriminate number: tell the difference between two things and three things, for example?

And it's not just looking behaviour and visual stimuli which we can use in the habituation paradigm. Babies will suck on a teat to keep a stimulus going. So if you present them with some type of sound, a song, say, babies will be interested, and suck hard for a while, and then gradually stop sucking as they get bored with it. Change the sound, and you can see whether the baby recognises something new, and starts sucking again, or thinks it's all the same as before, and goes on showing boredom. You can use this method to see whether babies can tell the difference between their mother's voice and another woman's, for instance, or between their mother tongue and other languages.

Recent research has begun to use a new measure in habituation studies: the baby's heart rate. Heart rate changes in response to the events around us. Events which startle may make the heart beat faster, where concentration or paying attention to something makes the heart rate slow and steady (Richards and Cronise, 2000; Kitajima, Kumoi and Koike, 1998). By measuring changes in a baby's heart rate we can make even finer analyses of the kinds of distinctions babies can recognise, and the things that interest or surprise them. Even more excitingly, we can measure heart rate in the unborn baby. Even a very young fetus will show a change in heart rate if there is a loud and startling noise, and an older fetus can show quite a complex pattern of heart rate change to progressively more subtle stimuli. Such patterns of fetal heart rate change can be used to explore what sorts of discriminations the unborn child can make, what kinds of stimuli the fetus can register and respond to (Kisilevsky, Fearon and Muir, 1998).

Studies of brain activity

Historically, our understanding of how the structure of the brain develops has come from post mortem studies of fetuses and young children who have died for one reason or another. Such studies are informative, but they cannot show us the brain in action. Furthermore, there is always the possibility that a fetus or child who has died of natural causes is abnormal in some way which may distort our understanding of normal brain development, or that the trauma which caused a violent death has damaged or altered the brain.

Recent developments in medicine have produced some powerful tools for making images of the living brain in action. For example, positron emission tomography (PET scan) can build up a picture of the structure and activity in a living brain. Magnetic resonance imaging (MRI) can do the same thing. And complex models of brain activity can be built up by recording the location and nature of electrical activity in the brain in response to the presentation of some stimulus ('event related potentials', or 'ERP').

These neural imaging techniques are mainly used in diagnosing problems and dysfunctions in the brain. However, they offer a means of studying how normal brains work, and how brain functioning changes through infancy and childhood. But not all of these techniques are appropriate for studying the way healthy children's brains work. For example, PET scans require the injection of a radioactive marker, and this is too invasive to be ethical in a child unless there is some specific medical advantage to that individual child. MRI exposes the child to unpleasant and perhaps frightening vibration and noise, and to a powerful magnetic field which may itself alter, perhaps damage brain development. Again, using such a technique on a child is only ethical where there is a direct need to do so, for that child's benefit. But ERP involves no more than placing electrodes on the skull to measure the tiny electrical currents in different areas of the brain. It is not invasive, and not unpleasant, and so offers a reasonable tool for looking at how normal brains develop.

Studies using measures of ERP offer the possibility of answering questions of a very much more detailed kind than we have ever contemplated before. For example: in adults, planful eye movements are associated with electrical activity in certain areas of the brain. At what age do infants show the same ERP before an eye movement as an adult does? In other words, at what age do infants begin planning eye movements (Csibra, Tucker and Johnson, 1998)? When do infants show the same ERP patterns as adults, in response to recognising or anticipating things (Ackles and Cook, 1998; Nelson, Thomas, de Haan and Wewerka, 1998)? When do baby brains respond differently to different aspects of language (Schafer, Shucard, Shucard and Gherken, 1998)?

ERP studies are very new, and very exciting. They offer a new way into understanding what the infant mind is like, and how it changes through development. Without doubt, this sort of technique will play a more and more important part in research in the coming decades. However, the technique is not without teething problems. For example, there are practical problems in collecting accurate ERP data from infants, which may distort the theories derived from such work (Hood, 2001).

Infant Minds: Current Research

So what exactly is a baby's mind like? How does it change and develop through the first few years? Of course, we don't yet have definitive answers to those questions. But we do have quite a few clues, theories and some intriguing questions. Let's look at two key areas of research (other aspects of infant minds will come up in later chapters).*

Understanding objects

Thirty years ago, as we've seen, Piaget and most other researchers believed that newborn babies had no understanding of what an object is, and had to learn this from experience with the world. That is to say, the common view was that newborns did not know that objects look different from different orientations or distances, did not know that objects are solid and can't pass through other objects, did not even know that objects have edges, or that they continue to exist when out of sight. According to Piaget, all this knowledge had to be *constructed* by each individual baby through their own interactions with the world. Recent research suggests that this is wrong, that in fact, babies are born with quite a sophisticated perception of objects and their properties.

Perceiving shape
For example, even newborn babies can recognise many two dimensional shapes. It is harder to demonstrate this than you'd think! The basic method is to use a habituation study such as was described above, letting the baby habituate to a particular shape, and then showing something different. The key question is: can the baby see the difference? Many studies have shown that they can (Slater, 1997) and, incidentally, that they can also distinguish colours and sizes of objects. But does this really mean that the baby can tell the difference between a square, say, and a triangle, or does it mean no more than that the baby can detect the difference between, say, a right angle and an acute one, or some other sub-component of the shapes? To say that the newborn baby can recognise shapes such as squares or triangles, we have to show that the child responds to the shape *as a whole*, rather than just to its component bits.

Clever studies by researchers such as Slater and his colleagues (1991) have shown that, in fact, newborn babies *do* process objects as wholes,

---

* Much of the work summarised in this section is reviewed in more detail in the collections of essays in Bremner, Slater and Butterworth (1997) and Rochat and Striano (1999). These two books would make an excellent follow up, as is suggested at the end of this chapter.

rather than seeing them simply in terms of their separate properties. Slater habituated newborns to two stimuli: a green (shown here as plain) diagonal bar, and a red (shaded) vertical one (Figure 2.4a). Then they offered two test stimuli, one of the two original stimuli to which the child was habituated (the red vertical, say) and a novel stimulus which might be either a red diagonal or a green vertical bar (Figure 2.4b). Which one will the baby be more interested in? If babies process stimuli in terms of their component

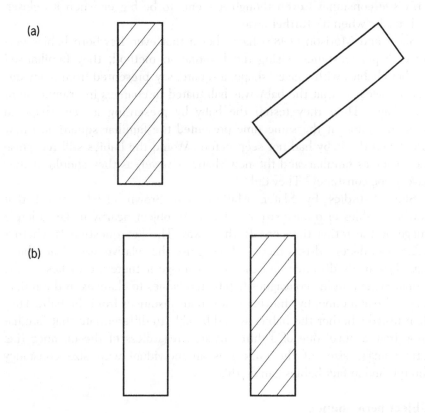

Figure 2.4 Compound stimuli
Source: After Slater (1997).

parts rather than as wholes, they should see both of these test stimuli as equally boring: they are already habituated to red and green, and to both vertical and horizontal orientations. It is only the *combination* of these component parts to make a new whole which is novel in one of the test stimuli. If babies see objects as wholes, they should recognise one of the test stimuli as new, and look more at that. And in fact, babies do look more at the novel test stimulus, showing that they see objects as wholes in the same way adults do.

Size and shape constancy

Another critical element of perceiving objects is recognising that an object is still the same shape (hence the term 'shape constancy') even though it looks different from different angles, and still the same size (hence the term 'size constancy') even though it seems to be bigger when it's closer, and smaller when it's further away.

Slater and Morison (1985) have shown that even newborn babies perceive shape constancy. Using the habituation method, they familiarised newborn babies with a given shape: a square, say, presented from many different angles, so that the baby was habituated to changes in orientation of that shape. Then they tested the baby by presenting a new shape (a trapezium), and at the same time presented the familiar square at a new orientation the baby had not seen before. Would the babies still recognise the square as familiar, and the new shape as novel, as they should, if they have shape constancy? They did.

Similar studies by Slater, Matlock and Brown (1990) reveal that newborn babies also have size constancy. An object nearby makes a larger image on the retina than one further away. The key question is whether babies can disregard this fact, and recognise the relative size of an object regardless of its distance and the size of image it therefore makes on the retina. Slater and his colleagues habituated babies to changes in the retinal image size of a cube, by showing it at various distances from the baby. They then tested whether the babies would be able to differentiate that familiar cube from a novel one of a different size, regardless of the distance (i.e. retinal image size) of the cubes, as an individual with size constancy should. And in fact babies can do this.

Object permanence

Piaget's claim that young babies don't realise that objects continue to exist when they are out of sight is startling. As we've seen, the claim is based on the observation that if you cover an object up with a cloth a baby under six months old will not look for it, as if it had ceased to exist. Even at nine months or more Piaget reported that if babies see an object hidden at position A and find it there, and then see it hidden again at position B, they search for it where they found it before, at position A. Piaget suggests that this is because the baby believes that the act of needing or looking for the object *makes* it come into existence in the expected position. Young babies think they are *creating* the object, rather than *finding* it, so they create it again where they created it before. This classic phenomenon is known as the 'A not B error'. Only in the second year of life do infants gradually construct the idea that the object has a permanent existence independent of their activities.

Piaget's observations are usually quite easy to reproduce. But do they really mean what he said they mean? Many researchers have argued that they do not. For example, Baillargeon, Spelke and Wasserman (1985) point out that Piaget's experiments require the child to have *two* quite separate abilities: first, understanding that objects still exist when out of sight, and second, the ability to search effectively for an object. Young babies may 'fail' in Piaget's tests simply because they don't know how or where to search for the vanished object, rather than because they think it no longer exists. Slater (1997) reviews clever new studies that test Piaget's claims in other ways, avoiding the need for the child to make a search.

For example, look at Figure 2.5. Here, the habituation display shows (to an adult eye) a solid rod behind a cube. This perception is strengthened if the top and bottom of the 'rod' move together as a single unit to right and left behind the cube, as the arrows indicate. But what do babies see? If they have no concept that objects exist when out of sight, one would expect them to see two separate short rods rather than one long one, because the occluded part of the rod that adults *assume* is there would not exist for the baby. So if babies do not understand that objects exist whether they can see them or not, then they should find the long whole rod more novel and interesting than the two short ones when presented with the test display. Newborn babies show exactly that response: they are more surprised by, and look longer at the long rod in the test display after habituating to the original stimulus (Slater, Mattock and Brown, 1990). This is true even when the stimulus materials are changed to make the fact that the rod is *behind* the cube much more salient (Slater, Johnson, Kellman and Spelke, 1994). These results suggest that Piaget may be right in thinking that newborn babies do not understand that objects exist when they can't see them. But this understanding develops far earlier than Piaget claimed. At two months of age, babies' reactions to the test materials suggest that they are unsure whether there were two short, or one long rod in the habituation display (Johnson and Nanez, 1995). But by four months of age, babies' responses show that they see one long rod in the habituation display, just as an adult would (Kellman, Spelke and Short, 1986).

Yet even studies like these cannot be taken simply at face value. Studies of babies' reactions to partly occluded objects (such as the rod in Figure 2.5) certainly show that there is an age change in the tendency to behave as if the occluded part of an object exists. But we must be cautious as to exactly what this means. Could it not be that there are age changes in the baby's ability to use the clues which tell an adult how to interpret occluded

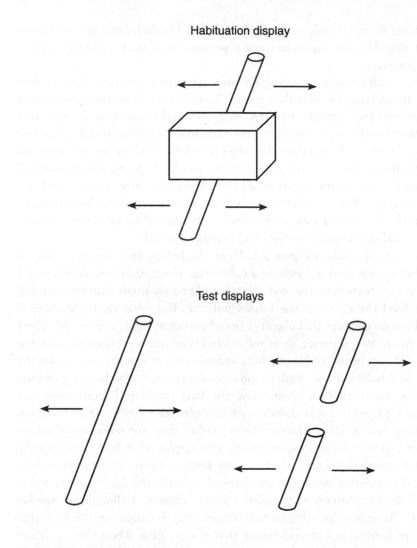

Habituation display

Test displays

Figure 2.5 Occluded rod display
Source: After Slater (1997).

items, rather than an age change in understanding that occluded items still exist? Adults interpret the rod as a single rod behind the cube on the basis of three clues: the similar appearance of the two visible parts of the rod, the depth cues showing the relative positions of rod and cube, and the fact that the two visible pieces of rod move together. Subtle studies (Slater, 1997) have shown that even very young babies can interpret these cues, but are less adept at drawing the right inferences than adults, and are more dominated by immediate visual cues (such as the fact that the rod is always seen as two pieces rather than one). So studies of how babies see partly occluded objects don't really give a definitive answer to the question of whether newborn infants *can't* understand that invisible parts of an object exist, or whether they merely *don't* interpret this type of experimental stimulus as an older individual would.

Nevertheless, data from this type of study show two useful things. First, that there is at least some degree of learning how to interpret objects in early infancy, whether it be learning to piece together the implications of clues as to what one is looking at, or whether it be getting a better grasp on the concept of the permanence of objects. But second, that even two-month-old infants can infer the existence of an invisible part of an object, refuting Piaget's claim that such understanding eludes even the nine-month-old.

A second type of study confirms the conclusion that, indeed, very young babies know far more about the existence and properties of invisible objects than Piaget supposed. These studies looked to see whether babies could tell the difference between possible and impossible events involving hidden objects. For example, Baillargeon, Spelke and Wasserman (1985) showed that by five or six months of age, babies are surprised and intrigued if one object, such as a toy car, seems to pass through another, such as a solid block, and that this is the case even when the solid block has been hidden by a screen after being placed in the car's way. They attend more to such impossible events than to possible ones (where the infant has been shown that there is no obstacle in the car's path before the screen is put in place, for example). Such results show that the infants were aware of the continued existence of the invisible block behind the screen, and understood that it should have been an obstacle for the car. Baillargeon and her colleagues have also shown that babies as young as six months know that a screen can fold down and compress a soft but not a hard hidden object, and that a screen will fold down further if the object behind it is small than it will if the hidden object is large (it folds until it reaches the object). In other words, these young babies not only represent the existence of objects they cannot see, but can also draw inferences about the physical and spatial properties of these objects.

Piaget, Gibson and modern theories about infants and objects

Overall, studies of infant perception suggest that Piaget's theory of how infants understand objects is wrong. First, even the newborn baby in fact already has an impressive understanding of the physical world, and of the principles governing the behaviour of objects in it. By two or three months, this understanding has become quite sophisticated and subtle. Very young babies not only understand a great deal about objects, they also have rudimentary concepts of causality, trajectory and number, and they can draw simple inferences (Spelke, Breinlinger, Macomber and Jacobson, 1992; Willatts, 1997). Babies of this age are far too young and immature to have acquired all this understanding through feedback from their own actions, as Piaget's theory proposed. So Piaget seems to have been wrong about what the newborn baby is like, about what the child develops in the first year of life, and about how this development takes place.

In fact, the data suggest that Gibson's theory is more accurate than Piaget's. Much of what a baby needs in order to understand objects is already pre-programmed at birth. Of course, much also remains to be learned (Slater, 1997; Bremner, 1997). Babies do show marked developmental change in how they perceive and interpret the world around them in the first few months of life (for example, in their understanding of occluded objects, as we have seen). But the data suggest that this learning can come from *observing* events, as Gibson's theory would suggest, rather than needing to be built up from direct experience of action, as Piaget argued.

However, it would be wrong to conclude that Piaget is wrong and Gibson is right. The situation is far more complicated because, although the young infant's *perceptual* system is very sophisticated, their ability to *use* the information it provides is quite limited. So, for example, in studies testing whether they can spot impossible events (such as those described above), infants as young as three months show that they understand that hidden objects still exist and still have functional properties. But they don't *use* this understanding in practical contexts, such as searching for a hidden object or retrieving a toy (Bremner, 1997; Willatts, 1997). Equally, Baillargeon and her colleagues have shown that eight-month-old infants will search for a hidden item, and can remember where a hidden item is for more than a minute. Yet at this age, babies still show the 'A not B' error and search for an item where they found it the last time rather than where they saw it hidden less than a minute ago. Thus there is an enormous developmental change in how effectively babies can *use* the rich information provided by their perceptual systems to guide their actions and their interactions with the world. Gibson's theory provides no explanation of what is involved in this crucial developmental change. It may well be a better account of perceptual abilities in infancy than Piaget's, but Gibson has little to say about how the child's interactions with the world develop.

How can we understand what it is that changes the infant from 'a sophisticated perceiver but limited actor' into a more coordinated and efficient user of information and solver of problems? Some researchers (Bremner, 1997) suggest that for perceptual information to be *useful*, it has to be explicitly integrated with the actions which it serves, and that creating such integration is the main developmental process in infancy. The idea is a complex one, perhaps easiest to grasp through analogies. If you have recently learned to drive, you probably remember how difficult it was, at first, to use all the information from your eyes, your ears and the motion of the car to drive smoothly. In fact, the first part of learning to drive is realising just how complicated that easy-looking activity is (how on earth did mum do it, whilst conducting a conversation, navigating, and refereeing an argument in the back seat . . . ?). But gradually, the information from your senses gets integrated with the actions needed to control the car. By the time you passed your test, you were no longer even noticing yourself working out when to start turning the wheel to get round an upcoming bend, as you had to at first: it was all 'automatic'. It is important to notice in this analogy that there wasn't any real change in what you were *able* to see: you could always perceive bends in the road, for example. The change is in how you used those perceptions in guiding your actions.

In effect, Bremner's suggestion is that the young baby is like a learner driver: he or she may have the equipment to make all the perceptual judgements needed for various tasks, but like the learner driver, has to learn how to use this information in guiding actions. And as with a learner driver, there is no way to integrate perceptions with actions without starting to try out the actions. It is only by becoming mobile, for example, that the child begins to need, and so to build up, perceptions as to which surfaces 'afford' safe walking or crawling, and which do not (Bremner, 1997). From this point of view, Piaget's emphasis on the importance of acting on the world in the development of an *intelligent* understanding of objects and the physical world in infancy seems right.

Nonetheless, Piaget's theory of exactly how acting on the world contributes to developmental change may be much too simple. His theory treats the infant mind as if it were a disembodied intelligence, like a computer riding in and controlling the body. Mental processes are supposed to construct themselves by reflecting on the result of the actions that they have directed the body to perform. This approach puts all the emphasis on *mental processes* as the force driving and shaping development. But the mental processes of the very young infant are far too limited to explain all the phenomena we see as the infant's behaviour evolves (Hopkins and Butterworth, 1997). In fact, it is doubtful that mental processes alone could ever fully explain the development of new mental structures (Thornton, 1999), as we shall see in Chapter 7. And, in fact, infant minds are not disembodied: they exist very firmly in bodies that have a certain size, that have certain properties, certain limitations, bodies which interact with a physical world.

'Dynamical systems theory' is a new approach to explaining how infant behaviour develops (Bremner, 1997; Hopkins and Butterworth, 1997; Lewis, 2000; Thelen and Smith, 1994). Rather than seeing mental processes as the key factor, as Piaget does, this approach proposes that infant behaviour develops as a result of interactions between many different factors. For example, learning to crawl to a toy is not a disembodied action (Adolph, Vereijken and Denny, 1998). The infant's behaviour will be constrained and shaped by the laws of physics (gravity and so on), the properties of the immediate environment (the distance to the object, for example) and the properties of the baby's own limbs (the fact that one cannot simultaneously crawl and reach out with both hands at the same time, and that there are limits on how far one can reach out without tumbling over), as well as by the infant's perceptions of the object, intentions or goals. Crawling itself may develop from a repeated process of reaching toward a distant desirable object, overbalancing onto the outstretched hand and moving forward almost accidentally through the action of gravity, to repeat the process until the object is achieved. Through sequences of events like this, babies can make new discoveries which they had no *intention* of making: they can discover crawling without having had any thought of doing that, for instance (Goldfield, 1994). Thus the interaction between many different factors can produce effects far beyond what could be produced by any one factor alone, and far beyond what the infant's initial mental processes could imagine or attempt. Dynamical systems theory is beginning to offer a new insight into the rich processes through which actions develop and contribute to the growth of intelligence in infancy.

Understanding people

Because of the great influence of Piaget's theory, and its emphasis on understanding the physical world, there has been much less research into an equally important topic: how babies understand the social world. As we've already seen, Piaget thought that babies made no distinction between people and other objects. But in fact, the social world is special and distinct from the physical world: interactions with people provide the key to the child's survival and development. And people are very different from inanimate objects.

Treating people as 'different'

From soon after birth, babies respond differently to people and objects (Legerstee, 1992; Poulin-Dubois, 1999). For example, newborn babies move their hands and arms in quite different ways when they interact with people than thay do when they interact with inanimate objects (Ronnqvist and von Hofsten, 1994). There is mounting evidence that, in fact, there may be innate mechanisms which lead babies to find people highly attractive, and to interact with them in special ways.

Habituation studies show that newborn babies can tell the difference between speech and other sounds, can tell the difference between their own mother tongue and another language (Mehler, Lambertz, Jusczyk and Amiel-Tison, 1986) and, within a few days of birth, can recognise (and prefer) their own mother's voice to that of another woman. Of course, the baby can hear sounds in the womb, so some of this responsiveness to language may be learned. Nevertheless, newborns show an impressive orientation to speech, suggesting that they may be innately programmed to respond to it. This hypothesis is perhaps best supported by the finding that, within hours of birth, infants will imitate vowel sounds spoken to them (Kugiumutzakis, 1986, quoted in Slater and Butterworth, 1997).

Very strong evidence that we are born pre-programmed to orient to people comes from studies of infants' responses to faces (Slater and Butterworth, 1997). There may well be developmental changes in exactly how infants perceive the human face: for example, newborn babies may tend to orient more to the outline of the face and to grosser features such as the shape of the hairline rather than to the details of internal features, as an older infant does (Bushnell, 1982). Nonetheless, in the first two days of life, babies have learned to recognise the basic features of their own mother's face (Bushnell, Sai and Mullin, 1989). As soon as twelve hours after birth, a baby prefers its mother's face to that of a stranger, sucking a teat more to see a video of the mother than of a stranger (Walton, Bower and Bower, 1992).

Most striking of all, within minutes of birth, babies are more interested in faces than in other things. Johnson, Dziurawiec, Ellis and Morton (1991) showed newborn babies each of the three stimuli shown in Figure 2.6. Each stimulus was the size of a human head. Johnson and his colleagues showed newborns one of these stimuli at a time, moving it back and forth in a small arc once the baby had begun to look at it, and measured how much the infant turned to follow the stimulus as it moved. Newborn babies tracked the most face-like stimulus the most, and the blank stimulus the least. The scrambled stimulus attracted more following than the blank one, but less than the face-like one. Johnson and Morton (1991) argue that the evidence suggests that there are special innate neural mechanisms specifically geared to orient newborns toward faces, and to let them detect similarities and differences between individual faces. For example, there may be built-in mechanisms which attract babies to the very general properties of faces (after all, the face-like stimulus in Figure 2.6 is not really so face-like: it's more of a *cartoon* of the general features of human faces). Such mechanisms would provide the baby with a good basis for learning about *specific* faces. Without such a built-in basis for learning, it is hard to see how newborns could learn to recognise their own mother's face so very quickly.

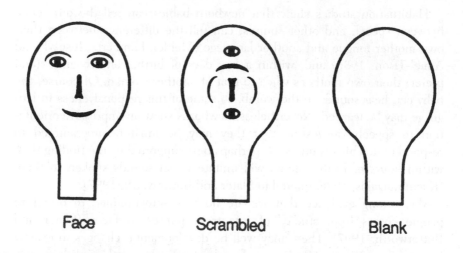

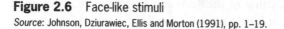

Figure 2.6　Face-like stimuli
Source: Johnson, Dziurawiec, Ellis and Morton (1991), pp. 1–19.

The idea that human babies are pre-programmed to be specifically social creatures, to treat other people as something special and different from inanimate objects is not surprising. We are a very social species. There is clear evidence that the young of many other species have innate mechanisms to support very early interactions with other members of their own species (Manning, 1972). Why should human beings be different, when successful bonding between parent and infant is so critical to the infant's welfare? The newborn human's rapid recognition and preference for its mother's face and voice is rewarding to the mother: a major asset to such bonding.

Interacting with others
In fact, there is still more intriguing evidence that we are pre-programmed not just to recognise other people as something special and different from inanimate objects, but to actually *react* to them in special ways (Poulin-Dubois, 1999; Rochat and Striano, 1999; Slater and Butterworth, 1997). Newborn babies will imitate not only speech sounds, but also facial gestures, such as poking out the tongue (Figure 2.7), or the expression they see on another's face (Kugiumutzakis, 1993). They don't imitate inanimate objects (Meltzoff, 1994). This ability to imitate seems to be innate: the newborn has not had time to learn to connect seeing someone else's tongue poke out with having a tongue of his or her own. But imitating others is not a reflex like a knee jerk: infants have to make an effort to imitate (Kugiumutzakis, 1993), and babies clearly modify and correct their imita-

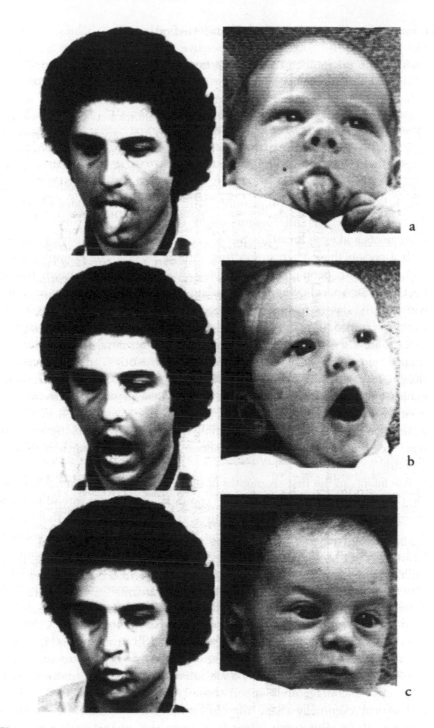

Figure 2.7 Examples of newborn babies imitating facial gestures
Source: Meltzoff (1981).

tions of the other face (Meltzoff, 1994). Furthermore, babies are more likely to imitate an adult who is responsive to the child than an actor who runs off a predetermined series of expressions (Kugiumutzakis, 1993).

What does this innate capacity for imitation imply? Trevarthen (1993a) believes that it is evidence that newborn babies are already able to recognise in some way that there is an important similarity between themselves and other people, and that they are already pre-programmed to engage in social interactions and communications. Trevarthen was the first to make very detailed analyses of babies interacting with adults or objects, making frame by frame analyses of video of such interactions. Such studies suggest that babies are born pre-programmed with two different modes of action: *doing* with objects, and *communicating* with people. A baby's physical movements and even breathing pattern are quite different when interacting with a person than when interacting with an object. For example, when interacting with people, babies adopt the same breathing pattern that is necessary for speech, but they breath quite differently when interacting with objects. Babies react socially to people, but not to objects (Legerstee, Anderson and Schaffer, 1998). And indeed, the very things that infants imitate are the things relevant to speech and communication: the lip shapes of sounds, certain vowels, facial gestures and expressions (Kugiumutzakis, 1993). As we shall see in Chapter 3, videos of young babies interacting with adult partners do indeed powerfully suggest that even in the first few months of life, babies behave very much *as if* they were taking part in a real conversation with the partner, taking turns to react, responding to the partner's emotions and so on (Trevarthen, 1993a, 1993b).

Are infants in the first six months of life truly social and communicative? Do they in any way understand what communication is, or intend to communicate? This issue is still very controversial. It is quite clear that babies are innately programmed with the basics for a limited sort of interaction with others, and with a strong predisposition to focus on people rather than things, as we have seen. These things make babies very attractive to adults, encouraging adults to interact with them. But many researchers argue that, although they have rudimentary processes for social interactions, young infants do not, in fact, make real, intentional communications at this age (Rochat and Striano, 1999; Poulin-Dubois, 1999). Rather, the adults around them simply *interpret* various of the baby's behaviours *as if* they were social and communicative. Such interpretations on the part of adults may act to encourage and support those types of behaviours in the child, and so may eventually shape the child toward more deliberate efforts at communication. But these researchers argue that at this early stage, the infant does not understand the very concept of communication. He or she is simply reflecting an innate predisposition to react in certain ways to people, predispositions which are not yet integrated with any under-standing of what other people are or with any focused plans of action or communication.

Understanding communication

Around nine months of age, infants seem to experience a sort of 'revolution' in the way they understand people (Poulin-Dubois, 1999; Tomasello, 1999). Now, for the first time, infants will follow someone else's gaze, looking around to see what that person is looking at. They will use shared gaze, pointing and sounds to make requests (such as getting an adult to pass a toy which is out of reach), or to bring something to the other's atten-tion (a dog in the distance, say). This new ability to share a focus of atten-tion with someone else (often referred to as joint attention), and to coordinate eye contact and shared attention with gestures such as pointing is the first step toward real, intentional communication (Butterworth, 1991; Poulin-Dubois, 1999; Camaioni, 1992).

What has changed, in the first nine months of life, to allow the infant to develop such deliberate interactions out of the innate predispositions present at birth? The key may be that the child has developed a concept of people as specifically *animate* agents, by understanding (for example) that people can have goals, and can cause their own movements and actions (are 'self-propelling') where inanimate objects only move when something else causes them to (Premack, 1990; Poulin-Dubois, 1999). This new understanding lets the infant recognise that only people can respond autonomously, *do things* for you (or for themselves). They further realise that, whereas to make an inanimate object do something you need to directly touch it and act on it, people (and maybe other animate creatures) can be made to move from a distance, by communicating with them (making noises, pointing and the like). These discoveries come from learning about how objects and people move, in the first nine months of life.

Even very young babies can tell the difference between the movement of an animate creature and that of an inanimate object using purely the kind of perceptual information available from 'point light' displays of the type shown in Figure 2.8. Here, each black dot represents a light on a dark ground. The lights in panels A and B are in fact lights placed on the head, neck, hip, elbows, hands, knees and feet of a human being, whereas the lights in panel C are randomly placed. Adults who see these displays static see them all as random patterns of light. But when the lights move (ran-domly in panel C as the arrows depict, or reflecting the movements of a human walker, as the arrows indicate in panel B), adults see random movement in panel C, but can recognise the human form in panel B and can specify its actions (dancing, walking, running, etc). In habituation studies, babies as young as three months of age prefer the patterns suggesting a moving person, which may imply that we are innately disposed to orient to animated movement (Berthental, 1993). But this, of course, does not necessarily mean that these young infants understand what they see as an adult does. And, in fact, there are some age-related changes in infants' reactions to such light displays which suggest that whilst at three months of age babies are responding only to an innate perceptual preference for animate motion, by five months of age they are responding on the basis of understanding the meaning of the animated light pattern (Slater, 1997). Through experience and observation, the baby comes not only to distinguish between animate and inanimate things (the difference between a human stranger, say, and a humanoid robot) but to understand, by about nine or ten months of age, that animate behaviour is goal directed, self-motivating.

Understanding the difference between animate creatures and inanimate objects in this way is obviously a huge step towards understanding the nature of communication. But it is easy to overestimate how big a step this actually is. You and I, as adults, understand that living creatures have mental states, feelings, desires, beliefs and so on. We believe that the goals and self-direction characteristic of living creatures derive from these mental

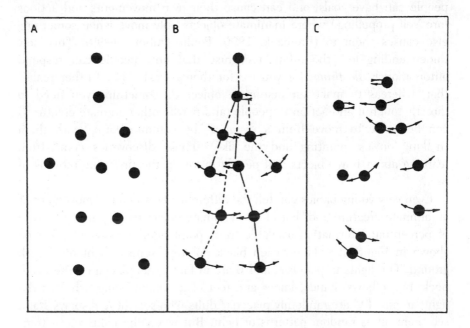

Figure 2.8   Point-light displays
Source: After Berenthal (1993). Reproduced after Slater (1997).

states. But the data suggest that the ten-month-old baby can recognise that living creatures have goals, but does not yet understand that these goals derive from mental states, or even that mental states exist at all, either in themselves or in others (Poulin-Dubois, 1999). Whereas you or I, when we communicate with others, understand that we are sharing ideas with another mind, influencing someone else's feelings, beliefs or desires, the young infant seems to be entirely unaware of this.

Babies can certainly discriminate between different facial expressions (happy, sad, surprise) within days of birth (Field, Woodson, Greenberg and Cohen, 1982), and are adept at distinguishing between specific expressions by seven months (Soken and Pick, 1999). But this does not necessarily mean that these young infants understand the emotional significance of these expressions. Take a parallel case: you or I might be very easily able to identify various different postural states shown by a scorpion, say, without having any insight whatever into what those postures boded for its behaviour. Is it more likely to attack when motionless and focused, or when scuttling rapidly across the floor? Do either of these behaviours signal a particular mental state in the scorpion? We don't need to know, in order to see the difference per se. And in fact, even adults are fairly unlikely to attribute mental states to scorpions. We may speculate about their immediate goals, but are normally indifferent to the possibility that the goal of stinging us may be motivated by feelings such as fear in the scorpion. Knowing that another creature is goal directed does not necessarily mean that we understand (or care) whether it has mental states.

It is difficult to discover exactly what babies understand when they recognise or copy someone else's facial expression. Such young infants cannot tell us what they think another person feels, and their capacity for responding to others is too limited to reveal empathy, say, or a sharing of the emotion they see. Even when older babies do react differentially to their mothers' expressions, they need not necessarily understand that the expression reflects a mental state, as opposed to treating it more simply as a signal: a warning of danger, perhaps, or a signal that a rewarding interaction is available. For example, by twelve months of age, infants can certainly use facial expressions as signals in this way. Sorce, Emde, Campos and Klinnert (1985) showed that babies would not cross the glass surface in Gibson's 'visual cliff' study (Figure 2.3) if their mothers' faces expressed fear or anger. But they would do so if the mother looked interested or happy. But data such as these can't demonstrate that the child understands that the mother *feels* fear or anger or happiness. And in fact, the majority of researchers believe that children of this age do not yet understand that others have feelings and beliefs or mental states. They do not yet have a *theory of mind*.

Awareness of the fact that others have mental states and feelings is a seminal development in the child. Such awareness lays the foundation for real communication, for a true 'meeting of minds'. It is yet another unique achievement of our species. We shall come back to this issue in Chapter 3.

In Summary

Recent research has very much overthrown traditional ideas of what baby minds are like, and where intelligence comes from. Babies are not born as blank slates, and they do not have to construct every aspect of intelligence for themselves, as was long supposed. In fact, it is hard to see how intelligence could possibly develop in that way. Without at least some initial basis for learning and making sense of the world, a baby could not learn at all.

In fact, there is now overwhelming evidence that babies start life with an impressive array of innate predispositions and processes already wired into their systems. We are born already programmed to see and learn about certain things in both the physical and the social world, to make certain discriminations, to find some things more interesting than others, to react in special ways to certain things. In other words, there is a powerful *biological* basis to our intelligence. Far more of the fundamental structure of the human mind is part of our species inheritance, of our evolutionary history than was supposed only thirty years ago. And indeed, analyses of our evolutionary history are increasingly influencing how researchers understand the patterns of change we see through cognitive development (Bjorklund and Pellegrini, 2000).

But these innate structures or tools of the mind are not yet *functional* at birth. To be useful and to support the growth of real intelligence, understanding and intentional behaviour, these innate processes have to be integrated into patterns of action, experiences of interacting with the world. They have to be made sense of. One might compare a newborn baby with an adult presented with a box of tools never seen before, and an unfamiliar object to mend. Each tool suggests certain actions (a spanner lends itself to fitting on nuts and bolts, for example, while a screwdriver lends itself to unscrewing screws) and elements of the object (the fact that it has nuts and bolts here and screws there) indicate where certain tools could be used. At first, each of the tools works well, one might even be fairly good at deciding which to use where, and even in using it effectively. But until one has had quite a bit of experience unscrewing this and rebolting that, one might have little or no idea what the object was, or what effect one's actions had on it. Only through using the tools is one likely to develop any meaningful understanding of the object, or learn to use the tools in a goal-directed way.

The analogy of a newborn baby as the possessor of a toolbox for inter-acting with the world but no meaningful understanding of the effects or purpose of those tools shows up both how much we have discovered about the origins of intelligence, and how many questions we have left to answer. Yes, we can say that (for example) communicating with others grows out of a biologically programmed predisposition to notice certain things, to treat people as special and to respond to them in certain ways. And yes, we can say that interacting with the world and all its complexities alters this basic predisposition, leading it to evolve into something else, something more deliberate and knowing. We are even beginning to understand how the physics of the universe, the dynamics of bodies and even chance events combine to shape and impel this developmental change. But we are still a very long way from understanding, for example, precisely what it is that changes as insight grows in the child's mind, or what it is that is critical to that change.

EXERCISES

1   Using a habituation technique, a laboratory in America finds that babies of six months can distinguish between classical and pop music. But a laboratory in France cannot replicate the results, with the very same pieces of music: their study suggests that babies cannot tell classical from pop music. What are the possible explanations for the different results? How could you test which explanation was the best?
2   What implications do the results obtained by Sorce, Emde, Campos and Klinnert (1985) have for Gibson's interpretation of his data in the 'visual cliff' task?

SUGGESTED READING

For a good introduction to Piaget's ideas:
   Piaget, Jean (1968) *Genetic Epistemology* (New York: Columbia University Press).

For more detail on the recent research covered in this chapter:
   Bremner, G., Slater, A. and Butterworth, G. (1997) *Infant Development: Recent Advances* (Hillsdale, NJ: Psychology Press, Erlbaum).
   Rochat, P. and Striano, T. (1999) *Early Social Cognition: Understanding Others in the First Months of Life* (Hillsdale, NJ: Lawrence Erlbaum).

For an excellent 'feel' for what babies are like, and how dramatically fast they change:
   Karmiloff-Smith, A. (1994) *Baby It's You* (London: Ebury Press).

Language, Communication and Sharing Experience

The most striking achievement of infancy is the development of language. From a starting point where he or she can do little but cry, the baby progresses with astonishing rapidity until, by the third birthday or so, this same child is fairly fluent: argumentative, able to explain events, share information, wheedle and cajole, fink on siblings, and generally engage in the rich interactions which language allows.

In adult life, learning a new language seems a daunting affair. A foreign sentence can seem utterly incomprehensible. We may be unable even to break it down into separate words or syllables, let alone establish what the words mean either individually or collectively. We put in hours and hours of effort, struggling to learn vocabulary, to master an apparently impossible grammar, twist our tongues into unnatural shapes to match the pronunciation. And as like as not, we end up with a product that native speakers find hilarious or quaint. And *all this,* despite the fact that we are already quite experienced linguists, have had decades of speaking our mother tongue! We already *know* what a sentence is, for example, that things have names, that verbs and nouns are different. And we can probably make enough sense of what's happening around us to work out word meanings, however strange the new vocabulary! If sophisticated adults struggle to learn a new language, how on earth can a newborn baby, so much less experienced in life, set out on this complex task, and be so very successful at it so quickly?

The Nature of Language

Let's start by thinking a bit about what language actually is. In adults, it is a means of describing the world, manipulating ideas (and other people), solving problems. Through language we signal our beliefs, needs, feelings, intentions and plans to others, coordinating our actions with theirs. We communicate with others, sharing ideas, influencing their beliefs, moods or desires and actions. But language is also a medium through which we think, through which we privately reflect on and direct *ourselves*.

Language is specifically, uniquely human. No other species has anything like it. It's true that other species also have means of communicating with one another, for example all mammal species can use body postures and vocal signals (growls, howls, mewing, etc.) to indicate threat, say, or sexual attraction, or the imperious 'feed me!' of the young. Birds have elaborate courtship and territorial songs and displays. Some species seem to have quite distinctive ways of giving complicated messages to others. Bees, for instance, whose dances tell other bees where useful pickings of pollen lie. Whales sing to one another in expressive ways. But the messages communicated by these means are very concrete, specific and fixed. A mating call is always a mating call, and *only that*. It has a particular practical function rather than a symbolic one. Other species do not take bits of one signal and combine them with bits of another to create new messages as we humans do.

By contrast with the communication systems of all other species, human language is an almost infinitely flexible symbolic system. It is primarily verbal, but functions just as well without sounds, in written or electronic text, Morse code, flag signalling systems, for example, or in the many sign languages used by the deaf. In whatever medium, human language allows for an infinite variety of new combinations, new messages and new meanings. We can produce and understand sentences we've never heard before (such as: 'the wise pink elephant baked his socks in the stove'). Language allows us to communicate not only concrete, present events and needs as other species do, but also to discuss complex, abstract ideas, and events distant in time and place, potential events, hypothetical events, impossible events. It is the richness and variability of the signalling system embodied in language which is unique to our species.

It is not just that no other species *happens* to communicate as we do: quite simply, they can't do it. All our efforts to 'talk with the animals' have failed. Yes, we can interact with many species in subtle and complex ways, sometimes using words: my own dogs (dachshunds) respond appropriately to about 40 words (most reliably, when these involve suggestions of shared food or a romp in the forest!). This is quite impressive, in that my words are definitely not a part of the dogs' natural signalling system: they don't resemble the dogs' own postural or vocal signals. But nonetheless, the overwhelming evidence is that both this responsiveness and the dogs' means of controlling me (fetching a lead and barking until I give in and take them for a walk, for instance) is based more on the processes of 'conditioning' which Pavlov (1927) and Skinner (1974, 1957) described than on any real response to language per se. Certain sounds have come to signal certain events, and the dog recognises the signal and anticipates the event, just as Pavlov's dogs learned to salivate on hearing a bell in anticipation of being fed. Or certain actions (fetching a lead) have become associated with particular rewards, and will be repeated when the dog wants that reward again, just as Skinner's pigeons learned to press a lever to get food. This is not language or communication as human beings use it, however seductive that idea may be to the proud dog owner.

Even our closest relatives, chimps, can't grasp the essential features of language. Chimps lack the vocal apparatus for speech, so researchers have tried to teach them sign languages. But despite huge and focused efforts on the part of their human helpers, over many years, chimps never get beyond using a few signs to refer to concrete, specific items or events. They create very few new combinations of 'words' beyond what they've been directly taught (Gardner and Gardner, 1980; Premack, 1986). Again, their best performances look more like the outcome of Pavlovian or Skinnerian conditioning processes than like human language.

And yet, every normal human child learns to talk, and to use language in powerful ways, in a remarkably short time and without the huge efforts devoted to trying to teach chimps sign language (or the efforts needed to teach human children basic mathematics, for that matter). Human babies seem to have a strong drive to master language. As Flavell (1985) put it: 'Draconian measures would be needed to *prevent* most children from learning to talk'! The force of his comment is underlined by studies of deaf children born to parents who can't use sign language. These infants, though not exposed to language, develop their own hand signal systems, systems which spontaneously show some of the structural and grammatical properties common to all natural human languages (Goldin-Meadow and Feldman, 1979). Language is definitely and definingly a human thing.

The development of language is one of the most variable phenomena of early childhood. Whereas some developmental milestones (such as pointing or sitting up unaided) are passed pretty much at the same age in all normal children, language develops at a very different pace across children. For example, one child may produce a first simple sentence at seventeen or eighteen months, where another perfectly normal child does not do so until the age of thirty months or more (Brown, 1973). But despite this variability in *timing*, the majority of researchers have generally agreed that the *pattern* of language development is the same for all children. The big steps happen in the same order, whether in a child of eighteen months or one of thirty-six months. How confident can we be that that conclusion is right?

Studying Child Language

The basic method for studying children's language is to record the things children say in more or less detailed diaries. Of course, there are some types of experiment one can do to find out what a child knows about language. A famous example is the 'wug' task (Berko, 1958) where one shows a child a picture of a cartoon bird, and tells the child that it is a 'wug' (Figure 3.1). The child is then shown another wug, told that there are two of them, and asked to complete the simple sentence: 'There are two . . . '. Here, a child who understands that a word gains an extra 's' sound when it becomes plural will say *'wugs!'* Such tasks can clarify what a child has already mastered, but they cannot tell us how that mastery came about. For that, we must study children's language in the natural contexts in which it develops, through diaries.

Diaries of child language are very difficult to produce. The process of learning to talk takes a lot of time, often taking months or even years for each step. One cannot record *everything* that happens to a given infant or group of infants over such long periods of time. That would be impractical (there would be far too much to record) and probably unethical (it might only be possible in some tasteless experiment like the scenario depicted in the film 'The Truman Show', where one individual is, unknown to himself, raised in a giant TV studio where his every movement is recorded by

Figure 3.1 Two wugs
Source: Berko (1958), pp. 150–77.

hidden cameras and all the people around him are actors playing parts dictated by the director).

Inevitably, because of the difficulties of producing diaries of a child's language, what we have are only *samples* of the language any given child produces or hears. Studies describing the sequence of language development rely on 'snapshots' of how the child uses language in certain relatively short periods of time. Furthermore, because the effort of recording and later analysing the sheer volume of what children say (and what is said to them), even in short periods of time, is so great, most studies of language development involve only a very small number of children. Many studies have looked at only two or three children, and others are case studies of just a single child. A sample of twenty children would be very large for a study of how language develops in natural contexts. And given the commitment that it takes from parents to make such recordings, most of the children who have been studied are from educated middle class families. Often they are from the families of the researchers themselves, either their children or grandchildren. So the children studied are not representative of the population at large.

These characteristics of studies of how children learn to talk mean that we must be cautious in assuming that language always develops in the same way in all children. Some researchers believe that it does not: for example, children usually produce nouns before they produce any other kind of word (Nelson, 1973), and this is so for children in many cultures (Gentner, 1982). But not all children produce nouns first. Some produce pronouns ('me') or pro-social words such as 'please' (Nelson, 1973). There is evidence that the subsequent path of language development differs for those who start out with the more 'referential' approach (nouns) from those whose first productions are more 'expressive' or socially oriented (Bates, O'Connell and Shore, 1987; Nelson, 1981). There may be other ways in which language development varies between individual children, or between one culture and another, which we do not yet know.

It would be impossible to overestimate the importance of always bearing in mind questions as to how good our data on any topic are. In the case of child language (as with every other topic), improvements in the detail, or the amount, or the accuracy of our data have played a leading role in the evolution of new theories and better understanding, as we shall see. No doubt new improvements in our methods will lead to even more new discoveries!

Controversy and Certainty in Child Language Research

The puzzle as to how infants learn language is far from solved. There are many different theories, and no one theory can explain all the data. Researchers disagree with one another about what the data mean, and what must be involved in the process of mastering language. Nevertheless, one conclusion has been accepted by almost everyone for a very long time: human babies do *not* learn to talk through the kinds of conditioning processes which lead dogs and dolphins to learn to respond to words.

Skinner (1957) proposed a theory of the development of language through such conditioning processes. But this theory simply does not fit the facts. For example: if babies learn language by learning to anticipate the meaning of particular word sequences through conditioning processes, we would expect them always and only to reproduce the particular word sequences they hear around them. Their early speech should be like adult speech in terms of its syntactical structure. But the first detailed studies of young children's speech show that this is not so, as you can see from the examples in Figure 3.2.

'I wented to the shops!' (excited greeting from a small boy to his grandmother)

'It's badder to feed them too much' (three-year-old discussing goldfish care – Bee, 1989)

'Nobody don't like me' (aggrieved small boy – quoted by McNeill, 1970)

'Allgone doggie' (my young neighbour as the dogs ran out of her garden)

'Where ball? (Slobin, 1979)

Figure 3.2 Examples of young children's speech

As these examples show, young children's language is not simply a copy of adult language, as Skinner's theory predicts it should be. In fact, it is creative in its own right. But this creativity is channelled and focused. Early child language has a *grammar* of its own, different from adult grammar (Brown, 1973; Slobin, 1979). Children the world over produce the same types of utterance, show the same strange but apparently rule bound forms in their early speech (Slobin, 1979). The simple principles of conditioning described by Skinner cannot possibly explain how this could be so.

Does Language Grow Out of the Child's General Intellectual Development?

One stark difference between human beings and other species is the sheer subtlety and complexity of our conceptual systems. Like the two children Mary and Simon, described in Chapter 1 of this book, we want to understand the world about us, and we develop elaborate – though not necessarily correct – concepts (such as Simon's theory that young creatures are *necessarily* smaller than adult ones, in that particular example) to help us do that. Does language grow out of this very general intellectual development? Some theorists have argued very strongly that it does.

Piaget's theory

Piaget (1955), for example, argued that conceptual development must come before, and provide the basis of, the development of language. As we saw in Chapter 2, Piaget believed that newborn babies have almost no understanding of the physical world around them, not even that objects exist when out of sight, and must gradually discover this through the first 18 months of life. To understand that a hidden object still exists, the child must have some means of *representing* that object in its absence. In other words, the child must be able to use *symbols* to stand for absent objects. According to Piaget, the discovery of object permanence requires the *construction* of the ability to use symbols, and it is this which is the key factor allowing the child to begin learning language, which is the symbol system *par excellence*. Piaget believed that language always remains subordinate to thought, so that one cannot learn the meaning of words, for example, if one has no pre-existing understanding of the concept of which the word is a symbol. Nor can one master the structure of grammar unless one has mental operations to support such a structure.

Piaget's theory seems to explain one puzzle about language: why it is that infants first begin to make progress with language in the second year of life, rather than from the very beginning. Piaget claims that the conceptual structures that language requires take about eighteen months to develop. But as we have seen (Chapter 2), recent research has shown that babies are born with a far more sophisticated ability to perceive and understand objects than Piaget thought, through innate mechanisms. It is clear that even very young babies have at least some ability to represent things which are no longer visible. They can *remember* things, for example the properties and location of an object when it has been hidden behind a screen (Baillargeon, 1986). Some researchers have argued that this means that even very young babies must have at least some ability to use symbols

(Mandler, 1988). So Piaget's theory does not in fact give us a satisfactory account of why language appears in the second year of life. Furthermore, there is nothing in Piaget's theory that could really explain how general intellectual development per se could produce the complex patterns we see as children master grammar and word meanings.

That Piaget's theory doesn't explain the development of language does not, of course, mean that the general thesis that we must understand a concept before we can learn the word for it is necessarily wrong. But nor is this thesis necessarily right, either. Some theorists have proposed the exact opposite: namely, that it is through learning the word that we develop a new concept or understanding of the world (Clark, 1973; Whorf, 1952). The evidence suggests that, in fact, we *both* learn words for the concepts we already have, *and* learn new concepts from learning new words, but that in the very first stages of learning language, understanding must come before the word.

Language from meaning

There is strong evidence that babies develop concepts, in other words that they have an understanding of the world, well before they begin to learn to talk. For example, very young babies group things together in ways which imply that they have extracted a general concept covering that particular collection of things (Bomba, 1984). And it is quite clear that the pre-verbal child already has an intelligent understanding of the daily routines and tasks of their lives (Macnamara, 1972). For instance, they take part in simple games ('Peekaboo!' and the like), and their reactions to familiar events such as meals, bathtimes, being dressed and so on suggest that they have a good expectation of what is coming next, and what the point of the activity is. Macnamara (1972) argued that the child's first breakthrough into language *must* depend on this pre-existing understanding of the world. Without any understanding of events, how could the child ever begin to associate particular words with particular meanings? And it is important to note that the child's understanding must be quite subtle, to allow the meaning of a given word to be identified. For example, suppose a mother proffers her child a beaker of milk and says 'tergl' (or some other unfamiliar word). How does the child know whether the word 'tergl' refers to the substance to be drunk, the act of drinking, the beaker, or all of those things? Indeed, how does the child know that the word 'tergl' refers to any part of the interaction at all, as opposed to being another kind of comment altogether (such as 'Wow!', or another emotional expression).

Bruner (1975a) suggested that children develop a good understanding of the characteristics of human interactions, the structure, meanings and intentions behind these interactions, well before they start to learn language, and that it is this understanding which allows them to learn the meaning of words. For example, at around nine or ten months, babies begin to follow another person's gaze to see what that person is looking at, and they begin to point at things themselves and to look back at the other's eye to check that that person is looking the right way (Poulin-Dubois, 1999, and see Chapter 2). 'The joint attention' established by making eye contact with someone else, indicating some object by then looking toward it and pointing at it is the prerequisite for, and the start of real communication between an infant and another person (Butterworth, 1991).

Ten-month-old babies understand pointing in two senses: instrumentally ('I want that') and demonstratively ('Look at that'). Now they are well placed to understand that a word uttered in the context of pointing probably refers to the object of mutual attention, and so they are able to connect that word with its meaning. Babies understand their first words at about this time, and produce their first word shortly afterwards.

A baby's first word is often not a conventional word, and is usually poorly pronounced, hard for anyone but the doting parents or a keen researcher to identify. For example, my son's first word was 'awa', which he used to mean various plants, but particularly those in bloom. This word probably wasn't his own invention (as some babies' first words are) so much as his best effort at saying a word he had often heard: 'flower', the middle part of which sounds very like 'awa'. Like most babies, he seems to have picked out and learned the part of the word where the emphasis falls (**flow**er). We can say that a baby really has produced a *word* rather than simply a noise when he or she uses one particular sound consistently to mean the same thing, or the same collection of things. Most of the first words children produce are nouns (Nelson, 1973; Gentner, 1982), as one would expect if their first insight into language came from understanding the dynamics of shared attention and pointing at things. Infants learn new words very slowly at first, taking several months to get a vocabulary of around ten words (Nelson, 1973). Gradually, vocabulary starts to expand faster, with the child reaching fifty words at around eighteen months on average, and having a vocabulary of several hundred words by the second birthday. And as their vocabularies grow, infants achieve an important insight: that objects, actions (and people) have *names* (Vygotsky, 1962). This insight leads to another breakthrough: the child begins to ask what things are called, rather than working everything out individually.

One thing that is quite interesting about children's early learning of nouns is illustrated by Figure 3.3. This is a picture of two 'glugabubs' and three 'plarks'. Which are the plarks? Like a small child you have almost certainly decided that the two 'birds' are glugabubs, and the three 'mammals' are plarks. But you *could* have decided that the three creatures looking to the left were the plarks, or that the three with black legs were plarks. Like us, babies take nouns to refer to the whole object rather than to any component part or transient feature. This makes learning nouns so very much easier that some researchers have suggested that it reflects an innate bias. Such a bias may be nothing to do with language per se. Rather, it may reflect the far more general tendency to see things as *wholes* rather than breaking them down into component parts or features (Koffa, 1935; Slater, 1997).

Once a child has learned a number of nouns, an understanding of human actions and interactions can also lead to the discovery of other parts

Figure 3.3 Two glubalubs and three plarks

of speech, such as verbs (Bruner, 1975a; Pinker, 1984). For example, suppose you know the word 'banana', you know the word 'Mummy', and you hear a sentence with an unknown element in the middle: 'Mummy *is eating* a banana'. If you can see Mummy *in the act of eating* a banana at the same time, and understand the basic idea that human speech refers to current events, you are well placed to identify the new part of the utterance as referring to your mother's *actions* on the banana, and hence learn the meaning of the verb. There is some evidence (Bruner, 1975a) that adults may help infants to make the correct deductions from such experiences by modifying their intonations (stressing the word 'eating', for example, and only using simple active sentences like my example, rather than more grammatically complex ones such as 'The banana is being eaten by Mummy'). By twenty-four months, infants are very good at inferring the meaning of verbs from understanding the dynamics of human actions in this way. For example, if a researcher holding a Mickey Mouse doll says 'Let's dax Mickey Mouse', and then does *two* things to it, one apparently by accident (and saying 'whoops!' to reinforce that) and the other apparently deliberately (and saying 'There!' to underline that), twenty-four-year-old infants will take 'dax' to refer to the deliberate action and not the accidental one (Tomasello and Barton, 1994; Tomasello, 1995).

Some researchers suggest that a progressively sophisticated understanding of the dynamics and structure of social interactions is sufficient to explain how children learn not just the meanings of nouns and verbs, but also the whole structure and rules of grammar (Bruner, 1975a). For example, understanding who is doing what to whom as mother eats a banana can be mapped onto the structure of the sentence which describes this event to reveal the grammatical word order for active English sentences: *subject, verb, object*. But many theorists believe that this cannot be the whole story of how children learn grammar. The structure of human interactions simply doesn't provide enough information to allow a child to discover all the subtle complexities of grammar.

One solution to this conundrum is the suggestion that infants are innately pre-programmed with at least some grammatical structures (Pinker, 1984, 1987), so that in some sense their brains are *expecting* to discover things like nouns and verbs and rule governed relationships between them. Pinker argues that understanding the meaning of a whole sentence activates the child's innate grammatical expectations: the *subject, verb and object* of the sentence are identified in terms of the innate expectations that such categories of word exist. Now the child is in a powerful position to start learning grammar properly. The innate grammatical structures include the expectation that, for example, some verbs are transitive and so must have an object (like the verb 'put': *she was putting* is not grammatical, while *she was putting the coat away* is), while some are intransitive and have no object (like the verb 'sleep'). Understanding meanings, mapping meanings onto innate grammatical structures and noticing how verbs with different meanings have different grammatical properties gives the child the basis for beginning to explore the specific grammar of his or her mother tongue (Pinker, 1984, 1987). Pinker calls this process 'semantic bootstrapping'.

That children can make discoveries about grammar through understanding the meaning of words and sentences seems very likely. However, some researchers have suggested that not all meanings can be discovered from understanding the events to which sentences refer (Gleitman, 1990). Many scenes can be described in different ways, using different verbs, for example 'the goose chased the hen' or 'the hen fled from the goose', which refer to the same event. One could not deduce the meaning of either sentence simply by observing the event. Here, specifically linguistic cues, such as word order or the use of the word 'from' indicating an intransitive verb which has no direct object, can help to make the meaning of the verb apparent. Gleitman argues that children not only learn about grammar from discovering meanings, but learn about meanings by drawing inferences from grammar, through a process of 'syntactic bootstrapping'.

The suggestion that children must understand the meaning of what they see and experience before they can identify the meaning of words is almost certainly right. It is also very likely that understanding the structure of meaning in the sentences they hear gives children a route into understanding grammar, as Pinker suggests, and also that understanding something about syntax in turn helps the child to identify word meanings, as Gleitman argues. Both semantic and syntactic bootstrapping processes occur not just in infancy, but right through childhood and into adult life as we encounter new ideas and new forms in language. However, the extent to which there is an innate basis for grammar is far more controversial.

Are We Innately Programmed to Learn Language?

That language must have some sort of innate basis is beyond dispute. As we have seen, language is specifically a human thing, part of our species endowment. And as we saw in Chapter 2, there is a great deal of evidence that babies are born innately predisposed to attend to language and to respond to it as something special. Newborn babies are attracted to speech and prefer it to other types of sound (Aslin, Pisoni and Jusczyk, 1983). Very shortly after birth, they can distinguish between their own mother tongue and another language (Mehler, Lambertz, Jusczyk and Amiel-Tison, 1986), implying quite a focused attention to the patterns of language. Newborn babies imitate the lip and tongue movements they see on adult speakers' faces, and will imitate vowel sounds (Kugiumutzakis, 1993).

Obviously, babies cannot be born with a predisposition to learn any one particular language. The data suggest that, in fact, they are 'ready' to learn any of the possible languages they may encounter. For example, young babies can 'hear' and tell the difference between all the phonemes that appear in every human language, and they produce all these sounds in their babbling, even though the adults around them can neither distinguish nor use all those phonemes. The classic example is the 'l' sound, which does not occur in Japanese, and which Japanese adults have enormous difficulty in either hearing or pronouncing. Japanese babies can easily discriminate the 'l' sound, and produce it spontaneously in their babbling.

Babies are strongly disposed to babble. From the first month of life, they start to produce repetitions of vowel sounds ('aaaaaaaaaaa!' for example). From about five months of age they begin to add consonants to these sounds, producing syllables such as 'ma' or 'da' (Bates, O'Connell and Shore, 1987). The same syllable is often repeated over and over: 'wawawawawawa', for example. Babies babble to themselves, alone in their beds, as well as in company with other people. There seems to be a strong drive to make sounds, to make patterns in those sounds, and to try different things out. And although this babbling at first includes all the phonemes ever found in human language, it gradually shifts toward the sounds typical of the infant's own mother tongue. By about nine months of age, the ability to discriminate and produce other sounds disappears (Mehler and Dupoux, 1994; Werker and Tees, 1984).

Even more intriguingly, there are some data which suggest that babies may be innately programmed to be sensitive to the grammatical structure of language. For example, Jusczyk *et al.* (1988, quoted in Karmiloff-Smith, 1992) found that four-month-old babies raised in an English-speaking environment could detect certain grammatical structures, *not just in English*, but also in *Polish*, a language they were not familiar with at all. By the age of six months, babies have lost this sensitivity to all but the language they hear spoken around them.

Thus there are very strong grounds for supposing that there is at least some innate preparedness for language in the newborn human. What is less clear is exactly what form this preparedness takes.

The problem of grammar

Up to about eighteen months of age (on average), infants produce only one word at a time. These single words may carry the meaning of a whole sentence, so that 'chocolate!' may mean 'Give me some chocolate', or pointing at a coat and saying 'Jack' may convey 'That's Jack's coat'. At this stage of learning to talk, infants are obviously not producing anything reflecting the syntactical structure of language in their speech. But they are already *sensitive* to that structure: for example, they can use word order in telling the difference in meaning between, say, 'John hugs Mary' and 'Mary hugs John' (Hirsh-Pasek *et al.*, 1988).

Somewhere between eighteen and thirty months, infants begin to use two words together, for instance: 'Daddy gone', 'Where doggie?' or 'Simon hat?' These sentences are very simple. Nonetheless, they already show a sensitivity to grammatical constraints. They already reflect grammatical rules, for example for word order, found in adult speech. Young infants produce grammatical forms such as 'little cat', rather than ungrammatical ones such as 'little it'. And from the earliest two-word utterances, infant speech is rule governed: it shows certain typical structures and forms, and these are found in all languages (Slobin, 1979).

Furthermore, the errors infants make in speaking are not random. Look back at Figure 3.2. The errors in the first few examples reflect overgeneralisations of grammatical rules. Such errors are typical of young children's speech (Brown, 1973). They suggest that from very early on, infants attend to grammatical rules and try to apply them. Extrapolating the usual rule for making a past tense ('I push/I pushed', 'I kiss/I kissed') yields the mistakes typical of the young child: 'I go/I goed', I sit/I sitted' and so on. Extrapolating the usual rule of adding an 's' sound to make a plural ('shoe/shoes', 'apple/apples') yields errors such as 'tooth/tooths', or 'sheep/sheeps'. And overgeneralising from regular adjectives ('small/smaller') to irregular ones creates 'bad/badder', 'worse/worser'. This focus on grammar is universal: all children, learning all languages, show the same sensitivity, and the same types of errors.

Now, the puzzle for researchers is this: where does the infant's evident focus on grammar come from? What drives it? This question dovetails with one which is implicit in work on semantic and syntactic 'bootstrapping', namely: how is it possible for a child to learn all the subtleties and complexities of grammar? Could a child possibly deduce the rules of grammar from understanding the meaning of words and the events to which they relate? Or do babies have an innate 'head start' in the form of preset expectations about grammatical structures? And if they do have such preset expectations, why does it take so long for babies to learn the basics of grammatical speech?

Understanding the origins of our grammatical skills is the key to understanding the development of language. For it is the existence of rules for structuring words and combining them with other words in constrained ways which gives language its infinite flexibility and power of communication.

Chomsky's theory

One of the most influential theorists on child language has argued that the rules for grammar are wired into human brains as part of our innate biological endowment (Chomsky, 1975, 1980). Of course, different languages have different grammatical rules, which seems at first to refute Chomsky's theory. Chomsky suggests that in fact, human beings are born with a 'universal grammar' which prepares us to expect and discover any of the possible principles of grammar which may exist in any natural human language. One language differs from another in relatively few ways. Experience with their own mother tongues allows infants to 'choose a setting' for each of the parameters on which one language differs from another.

Chomsky argues that the young child's focus on rules for combining and modifying words, and the regular patterns we see in the development of language across children are evidence for the existence of an innate mechanism for discovering grammar. McNeill (1970) described this mechanism as the 'language acquisition device'. According to Chomsky, mastery of all the intricacies of grammar would not be possible without such an innate mechanism, because the experience of language which the young child is given is simply not adequate to allow the deduction of anything so complex. It is the language acquisition device which prevents even very young speakers from making certain types of grammatical error. The child is not *learning* grammar at all: rather, he or she is using examples from adult speech to set the parameters appropriate for the relevant language. Chomsky explains the timing of language development and the lengthy delay in the infant's first production of anything grammatical as due to maturational processes. That is to say, Chomsky argues that every step in the mastery of language is controlled by a preset developmental programme which unfolds at a certain pace, determining when each next step will be taken.

How plausible is Chomsky's theory? Many researchers agree with the main principles of this explanation of how children learn language, but many others don't. Critics of Chomsky's ideas argue that it is next to impossible to adequately specify the principles of the supposed 'universal grammar', or the parameters differentiating one language from another. How plausible is it that something so complex could be an evolutionary 'given' in our brains? And Chomsky's emphasis on language as the product of maturational processes predicts far less variability in how children acquire language than seems to occur (Maratsos, 1983). Furthermore,

Chomsky's claim that language must be innately specified because adults do not teach children grammar, and children's linguistic experiences are too simple to allow them to learn grammar for themselves may be wrong, as we shall see below.

Do Children Construct Language for Themselves?

Until very recently, the majority of researchers believed that children must have at least some innate representation or expectation of the grammatical structure of language (Chomsky, 1980; Pinker, 1984). But new and more detailed studies of young children's speech suggest that this may not be so. Babies may be born with no innate mechanisms for learning grammar at all (Lieven, Pine and Baldwin, 1997; Tomasello, 1992, 1998).

As we have already seen, there is very strong evidence that babies are born predisposed to find language attractive and interesting and to imitate speech-like sounds and mouth movements. And they are powerfully predisposed to be social, to treat other people as something special, and to interact with others in certain ways (Tomasello, 1999). More generally, as we saw in Chapter 2, babies are very well equipped to monitor the world around them, to notice new things and to recognise familiar patterns of events. Some researchers suggest that these basic skills and predispositions are enough to account for the development of language, and that there is no more specific innate factor contributing to the acquisition of grammar (Lieven, Pine and Baldwin, 1997; Tomasello, 1998).

One key factor supporting the idea that children must have innate processes for mastering grammar was the observation that they overgeneralise rules and so produce errors like 'wented', 'sheeps', 'badder'. Such errors were taken to imply that young children were mapping specific words (went) onto innately given representations of parts of speech (verb) and extrapolating rules from one verb to another on the basis of this mapping. But recent more detailed studies of young children's speech show that generalisations of this sort are not as common as we used to think (Lieven, Pine and Baldwin, 1997). In fact, children seem at first to learn each specific word or group of words as a separate, concrete unit. Each verb is learned separately, and what has been learned about one verb is not generalised to another verb (Tomasello, 1992).

Researchers such as Tomasello and Lieven suggest that in fact, young children have no representation of the parts of speech at all. They have no expectations of categories such as noun or verb, as Pinker (1984) suggested, and do not identify such categories as they learn to speak, still less formulate abstract rules for grammar. Rather, they gradually construct utterances from the specific concrete words or phrases they have learned. The infant's first two-word sentence ('where daddy?' for example) may be learned as a specific, concrete whole unit. As other related concrete phrases are learned ('where milk?' 'where sock?' and so on) the child gradually abstracts a more general template for now *creating* new utterances around a key word: 'where . . . ?' This abstraction owes nothing to grammatical processes or insights per se. It is a reflection of the child's very general cognitive ability to detect patterns and regularities. But the creation of such a template provides the child with a frame into which new words can be slotted to create utterances which have *not* been concretely learned by rote (Lieven, Pine and Baldwin, 1997; Tomasello, 1998).

Detailed diaries of infants' speech suggest that early language is gradually built up around verbs, each of which is learned separately, and each of which becomes a key word in a template with several slots to fill (Tomasello, 1992). For example, learning *Mummy eating banana* provides the template 'X eating Y' into which any other words the child has learned can be inserted. Entire phrases learned as specific concrete wholes ('hungry mummy' or 'lots of beans', for example) can be put into these slots, so gradually building up more and more complex utterances. Although these more complex utterances may, from an objective point of view, contain subclauses and sophisticated grammatical structures, there is no sense in which these grammatical structures are represented in the child's mind, nor any need for grammatical principles to play a role in generating the utterance. In fact, some researchers suggest that even adult language may be *constructed* in this way, rather than reflecting any process drawing on a representation of grammatical rules per se (Lieven, Pine and Baldwin, 1997; Tomasello, 1992, 1998). Perhaps only trained linguists actually represent the grammatical structures of language at any level.

Of course, children do make errors of overgeneralisation ('wented', etc.). But these errors occur *after* the child has already been producing the correct version of the word (saying 'went', for example). This pattern of events suggests that children do initially learn irregular verbs (and other parts of speech) concretely by rote from their experience of hearing adults talking. It is only later that they begin to generalise from one verb to another. Such overgeneralisations need not imply any specific focus on grammatical rules per se. Rather, they may reflect the very much more general cognitive tendency to extract generalisations from a collection of concrete examples (Bruner and Kenney, 1965).

This new approach to understanding how children learn language makes language far less of a special, separate process than is implied by Chomsky's theory. It integrates language with the child's general cognitive and social processes. And in stark contrast to Chomsky's theory, this approach suggests that young children's everyday experience of language is sufficient to allow them to learn to produce grammatical speech.

Learning to Talk through Social Interactions

Infants are highly predisposed to be social, as we have already seen in this chapter and in Chapter 2. By about two months of age, a baby interacting with a familiar adult partner looks very much like someone taking part in a 'conversation'. Infant and adult take turns to 'speak' as if replying to one another's comments (Trevarthen, 1993b). The pair watch each other's faces and copy one another's expressions (Stern, 1985). The baby makes speech-like sounds, and in turn the adult either repeats these back or speaks in a simple, repetitive, sing-song way (Trevarthen, 1993a). Such interactions have all the characteristics of real conversations except an actual linguistic exchange. Bateson (1979) called them 'proto-conversations'.

What exactly is happening during such proto-conversations? Some researchers (Reddy, Hay, Murray and Trevarthen, 1997; Trevarthen, 1993a, 1993b) believe that the infant is actively engaged in a real social interaction, a real communication with the adult partner. Other theorists have suggested that in fact, the baby has no real intention of that sort. Rather, adults interpret slight gestures from the child *as if* they were interactive and respond accordingly. From this point of view it is the adult who creates the turn taking and the appearance of responsiveness, by matching his or her behaviour to that of the child (Schaffer, 1984). This issue is still controversial. The likelihood is that infants do have some predisposition to take part in such proto-conversations. But much more interestingly it is clear that adults are strongly predisposed to take part in proto-conversations with babies too *and that their behaviour in so doing encourages and shapes the baby's behaviour toward a conversational exchange.* And that is just as true whether the baby starts out intending to interact with the adult or not.

Our adult tendency to take part in proto-conversations with babies is far from the only way we help children master language. Adults speak to children in special ways quite different from normal adult to adult speech. In talking to a baby or small child, we use *'motherese'*. We speak more slowly than normal, in a higher pitched voice, using very short, simple sentences and making much clearer pauses at the end of sentences (Jacobsen, Boersma, Fields and Olson, 1983). Sentences in motherese are more grammatically correct than is usual in everyday speech. There is a strong tendency for the adult to repeat things a number of times, and to repeat back what the infant has said. There is a tendency to expand and correct what small children say in repeating things back to them: for example, the child says 'teddy hat!' and the parent replies, 'yes, that's teddy's hat'. Adults speaking to children use a small and simple vocabulary referring to events or people which are immediately to hand.

One of the most interesting things about motherese is that most people don't have to learn to modify their language to speak to babies in this way: it comes naturally. In fact, it is almost impossible to inhibit the urge to use motherese! Child-rearing gurus at one time frowned on motherese, believing that showing children such simplified speech would retard their mastery of language. But the evidence is that nothing could be further from the truth. The simplified forms, direct reference and repetitions of motherese are ideally shaped to help a child make the first connections between events in the world and word meanings, and to build up simple concrete phases in the way described by Lieven and Tomasello.

Adults gradually modify their motherese, using the child's progress as an indication of when to step up to a slightly more sophisticated form of speech in talking to the child or in repeating back better versions of what the child has said. By this means they gradually lead the child to more complex and correct forms of language. This type of symbiotic interaction between adult and child is a powerful support to the child's learning, both taking into account the current level of skill and stretching toward the next (Wood, Bruner and Ross, 1976, and see Chapter 7).

Through the sensitive interactions described here adults undoubtedly do teach children a very great deal about language, although their intention may be more to encourage interactions than to teach language per se. New studies are exploring in more detail exactly how far the language children hear through motherese can account for their early efforts and progress. We will have to wait for the results to be sure, but it seems likely that such social interactions can indeed provide a rich enough input for learning language if one is constructing it from concrete building blocks (Lieven, Pine and Baldwin, 1997, Tomasello, 1992) as opposed to trying to fathom the abstract rules of grammar.

Correction and Self-correction in Learning Language

Figures 3.4 and 3.5 illustrate several interesting phenomena about child language: on the one hand, children can be remarkably impervious to correction over their grammatical mistakes, whether the would-be corrector is an adult (Figure 3.4) or another child (Figure 3.5). On the other hand, they are remarkably interested in *getting language right* (as the six-year-old in Figure 3.5 shows). The conversation quoted by Bee (1989) is really a debate about language itself, an early excursion into linguistics.

Child:	*Nobody don't like me.*
Mother:	*No, say 'nobody likes me'.*
Child:	*Nobody don't like me.*
Mother:	*No, now listen carefully, say: 'Nobody likes me'.*
Child:	*Oh! Nobody don't likes me.*

Figure 3.4 The child's resistance to linguistic correction
Source: McNeill (1970).

This interest in getting language right is manifested right from the start of the infant's learning to talk, first in improving pronunciations, and then in expansions which improve on an utterance, for example: *'Want more. Some more. Want some more'* (Braine, 1971). Such expansions are called 'replacement sequences', and may make up quite a large proportion of the child's utterances between twenty-four and thirty months (Anisfeld, 1984). These early self corrections probably reflect the sheer difficulty of producing language. For instance, the longer sentence *'want some more'* may be too difficult to produce all in one go, so the child *builds it up* from smaller segments (Anisfeld, 1984).

If children are so concerned to get language right, why are they so impervious to corrections to their grammar? Chomsky and his followers argued that this was because the child is not *learning* grammar from other people so much as priming an innate programme for producing grammatical speech. For Chomsky, grammar develops according to an innate agenda, and not as the result of tuition. But this is not the only possible explanation. If children learn about language primarily from others, and construct grammatical utterances bit by bit in the way Lieven, Pine and Baldwin

6-year-old:	*It's worse to forget to feed them.*
3-year-old:	*No, it's badder to feed them too much.*
6-year-old:	*You don't say badder, you say worser.*
3-year-old:	*But it's baddest to give them too much food.*
6-year-old:	*No it's not. It's worsest to forget to feed them.*

Figure 3.5 Children's interest in linguistic form
Source: Bee (1989).

(1997) and Tomasello (1998) suggest, then in a profound sense they are not learning about grammar per se at all. It may be hard for children to fit grammatical corrections into the concrete usages they have already learned, if they have no representation of grammar per se.

Very young children find it hard to explicitly reflect on language. They begin to extract general principles (like the rules for making a plural: one wug, two wugs). They become, by about three or four years of age, fairly fluent speakers. But even four- and five-year-olds have difficulty in thinking about language as a thing in its own right, or thinking about the structural features of language (Karmiloff-Smith, 1992). For example, children of this age can use the words 'the' and 'table', but they will say that 'the' is not a word, though 'table' is (Karmiloff-Smith, 1992). And young children have difficulty in understanding that names are arbitrary symbols, as opposed to being in some way reflections of the objects they represent. Even six-year-olds can be stumped by questions like: 'What sounds would cats make, if they were *called* dogs?' (Osherson and Markman, 1975). These young children's efforts with language are aimed at making better or more accurate sentences, in other words, at achieving what Karmiloff-Smith calls 'behavioural success' in speech. But they do not make self-corrections suggesting any real reflection on the structural or grammatical properties of language per se (Karmiloff-Smith, 1992).

Metalinguistic awareness (that is, the ability to directly reflect on language) starts to develop at about six years, and continues right through childhood and beyond (Karmiloff-Smith, 1992). Six-year-olds begin to correct their own utterances (and other people's, as figure 3.5 shows) to reflect strictly linguistic criteria, and by the age of ten, children may be able to articulate very clearly why they have used certain words rather than others. Karmiloff-Smith (1992) gives this example: an experimenter hides a child's watch and then asks the child what she did. Six-year-olds may make self-corrections like this, in replying: *'You hid my wat . . . the watch'*. Ten-year-olds may say *'the watch'* from the outset. Karmiloff-Smith quotes one ten-year-old's explanation of why 'the' is better than 'my' watch:

> Well . . . *'my* watch' because it belongs to me, but I said 'you hid *the* watch' because there are no other watches there. If you'd put yours out, I would have had to say 'you hid *my* watch' because it could have been confusing, but this way it's better for me to say 'you hid the watch' so someone doesn't think yours was there too. (Karmiloff-Smith, 1992)

Both the self-correction of the six-year-old and the comment of the ten-year-old in this example reflect a degree of awareness of the way specifically linguistic considerations convey meaning, an awareness which is not evident in younger children. Between six and ten, this awareness has become very explicit. However, metalinguistic awareness continues to develop well beyond the age of ten, fostered not only by the child's own efforts but by explicit teaching of grammar in schools. It can be patchy even in adults: for example, you use subjunctives easily in your speech. Can you define what a subjunctive is?

How and why does metalinguistic awareness develop? Karmiloff-Smith (1992) argues that intellectual development as a whole always involves first getting a particular skill right and then reflecting on it, discovering patterns and regularities and so making explicit what was implicit in the structure of the skilled performance. Each new level of skill mastered provides the basis for new reflections and new discoveries, which themselves feed into changes in the child's skill, in a recursive cycle. In a real sense, the beginnings of metalinguistic awareness provide the child's first step into an explicit representation of the rules governing the shape and structure of language, in other words into grammar.

Communicating with Language and Theories of Mind

Right from their earliest words, babies use language to communicate their needs, ask for things, point things out, complain, solve problems, control others. And as we have seen in this chapter, there is a sense in which the infant's understanding of the structure and dynamics of social interactions is almost certainly critical to their ability to first identify word meanings and break into the language game (Butterworth, 1991). But do infants understand that they are communicating with another mind like their own? In other words, do they have a 'theory of mind'?

Understanding that others have minds, and that they have mental states such as beliefs, desires, feelings and intentions is vital to a full and proper adult social interaction. Imagine what it would be like trying to have a relationship with a being that had no such mental states. However good such an entity was at responding like a human being, you would be interacting with something more like a mechanical device, a robot, rather than a living entity or a person. The fact that we believe that our mothers or our partners, say, *feel love* for us, *want* to be with us, *believe* that we are worthwhile is what makes relationships with them valuable. The fear that some important other *does not* have such sentiments toward us is a major cause of human misery. It is our understanding that other people, and even in a more limited way pets such as cats and dogs have feelings, desires, beliefs and intentions which makes our interactions with them have the special quality of social interaction and communication.

The power of an understanding of minds and mental states is made clear by studies of autistic children and adults. These individuals are very poor at all forms of social interaction and communication (see Chapter 8). Their language development is either very delayed, or almost non-existent. Their non-verbal communication is equally poor, so that (for example) they don't make eye contact as normal individuals do, and they neither interpret nor produce other forms of communicative gestures or body postures (Mash and Wolfe, 1999). Autistics also perform very poorly on all tests of their understanding whether people have mental states. It may be that this inability to understand other minds is the primary deficit responsible for the strange a-social world of the autistic (Baron-Cohen, Tager-Flusberg and Cohen, 1993).

Some researchers have suggested that the discovery that other people have minds may be the key factor in the development of efforts to communicate, first through shared attention to objects, joint attention, pointing and the like, and then through language. But this idea is problematic. It is true that babies produce their first words at about the same time that they discover that they can share attention with another person (Poulin-Dubois, 1999), and they undoubtedly use words to get people to do things for them. But shared attention and using language to control others need not imply that the child understands that others have minds, or even that they themselves have minds (Poulin-Dubois, 1999). For example, if I say 'fetch!' and turn my head to 'point' it at something, the brighter of my two dogs will look in the same direction and retrieve an object lying roughly where I was looking. This same dog will fetch *me*, by barking till I follow him, for example to discover his water bowl is empty if he is thirsty. No one suspects him of understanding that I have a mind, or of having any thought as to what my mind might be like! Of course, human language is a great deal more subtle and sophisticated than barking. Could children learn to talk without understanding that others have minds, or that they are communicating with another mind?

Measuring children's understanding of mental states

When do babies realise that they themselves, or others, have minds? This is a surprisingly hard question to answer, and one which has generated a great deal of research and controversy. The problem is: how can we tell whether babies understand that others have beliefs, desires, feelings, intentions? What evidence would we need, to say that they have?

A great deal of the young infant's behaviour seems to suggest that he or she does know at least something about other minds. As we've seen, a baby of nine or ten months will look to see what someone else is looking at

(Butterworth, 1991), and by eighteen months, infants will pull away hands covering another person's eyes, if they want to show that person something (Lempers, Flavell and Flavell, 1977). At this age, infants will point things out to someone else just once, rather than repeatedly, as if they understand that the other person will know about it after seeing it once (Flavell and Miller, 1998). At about this age, too, infants recognise and respond to different emotional expressions in others, and will comfort another child who seems distressed (Flavell and Miller, 1998), or will do things apparently deliberately aimed at annoying other people (Dunn and Munn, 1985). All these types of behaviours seem to suggest at least some understanding that others have feelings, see things, know things, and some researchers take this as evidence that even at eighteen months, the infant does have at least a rudimentary grasp on the existence of minds and mental states. However, this view is controversial. Other researchers argue that none of these behaviours necessarily requires any such understanding. For example, the baby does not need to know that the mother *feels* happy to recognise that a happy expression on her face bodes well: this connection could be learned more mechanically, from noticing the association between events and the mother's expression (Perner, 1991). Equally, learning to share attention with someone else is a powerful basis for interacting with the world, but it does not necessarily imply that the infant understands that the other person *knows* what he or she is looking at (Poulin-Dubois, 1999). A robot could be programmed to respond to cues from the direction of looking, without having any representation of what it then 'saw', still less what the other saw or understood.

A more stringent criterion for saying that children recognise the existence of minds would be to provide evidence that they understand that the *state of the world* can be different from the *state of the mind*. Understanding this would, necessarily, imply that the child understood that minds exist, and something about the character of the mind. But what evidence do we need to say that children understand this distinction?

Leslie (1987) argues that 'pretend play', where an infant pretends that a cup is a boat, say, or that the arm of a chair is a horse must involve such an understanding. To engage in pretend play, the infant must know that objective reality (that the object to hand is a cup) and subjective reality (that it is a boat) are different. So Leslie argues that once infants begin pretend play at around eighteen months, they must have some understanding of the existence of minds.

Few researchers would agree with Leslie's conclusions (Harris, 1991; Perner, 1991). Pretending that a cup is a boat must certainly imply that the child has two models of reality at the same time (that the object is a cup, and that it is a boat). But Leslie's critics argue that understanding that there can be alternative versions of reality does not necessarily mean that the child understands that one of these 'realities' is a state of mind, or that minds exist at all (Perner, Leekham and Wimmer, 1987). Both might be construed as alternative states of an outer reality.

Perner and his colleagues have developed various ways of testing whether or not children understand that people have mental states. A classic type of study involves a child watching the experimenter hide some chocolate. A boy called Maxi also sees this, and then leaves the room. In his absence, the experimenter retrieves the chocolate and hides it somewhere else. The child is then asked where the chocolate really is, and where Maxi will think it is when he comes back (Wimmer and Perner, 1983). Answering this question correctly requires the child to understand the difference between the real state of the world (where the chocolate is) and Maxi's mental state, that is his belief (where it was originally hidden). The child must also realise that Maxi's mental state, rather than reality, will determine where Maxi will search. This type of task is called a 'false belief' task. Typically, three-year-old children fail in tasks like this, whereas four-year-olds succeed (Wimmer and Perner, 1983; Perner, Leekham and Wimmer, 1987).

What can we conclude from this developmental change in children's response to the false belief task? One interpretation is that three-year-olds don't understand that others have mental representations of the world that direct their behaviour, and that can be different from reality. But this is not the only possibility. For example, it may be that three-year-olds are less used to dealing with 'hypothetical' tasks like this, which are not connected with the child's own interests and activities, and so simply fail to take the task seriously. Or the younger child may misinterpret the question 'where *will* he look . . . ?' and take it that the experimenter meant to ask 'where *should* he look . . . ?' (Siegal and Peterson, 1994). Or three-year-olds may be more influenced by where the chocolate really is than where Maxi thinks it is because reality is more salient than Maxi's false belief. After all, they have *seen* where the chocolate is, but must *infer* what Maxi thinks, which is more effort (Flavell and Miller, 1998). In sum, three-year-olds might fail in tasks like this for many different reasons besides a lack of awareness of other's minds.

The problems of just how to study children's theories of mind and how to interpret different types of data are areas of continuing controversy, and are among the biggest issues for research in developmental psychology.

Developing a theory of mind

It is most unlikely that children have *no* understanding of mental states at one minute, and a good understanding the next. Rather, this understanding must come on gradually, bit by bit. Understanding what the human mind is like is a complex, multi-faceted process. For example, understanding that people have feelings is quite different from understanding that they have beliefs. And we can understand each of these things on many different levels: in everyday life we need only a sketchy grasp on how minds represent reality, or how emotions work, compared with the elaborate detail with which psychologists hope to answer these questions.

Exactly how children's theories about minds develop is still unclear. There are literally hundreds of studies on the subject, and many disagreements between researchers as to what is or is not a good measure, or how the data we have should be interpreted, as we have seen. However, it is possible to sketch a provisional account of development.

Infants come to recognise that people have desires and emotions well before they understand that minds also have beliefs. Even before their second birthday, children will talk about desires and emotions (Astington, 1993; Wellman, 1993). A very detailed analysis of infants' spontaneous conversations shows that comments about desires and feelings first start at about eighteen months, and that by about two years of age children use these terms in ways which imply that they have a degree of real understanding that these are mental states, distinct from reality (Bartsch and Wellman, 1995). In fact, any demand ('I want') for something not available at this moment implies some such distinction. Bartsch and Wellman also found evidence that two-year-olds already know that what one person desires may be different from what another wants.

Experimental studies confirm that children have gained some real understanding of desires by the age of two. For example, they understand that how people feel reflects the relationship between what they want and what they get (Hadwin and Perner, 1991; Yuill, 1984). They know that people are pleased or happy when they get what they want, and sad or angry when they don't.

This early understanding of desires and emotions is quite sophisticated, in that two-year-old children already understand that people are motivated by these feelings, and that their actions reflect these motivations. But their understanding is also quite limited, in two ways. First, the range of emotions and desires that two-year-olds understand is initially small, and the kinds of evidence they use in inferring these states is naive (Gnepp and Hess, 1986). For instance, even a four-year-old does not know that disappointed people may hide their disappointment by smiling. Such understanding is still weak at six years, and increases up to age ten years. And second, at two years of age children may know that others have desires and feelings but they do not yet understand that these mental states involve beliefs about the way things are or the way things might be. They refer to desires, rather than beliefs, in explaining why they or someone else did something.

Children first start talking about beliefs at about three years of age (Bartsch and Wellman, 1995), and begin to differentiate between intentional and unintentional actions (Shultz, 1980). But their understanding of these things is shaky (Astington, 1993). For example, three-year-olds confound intentions and desires: they seem not to understand that desires can be met by chance, rather than by intention. They don't understand that intention and desire are different things, and can only really identify some action as deliberate when it fulfils a desire. Only at the age of four years is there the start of an understanding of intentionality as involving a plan, as distinct from a desire.

Three-year-old children do quite poorly on tasks designed to measure false belief, as we have seen (Perner, 1991), whereas four-year-olds perform much better. In effect, three-year-olds behave on such tasks as if they did not know that another person can have beliefs which are different from reality, and that these false beliefs will direct that person's behaviour, while four-year-olds appear to understand these things. Different ways of measuring this all achieve the same result. For example, the classic false belief task involving Maxi and the moved chocolate produces the same age effect between three- and four-year-olds as tasks where the child might be shown a box which has every appearance of being a chocolate box, but in fact contains pencils. Three-year-olds expect others to know what they know about the contents of such a box (that it contains pencils), where four-year-olds realise that others will expect the box to contain what it appears to contain (chocolates) until they themselves get a chance to look in it. Furthermore, four-year-olds are far better than three-year-olds at doing things to deliberately create false beliefs in others: misleading them as to where an object is to win a game, for example (Russell, Mauther, Sharpe and Tidswell, 1991).

Thus, even if there are questions about the way the results of false belief tasks should be interpreted, it is clear that there is some sort of major developmental change between three and four years in children's ability to recognise false beliefs in others. The four-year-old's knowledge is, at the very least, more robust and more certain than the three-year-old's. This understanding of other minds as having beliefs that influence their behaviour continues to grow through childhood, and into adult life (Frye and Moore, 1991). For example, even at eight or nine, children are only just beginning to understand how pre-existing beliefs affect how others interpret ambiguous events. And even in adult life, our understanding of others' beliefs and their relation to behaviour is still growing and changing, as anyone who has had a lover's tiff can probably testify!

How do children first come to discover that others have minds, that they themselves and others have mental states? The truth is that we don't know. We don't even know for sure whether this is a uniquely human thing. For example, some chimp behaviour seems to be aimed at deliberately deceiving other chimps, pretending there is no food when there is, for example, or pretending to leave but hiding and watching another animal (Byrne and Whiten, 1988, 1991). This seems to imply that a chimp understands that another chimp can have a false belief. But even adult chimps have difficulty with the simplest experimental tasks which more directly test whether they realise that another individual can have a false belief, and may solve such problems by learning mechanical associations rather than understanding anything about mental states (Povinelli and Eddy, 1996).

That there is some sort of innate basis for our human understanding of mental states seems very likely. Developing such an understanding fairly early in childhood is characteristic of our species. Those individuals who don't develop this understanding are severely abnormal: autistics, as we have seen, and psychopaths, for example. But the nature of these innate mechanisms is unclear. Leslie (1994) believes that the ability to understand other people's minds reflects the maturation of several different neurological systems, which then provide the child with pre-set mechanisms for understanding various different aspects of minds. This idea is very controversial. And even if there are pre-set 'modules' for processing mental states, we still need a theory to explain how children develop a specific understanding from their experience.

Perner (1991), by contrast, suggests that children's understanding of minds grows out of their developing capacity to represent objective reality. According to this theory, very young children have too little processing power to represent more than one version of reality at a time. So the one-year-old, say, can only represent the present state of events. As they become more sophisticated in processing information, children become able to represent two versions of reality: the past and the present, say. This creates the processing power to allow the child to also represent two alternative versions of the present: *his own*, for example, and *mine*. Thus it is the increasing power of the child's general cognitive processing which lays the basis for representing other minds, and coming to realise that each individual's actions will reflect their own minds and beliefs. Ever growing sophistication in the ability to represent alternative realities creates an ever growing sophistication in understanding the minds of the older child and adult.

Perner's very cognitive account of how children discover minds explains both the limitations on the younger child and the greater prowess of the older individual. But it doesn't really explain how we come to invest our representations of other minds with the warm subjectivity which we experience in our own minds. My experience of *me* is not of a clinical collection of beliefs and motives, but an altogether more organic thing. Harris (1991) suggests that children come to understand that others have minds by introspecting on their own subjective experience of themselves, and then imputing such states to others. This involves mentally 'simulating' what someone else's mental state is like (Harris, 1991). According to this theory, the child's understanding of minds grows through the development of the ability to make better simulations of this kind.

Theories of mind, communication and talking

Human babies are pre-programmed to orient to other people, to imitate them, and to engage in 'proto-conversations' with them, as we have seen in this chapter and in Chapter 2. Thus the earliest bases of communication need not rely on an understanding of other minds or mental states at all. And babies learn their first words at an age where there is little evidence that they understand much, if anything, about other minds. The very beginnings of language may not require much of a theory of mind, either.

And yet, it seems most unlikely that mature language and social communication could develop *without* a growing understanding of mental states and minds – as we have seen in the case of autism. But it would be wrong to conclude that learning to talk necessarily *follows on* from discovering minds. Several studies have shown that language itself plays a role in *developing* the child's theory of mind. For example, children whose parents often talk to them about feelings at age thirty-three months do better than those whose parents discuss such things less, when tested at forty months on false belief tasks and other measures of their understanding of mental states (Dunn *et al.*, 1991). Three-year-olds who take part in many discussions of feelings perform better than those who don't on tasks measuring their ability to infer someone else's feelings at age six years (Dunn, Brown and Beardsall, 1991). And even in adult life, we go on learning more about other people's feelings and beliefs by talking to them. Overall, then, it seems likely that there is a very complex interdependency between coming to understand mental states and mastering language, with each feeding into the other rather than either unequivocally leading the way.

Talking to oneself

Despite its strongly social origins and orientation, not all speech is social. From quite an early age, children talk to themselves, commenting on their actions or anticipating events, giving themselves instructions (Vygotsky, 1962). Two-year-olds playing alone will do this. In young children, this a-social speech may be a reflection of the child's very general tendency to play with language, to try things out. But by about five years of age, children clearly use language to direct their own attention and structure their thoughts and their problem solving (Vygotsky, 1962). The extent to which children talk to themselves out loud gradually decreases until it is comparatively rare, by the age of ten. What was said aloud becomes silent, internalised (Vygotsky, 1962, 1978).

This process of internalising speech raises a number of issues yet to be resolved. Vygotsky believed that speech becomes, in important ways, the medium of our thoughts, the main vehicle through which we understand the world. The child's earliest understanding cannot be based in language, as we have seen, because understanding must precede and provide the basis for the child's first words. But Vygotsky argued that children discover, at around five years, the power of speech in structuring thought and that the process of talking to oneself reflects this discovery.

The idea that language becomes the vehicle of our thoughts has far-reaching implications. Some theorists have argued that the language we speak actually determines the way we see the world, the distinctions we make and the concepts we form (Whorf, 1952). Others refute this idea, arguing that language always reflects our understanding of the world, and grows and changes to reflect the evolution of that understanding. Most likely, language is both shaped by, and itself shapes our minds. But it is not the only factor which shapes how children's minds develop, as we shall see in the remaining chapters of this book.

In Summary

The task of explaining how babies learn to talk is hard. We must explain not only how the child discovers his or her first word, but how this leads on to the development of properly grammatical speech with all the subtleties and complexities that that implies. And it is not enough to say: 'children learn to talk by listening to others talking' (for example), or 'language develops because we have innate mechanisms to help that happen'. We must explain just how it is possible to learn language from experience, or just how it could be that innate processes could contribute to this process.

Recent research suggests that babies are born predisposed to attend to language, to orient to people and to take part in social interactions. Understanding the dynamics of such interactions, and critically the meaning of shared gaze and pointing, gives the child a route into the vital discovery that things have *names*. And learning the names of things gives the child a basis for discovering verbs, for gradually identifying the meaning of whole sentences. Understanding meanings must come before language can begin to develop.

The power of language, its infinite flexibility and variety comes from grammar: from the rules for structuring and combining words to create endless new meanings others can comprehend. For a long time, the dominant theory has been that grammar is so very complex that children could not master it without a very substantial 'leg up' from evolution. It was believed, therefore, that there are innate structures in the mind which somehow prime the baby to 'expect' the particular syntactical structures which characterise human languages, and that grammatical speech develops from mapping meanings onto these innate grammatical expectations. In the past decade, new and more detailed studies of what young children's speech is actually like are undermining this view, suggesting that children have no innate expectations about grammar at all. Rather, these new data suggest that children learn to talk by learning very specific phrases as wholes from what they hear spoken, and then learning to fit these together bit by bit in ways that 'happen' to build up complex grammatical structures without the child having had any intention or awareness of doing so.

The theory that children build up grammatical structures in speech without having the intention of doing so, nor any awareness of what they have done or of grammar per se is fascinating. It has parallels with new theories about the infant mind which we met in Chapter 2, which suggest that babies learn complex motor skills such as crawling or reaching without having the intention of doing that, and with theories about the origins of new ideas in later childhood, which we shall meet in Chapter 7. What makes these ideas particularly interesting is that they explain the complex phenomena of human intelligence in terms of processes that have their parallels in nature as a whole. The origins of the grammatical structure of language are explained in terms of processes similar to those invoked to explain the complexity of an ants' nest, or the intricate physical structures of the human body itself. These new theories are beginning to build up a psycho-biological account of the origins of human intelligence which, for the first time, begins to answer the question which began this book: how can all the sophistication of human intelligence develop in what starts out as a single cell organism, the fertilised egg?

Once language has begun to develop, the child's general cognitive tendencies to look out for patterns and to group things in categories leads first to a focus on getting language right, and later still to an effort to reflect on and look for regularities in language itself. This metalinguistic awareness provides a basis for an explicit understanding of the rules of grammar, perhaps even the first recognition that grammar exists as such at all. If language begins as a tool embedded in the child's concrete actions, it gradually becomes an abstract object of reflection and the means of reflecting on and directing the self, certainly *a* vehicle for thought, if not the only one.

EXERCISES

1 Find a friend who speaks a language that you don't speak. Ask them to try to explain something to you, entirely in that language. Choose something practical, such as how to cook a new recipe (and actually do that together). How much can you learn about their language in the process of cooking? What did you learn? How did you learn it? What sort of clues did you use? What sort of phrases can you now produce in that language?

2 What problems are there in devising studies to check whether the sequence in which children's speech develops is very similar across all social backgrounds? How could we get round those problems?

SUGGESTED READING

For a good flavour of a study of early language:
Tomasello, M. (1992) *First Verbs: A Case Study of Early Grammatical Development* (Cambridge: Cambridge University Press).

For an excellent overview of recent research in language acquisition:
Karmiloff, K. and Karmiloff-Smith, A. (2001) *Pathways to Language: From Fetus to Adolescent* (Cambridge, MA: Harvard University Press, The Developing Child Series).

For a collection of essays on current issues in child language:
Berko-Gleason, J. (1997) *The Development of Language*, 4th edn (Needham Heights, MA: Allen & Bacon).

For a review of work on the development of theory of mind:
Astington, J. (1993) *The Child's Discovery of Mind* (Cambridge, MA: Harvard University Press).

Reasoning and
Remembering

4

If language is one thing that defines the human species, then the ability to reason, to draw inferences and to reach conclusons that 'go beyond the information given' as Bruner (1975b) has put it is another. This ability to analyse the implications of what we know, to extrapolate and to draw conclusions from a few facts and so to uncover new and unexpected ideas is the foundation of all our science, our philosophy, our technology and our culture.

Our human ability to draw inferences is astonishing and impressive. How does such an ability arise in a child? What basic mental processes serve this skill? These issues are explored in this chapter and the next. First: no reasoning would be possible without a basic ability to acquire information about the world and remember it. So let's begin by looking at how memory develops.

The Development of Memory

Right from birth, infants have a powerful ability to *recognise* that some situation or event is familiar, has happened before (Schneider and Bjorklund, 1998). If this were not so, there would be no possibility of learning from experience, since each event would appear to be new, unique, and unconnected with anything else. Recognition is the most basic function of memory. The clearest demonstration that even a newborn baby can recognise that something is familiar is, of course, the 'habituation' study used to test infant perception (for example Slater, 1997; this procedure is described in Chapter 2). A newborn could hardly become bored (or habituated) to a sequence of squares, say, if he or she could not recognise that each successive square was like the ones before!

Does the ability to recognise the familiar change with development? This is rather a hard question to answer. For example, some researchers have argued that babies get better at recognising things as they get older, because whereas a newborn baby may need quite a few trials to habituate to a given stimulus, such as a square, an infant of five months or so may habituate after only one or two exposures to the stimulus (Fagan, 1984). But this difference in habituation need not necessarily reflect a difference in the power of recognition per se. It could equally well be, for example, that the older baby has had so much more time to experience the world than the newborn that the stimuli used in habituation tasks are generally less novel, and so less interesting to the older infant, thus yielding a lower threshold of habituation or boredom.

Some research suggests that children's ability to recognise that they have seen some item in a given context before is as good as an adult's, by the age of four years (Brown and Scott, 1971; Brown and Campione, 1972). Other studies suggest that this is true where the items to be recognised have a fairly simple structure, but that there is still a developmental difference where complex stimuli are involved (Nelson and Kosslyn, 1976; Newcombe, Rogoff and Kagan, 1977). Either way, the young child's powers of recognition are impressive: four-year-olds may recognise over a hundred items as having been present in a given test situation.

Far harder than recognising familiar things, even for an adult, is recalling things (Shepard, 1967). It's not hard to see why this is so: recognition involves comparing some event to one's memory, seeing if it is familiar, or familiar in this context, or not. By contrast, to recall something involves retrieving a memory from wherever it has been stored. In other words, it involves a search of memory to locate that item, and then the reconstruction of the stored material.

There is a clear developmental change in the ability to recall events. Even very young babies can recall absent objects (Baillargeon, 1986). And by two or three months of age, they can recall how to make a mobile move (Rovee-Colier, 1984, 1987). Three-year-old children can recall events that happened nearly two years before (Perris, Myers and Clifton, 1990). And few two-year-olds have much trouble remembering promises made to them, or in deliberately remembering to remind Mother to buy them sweets (Somerville, Wellman and Cultice, 1983). Nevertheless, younger children consistently recall much less in experimental memory tasks than do their elders (Kuhn, 2000). For example, if you show children a tray with, say 12 objects on it, cover it up and ask for recall ('Kim's game'), a four year old might remember one or two items, while an eight-year-old might remember eight or nine (Brown, 1975). The ability to recall things improves steadily between three and twelve years of age. This developmental change reflects a number of different factors.

Knowledge and recall

How much we know about the world has a major effect on what we can recall. It is generally easier to recall familiar things than unfamiliar ones. The younger the child, the less knowledge of the world he or she has, and the smaller, therefore, the range of things which are familiar, and hence easy to recall. For example, memorising a list of animal names may be much harder for a three-year-old who has only just learned these names than for a ten-year-old to whom a wide range of animals have been familiar for years. Effects of this type are not specific to children. Even adults perform more poorly when asked to recall a list of unfamiliar items, compared to their recall for more familiar things (Baddeley, 1976).

A far more powerful effect on memory comes from the specific knowledge that the individual has about the topic or domain in which things are to be recalled. Rich knowledge in a domain leads to a more integrated causal understanding in that area, to the development of powerful ways of structuring and using information (Carey, 1985; Chi and Ceci, 1987). Such 'domain specific knowledge' has a radical effect on how we think in that area, and how we recall things, as we shall see in Chapter 5.

For example, rich knowledge allows an expert in some domain to see patterns and connections which are quite invisible to a novice who lacks that knowledge (Chi, Feltovich and Glaser, 1981; Chi, 1978; De Groot, 1965). The effect on recall is vividly illustrated in recall for the position of pieces on a chess board. If you are new to the game of chess, you will probably recall the exact position of only a few pieces, perhaps about seven (Miller, 1956) and will recall about the same number of pieces however the boards are set up. You will have treated each piece as a separate entity. But if you are an expert, you will recognise familiar and meaningful patterns among the pieces if they are arranged as might occur in a game of chess. You are probably able to recognise seven patterns, and so may well recall the position of all the pieces. But an expert will do just as poorly as a novice in recalling the position of the pieces if they have been randomly placed on the board. Expert knowledge cannot help structure a representation in this case (De Groot, 1965). The fact that children's weaker recall reflects less rich knowledge rather than age per se was clearly shown in a classic study by Chi (1978): child chess experts in her study were shown to recall much more than adult novices to the game.

Overall, the younger the child, the less knowledge he or she will have in any area. On this basis alone we would expect to see developmental changes in what, and how much children recall in any task. Thus in a profound sense memory is not a separate function of the mind, but an integral part of the process by which we process information and store knowledge

(Kuhn, 2000). Traditionally we have tended to think of memory as if it were a box in which we stow things. But as Kuhn points out, this very passive view of memory is not an accurate reflection of the way our minds work. We remember best what we understand best, as any student revising for an exam knows: what makes sense can be learned almost effortlessly, as part and parcel of the very process of understanding it. But what we cannot understand must be bludgeoned into the mind by rote, and is far harder to reproduce at all, let alone in a useful way.

Furthermore, retrieving things from memory involves actively *reconstructing* our understanding, rather than simply locating a stored file. This fact was first demonstrated by Bartlett (1932), who showed that our recall of a story evolves over time, drifting in the direction which makes the most sense to us. His classic experiment involved reading a North American Indian legend ('The war of the ghosts') to British students unfamiliar with the cultural assumptions implicit in the events depicted in this story. Rather than recalling this material verbatim, students recalled the gist, and the content of the gist recalled changed over weeks of repeated recall until the alien elements had been more or less transformed into things more familiar to an English mind.

Memories are not static: they change dynamically, reflecting our changing understanding, so that we revise old memories in the light of new knowledge. Thus children's recall of a display of different length rods presented in a descending series may change from one which in no way reflects the seriation by length present to a recall which does reflect it, some months later, even though the display has not been seen again in the interval (Piaget and Inhelder, 1973). The change in what is recalled comes from the change in the child's understanding of seriation, which retrospectively 'updates' the memory of the display. Despite controversy, this surprising effect has often been replicated (Liben, 1977). And memories are not verbatim: if a character in a story does something which implies using a tool, we assume the existence of the tool, and are very bad at telling whether it was really mentioned or not (Kuhn, 2000).

Deliberate and incidental recall

Powerful as the effects of changing conceptual understanding are on the child's memory, domain specific knowledge is not the only factor contributing to developmental change in recall. There are also clear developmental changes in the ability to recall something *as an end in itself*.

Everyday recall

In normal everyday activities, learning or memorising is very seldom an end in itself. For example, in following a recipe for making stew, the aim is to create the stew, not to memorise the ingredients. Nevertheless, next time you want to make that stew, you may find that you can recall the recipe anyway. In such everyday contexts, memories are almost incidentally embedded in a meaningful, functional pattern of activities and goals, which serve not only to structure our learning in a useful way, but also provide a rich constellation of cues for recall. There is evidence that children can recall things far better in the course of their everyday activities than they can in formal experimental tests of recall. For example, children recall far more of a list when it is presented as a shopping list than when it is presented without any context or purpose (Istomina, 1975). And children are far more likely to mobilise their memories effectively when addressing a problem with personal relevance than when taking part in an experiment with no personal relevance to themselves (Thornton, 1996). Even the use of deliberate mnemonics for recall is more common in meaningful contexts than in pure laboratory tests of memory (Bjorklund and Zeman, 1982). The same is as true for adults as for children: recall is far easier in contexts where we have real goals and purposes (Ceci and Liker, 1986; Saxe, 1988).

Is the young child's everyday recall, embedded in real goals and activities, as good that of an adult? It's hard to answer this question, since other factors (such as differences in knowledge between younger and older children and adults) cloud the issue. However, there is one phenomenon which suggests that there are developmental changes even in recall for everyday events, at least in early childhood. This is the curious phenomenon of early childhood amnesia (Pillemar and White, 1989). What can you recall from the first three years of your life? For most of us, the answer is: more or less nothing (Perlmutter, 1986). For example, Sheingold and Tenney (1982) asked adult students to recall the events on the day that a younger sibling was born. Students who had been three years old or more when the sibling was born could recall quite a lot about that day. But those who had been less than three years old at that time recalled almost nothing. This complete forgetting of early infancy is intriguing. It is not simply a matter of the passage of time: people in their twenties cannot recall the birth of a sibling eighteen years earlier, whereas people in their sixties normally have very clear recall for important events such as the birth of a child, forty years earlier. Two twenty-five-year-olds may have quite different recall of a sibling's birth, as a function of their age when the sibling was born. The probable explanation for this early childhood amnesia is that memories for everyday events are encoded in 'scripts' or stories which depend very much on language (Nelson, 1996). It is as if we must be able to tell ourselves a 'story' about the structure and events of a normal day, before we can encode deviations from this 'script' on special days (Nelson, 1986, 1996). Before the age of three years, the child has too little language to encode such scripts linguistically, and so stores them in some more non-verbal, sensori-motor way. As memory is progressively more influenced and structured by language, these early memories become harder to retrieve, and so are effectively lost (Sheingold and Tenney, 1982; Spear, 1984). Such a developmental change in the way everyday events are encoded might well be expected to influence many aspects of recall in early childhood.

The fact that recall is generally so very much better in the context of meaningful activities than it is in tasks where the sole purpose is to test memory implies that to understand the development of memory properly, research should focus less on lab tasks, and more on how children remember things in natural settings (Rogoff, 1998). This change in the direction of research is gradually coming about, for example, through studies of children's memories for events in their own lives (Johnson and Foley, 1984; Chance and Goldstein, 1984), or studies of recall of material learned in school (Pressley, 1995). Tests of everyday memory give a different picture of developmental change from that provided by lab tasks, so long as the context does not require *deliberate* memorising. But even natural settings often present the child with the need to learn things, and here, the results from lab studies and natural contexts are more in line.

Deliberate recall

Developmental differences in recall are far starker in experimental tasks where material is to be learned deliberately solely for the purpose of recalling it (Flavell and Wellman, 1977) than in everyday contexts. The reasons why young children are particularly poor at recalling things in formal tests of the ability to memorise things are probably manifold.

One likely factor is that young children do not understand the point of memory tasks (cf. Donaldson, 1978). For example, my son (then aged three years) took part in a memory experiment run by one of my students. She showed him a tray with twelve things on it, covered the tray with a cloth, and asked him what was on the tray (this is 'Kim's game'). To my intense embarrassment, he failed to recall even the normal few items one would expect of a three-year-old. He just stared at her and at the covered tray, flummoxed. I took him later that day to buy some shoes. In the car on the way, he said: 'Mummy, why did that lady want to know about the things on the tray?' Ever the psychologist, I asked: 'What things?' whereupon he recalled nine of the twelve items! When I asked him why he had not answered her question at the time, he told me that it was because *she already knew the answer, as she had seen the tray for herself, and could lift up the cloth if she really wanted to know!* And quite right, too. Memory tasks may seem perfectly sensible to the adult mind, but may appear so pointless or absurd to the young child that he or she does not really participate.

But a key factor limiting young children's recall in formal tests of memory is that, even when they understand the aim of the task, they are far less likely than their elders to use effective strategies for memorising and recalling the material in such tasks. For example, suppose I ask you to memorise the list of things in Figure 4.1. What would you do? You might read the list passively, and hope for the best. Far more likely, you would work through the list from top to bottom, *rehearsing* the items as you go (for example kettle, fridge, potatoes! kettle, fridge, potatoes *spoon*! Kettle, fridge, potatoes, spoon, *apple,* and so on). Or you might notice that the list can be simplified by restructuring it into groups of items (a group of vegetables, a group of utensils and so on) and then separately memorising each subgroup. Or you might try to make a single picture incorporating all the elements into one meaningful pattern (for example, visualising a kitchen and placing all the items in it). All of these are effective strategies which would greatly improve your recall of lists such as this.

However, four-year-old children seldom spontaneously use even the simplest of these strategies, namely rehearsing material to be recalled (Baker-Ward, Ornstein and Holden 1984). Whereas only 10 per cent of five-year-olds seem to spontaneously use rehearsal, the majority of seven-year-olds and nearly all ten-year-olds do so (Flavell, 1985). And even where the majority of five-year-olds do spontaneously rehearse material to be recalled, their rehearsal attempts are less structured and less efficient than those of twelve-year-olds (Kunzinger, 1985; Ornstein, Naus and Liberty, 1975).

Why does this developmental effect occur? Flavell (1985) suggested that the very young child simply lacks the capacity to use mnemonic strategies, in other words, that there is a 'mediational deficiency' in childhood, such that children *cannot* use certain mnemonic strategies at certain ages. There is some evidence to support this view: for example, Ornstein, Medlin, Stone and Naus (1985) found that seven-year-olds could be taught to use the strategy of grouping items for recall, but only if all the items to be recalled were visible at once, which reduces the effort needed in learning

KETTLE	FRIDGE	POTATO	SPOON
APPLE	CARROT	DISHWASHER	BANANA
FREEZER	SAUCEPAN	FORK	CABBAGE
BOWL	KNIFE	ORANGE	SINK

Figure 4.1 Items for recall

(we shall return to the issue of memory capacity shortly). However, the bulk of research suggests that even young children can be taught to use rehearsal effectively, and to benefit from organizing a list into groups (Brown, Bransford, Ferrara and Campione, 1983; Kail, 1990). But if the experimenter stops encouraging a child below about eight years of age to use a mnemonic strategy, the child stops using it, and recall declines again (Flavell and Wellman, 1977). Thus there is some sort of developmental deficit affecting the child's tendency to produce a mnemonic strategy (a 'production' deficit). Researchers such as Flavell and Wellman suggest that this reflects the fact that young children have too little knowledge about how their own memories work or what the limitations on their memories are to recognise the power and usefulness of mnemonic strategies, or to understand when and where to use them.

Meta-cognitive awareness

The suggestion that children's poorer performance in tests of memory reflects a lack of understanding of the limitations of memory or the power of mnemonic strategies was a seminal insight. It drew attention to the fact that the proper exercise of human intelligence depends not simply on *possessing* certain mental tools, but on *knowing enough about those tools* to be able to control and deploy them effectively and deliberately. In sum, it depends not merely on *cognitive* processes such as memory, but on the *meta-cognitive* processes which direct them. Put another way, becoming more expert in memorising (or any other cognitive function, such as drawing inferences) requires the child to acquire specific knowledge not just about the material to be recalled, but about memory (or other) processes themselves (Brown *et al.*, 1983; Schneider and Pressley, 1989).

Such meta-cognitive awareness develops gradually. There is evidence that even very young children know that one must do something to help recall. For example, DeLoache, Cassidy and Brown (1985) found that two-year-olds will point to, or repeatedly glance at the hiding place of an object they have been asked to find later (these are both forms of rehearsal). Four-year-olds know that long lists are harder to recall than short ones (Wellman, Collins and Glieberman, 1981). Nonetheless, even seven-year-olds still overestimate their performance in memory tasks, and underestimate the effort needed to memorise things (Kreutzer, Leonard and Flavell, 1975). And seven-year-olds rely more on external strategies to support memory, such as writing things down, rather than on mental strategies, such as grouping like things together (Fabricius and Wellman, 1983).

One source of children's growing meta-cognitive awareness is likely to lie in their own experience. Increasing experience with memory tasks, for example, would clarify how hard such tasks are, and provide the child with a better understanding of the powers and limits of memory. Likewise, experience of particular mnemonic strategies is a source of information about the effect and utility of such things, and the contexts in which they are most relevant. However, it is also likely that the acquisition of meta-cognitive awareness has an important social dimension. Children are explicitly encouraged by others to recall things, and to learn to do so deliberately (Rogoff, 1998; Schneider and Pressley, 1989). Schooling in particular requires children to learn how to memorise things effectively, as an end in itself. It seems highly likely that this social demand is associated with more or less direct support for the development of meta-cognitive awareness and strategies for learning and mental control, as we shall see in Chapter 7.

Does the basic capacity of memory change in childhood?

Despite the power of knowledge and meta-cognitive strategies in structuring recall, there are still grounds for supposing that there may be other, more neurological bases for developmental change in children's memories. The physiology of the brain, and particularly its efficiency in transmitting information continues to mature through infancy and early childhood. Might this not affect the child's ability to store and recall information? Specifically, might such effects mean that there is a physiological change in the *capacity* of the child's memory, through early development (Rabinowicz, 1980; Thatcher, 1992)?

To explore this idea, we need to consider the structure of memory processes. There are, in fact, very many different theories of what memory processes are like, dividing these processes up in various ways to reflect the different functions memory serves. For example, there are some things which we recall for a very long time, such as our teenage adventures, or a poem, or the meaning of words or other symbols. Then again, there are things which we 'hold in mind' for a short while, and rapidly forget. Do these 'long term' and 'short term' memories reflect different aspects of a single process, or do they reflect different processes? Are long term memories all jumbled together in one store, or are there special stores: a 'semantic' memory, say, for meanings and concepts, and an 'episodic' memory for remembering the particular episodes of our lives? These issues are complex, and beyond the scope of this book. But whatever position theorists take on the detail of such questions, there is general agreement that, somewhere, there is a 'central processing unit', or a 'working memory' which can only hold a certain amount of information at any one time. The amount of information this working memory can hold limits the complexity of the problems we can solve. If the demands a task places on this working memory (the mental or 'M demand' of the task) exceeds the capacity of the memory (its mental or 'M space'), we will not be able to hold enough information in mind to solve the problem (Pascual-Leone, 1970; Case, 1985).

An individual's M space can be calculated in various ways. For example, it can be assessed by 'digit span', the number of digits an individual can accurately repeat back (Case, 1985; Dempster, 1985); or by a counting span task, which requires the child to use working memory more dynamically, for example, by counting the number of spots on a card and recalling that while counting the spots on the next card, and so on (Case, 1985). By either method, there is a marked developmental increase in M space through childhood. For adults, M space is about seven items (Miller, 1956). A young child may have an M space of only three items. Digit span as measured in such tasks increases between the ages of three and ten years (Case, 1985; Dempster, 1985).

Some researchers believe that changes in M space account not only for developmental change in memory tasks, but also for developmental change in the range of problems that the child can solve. For example, some studies have shown that one can predict the patterns of children's success and failure in problem solving and memory tasks at different ages by comparing the M demand of various tasks with the M space characteristically available to the child at each age (Case, 1985; Pascual-Leone, 1970). Thus developmental changes in M space could explain why some strategies are simply beyond the child.

What exactly is involved in the development of M space? Is there literally a change in the *physical* capacity of working memory, perhaps some sort of physiological change? Some researchers believe that there is (Cowan, Nugent, Elliot, Ponomenev and Scott Sault, 1999). But many believe that the evidence pupporting to suggest that conclusion can be interpreted in other ways (Dempster, 1985).

In many ways, the idea that there is a fixed M space seems to be contradicted by the evidence. For example, Lindberg (1980) found that children could outperform adults in memory tasks using items familiar to the child but not to an adult, which is hard to understand if the adult has the larger M space. And the amount of information an individual can process, at any age, seems to reflect their expertise with that particular type of information rather than anything else (Chi, 1978), and to vary across different domains of knowledge reflecting relative expertise (Chi and Ceci, 1987). This does not fit with the notion of a physiologically limited working memory space with a fixed capacity. For example, one may be able to hold, say, the position of only seven separate chess pieces in mind on a jumbled board, but be able to recall all of the contents of seven groupings on a list like that in Figure 4.1, which is a great deal more information in absolute terms. This raises questions as to what a 'limited mental capacity' could be. What kind of bucket, for example, could have a *total capacity* of either seven separate drops of water, or seven cups? Fixed capacities ought to constrain the volume of material to be held, and not be affected by the size of the packages it arrives in.

Overall, the notion that there is a physiological limit to mental capacity which changes through childhood does not seem to fit the data, nor to illuminate our understanding of development very much. Case (1985) has tried to deal with the difficulties inherent in the notion of a fixed capacity M space by arguing that greater knowledge and expertise make certain aspects of a task *automatic,* so that they require less attention, or less effort to do. For example, when you learned to write, forming each letter took effort and concentration and involved a number of separate elements to remember (/, then \, then - to make A, for instance). But now, not only do you form each letter as a single unit, but you are unlikely to be aware of forming the individual letters that make up words and sentences at all. The task of writing has become automatic, and takes up less processing effort (M demand) than it did when you first learned to write, so there is more mental capacity (M space) left over for other things.

Case's thesis is interesting, in that it points out that there are developmental changes in the efficiency with which children can process information, and that these changes may influence success and failure across a wide range of memory and problem solving tasks. But it is important to note that the constraint on working memory which Case postulates is not really a physiological constraint on *memory* per se at all: the M demand a child can cope with is not 'set' by a limit on the capacity of working memory: rather, it reflects his or her specific level of experience and expertise in the task in question. Thus, whilst the concept of M space can describe developmental change in performance, it is not explaining anything about why that change occurs: to understand that, we have to look more directly at the child's knowledge and strategies.

Furthermore, since individuals may acquire experience and expertise in different areas at different times, any measure of M space based on, say, digit span cannot predict *individual* performance in any specific task, even if it can predict the *average* performance over many children. The amount of M demand an individual can manage varies from task to task, reflecting knowledge and experience rather than a fixed mental capacity. So measures of M space predict less than they appear to do.

The Development of Reasoning

The ability to remember past events is critical to all learning. Every organism shares some degree of our capacity to learn and remember, though none may share our propensity for remembering or reminiscing as an end in itself. And our ability to use what we recall to draw inferences and reason may be as unique as our language. From gossip to moving ourselves from A to B, from the prosaic to the sublime, we humans employ extraordinary and impressive powers of reasoning. Even in early childhood, reasoning is a crucial part of our lives. Consider this comment, quoted by Deloache, Miller and Pierroutsakos (1998):

> *Laura (three years) removing opened can of soda from refrigerator, to mother*:
> Whose is this? It's not yours 'cause it doesn't have lipstick

Or this impassioned plaint, from a two-year-old child (quoted from Thornton, 1995):

Child (very aggrieved):	Jack broke my car!
Mother:	I'm sure he didn't . . .
Child:	He did! He did! Harry didn't go there [the playroom] – Jack broke my car!

It is revealing and instructive to work out the sequence of inferences implied by these exchanges. And it is equally illuminating to note, for a few hours, the occasions where you or those around you draw quite complex inferences in the course of everyday activities, and what these powers of reasoning are used for.

Where does this ability to reason come from? How can it develop in an infant mind? For that matter, how is reasoning possible at all? What sort of processes do we use to do it? And why does it sometimes go so horribly wrong? How can a species so gloriously intelligent as we so frequently add two and two and make five?

For two thousand years, there has been a general (if rather vague) consensus on the answer to these questions. This holds that there are two types of reasoning: *logical* reasoning and *illogical* reasoning. Logical reasoning is supposedly human reasoning at its best and most powerful, while illogical reasoning is sloppy and poor. This view began with the ancient Greek philosophers such as Aristotle, and still pervades everyday ways of thinking about intelligence. How often have you heard someone criticise another person's reasoning by saying (for instance) 'he just doesn't think logically', or 'that isn't logical'? But everyday conceptions of what it means to say that reasoning is or isn't logical are sometimes based on a misunderstanding of the nature of logic itself. And the very assumption that human reasoning is logical may be wrong, as we shall see.

The Nature of Logic

Suppose I say to you:

> You have to study ten hours a day to do well in a psychology exam.
> Joe is only putting in half of that,
> so he won't do well.

Is my conclusion correct? Is it logical? We have a strong tendency to believe that pieces of reasoning which come to false conclusions are illogical. In the case of my example, many people would argue that the conclusion is wrong, and therefore illogical: there is no reason why Joe should not do well, because (you will be relieved to know!) there is no evidence that one must work ten hours a day to do well in psychology exams. Indeed, my conclusion may well be *factually inaccurate*. But it is nonetheless *logically correct* or *valid*.

Logic is an abstract system of principles for deducing *necessary* conclusions from the information (or 'premises') available. The crux of whether or not a conclusion is logically valid or otherwise is whether or not that conclusion *necessarily* follows from the form of the 'argument'. Here, the form of the argument is:

> If X is true, then Y will occur.
> X is true.
> So Y will occur.

Expressed in this abstract way, it is easy to see that the conclusion (Y will occur) *must* necessarily be true, given those premises. It must, therefore, be logically valid. The factual accuracy of any statement inserted in place of X and Y does not affect the *logical* validity of the conclusion one jot, even if it is plainly untrue, as in this case:

> If birds have green feathers, they can't swim.
> The mallard duck has green feathers,
> so it can't swim.

This 'argument' is logically valid, but factually inaccurate.

Obviously, a process of reasoning which completely disregarded the truth or otherwise of its conclusions would be of little use. It certainly wouldn't be very practical or intelligent! The factual accuracy of the premises 'fed' into a logical argument are always important in determining the calibre of reasoning in real contexts. But the peculiar power of logic comes from the fact that the abstract principles which determine the purely logical value of an argument can be applied in every possible situation. Logic thus provides an extremely general device for drawing inferences in any area of reasoning, and for assessing the validity of those inferences. This feature of logic is what led the ancient philosophers to identify logical principles as the rules for good reasoning. And indeed, it is easy to see how useful it would be to have such a very general basis for drawing inferences.

How could the ability to draw logical inferences develop in children's minds? What does this ability actually involve? How can we study such questions? As with so many areas of research into the development of intelligence, the most influential theory of the twentieth century, which still influences research today, is that of Piaget.

Piaget's Theory of the Development of Reasoning

As we have already seen in Chapter 2, Piaget's theory of cognitive development is enormously influential for two reasons: it was the first theory ever to provide any sort of explanation of how intelligent reasoning could arise in what starts out as a very limited biological entity. And Piaget's descriptions of the way reasoning changes were extremely acute in many ways, and still form the starting point of what other researchers must explain. Even when Piaget's own explanations of the phenomena he noted are wrong, the issues he raised must still be addressed. A full account of his theory is far beyond the scope of this chapter: the book by Margaret Donaldson suggested at the end of the chapter provides an excellent summary.

According to Piaget, the development of intelligent reasoning through childhood reflects the gradual development of logical structures in the mind (Inhelder and Piaget, 1958, 1964). As we have seen in Chapter 2, and will discuss further in Chapter 7, Piaget believed that each child had to *construct* this basic framework of intelligence for him or herself, starting with only a few special reflexes, through the operation of biological processes of adaptation. By *acting* on the world and reflecting on the relationship between actions and their consequences, Piaget believed that the child gradually built up a logical framework for reasoning. This developmental process passes through three stages. The first of these, the *sensorimotor* stage occurs between birth and about eighteen months, and is discussed in detail in Chapter 2. These first eighteen months of life are spent constructing the basic mental structures for perception and memory, coming to see the world as separate from the self, with properties of its own, and to be able to represent and remember those properties in their absence.

Real reasoning begins to develop through the second stage of development, the stage of *concrete operations,* which runs from about eighteen months to eleven years of age. This long period is divided into two sub-stages: the *pre-operational* period and the *concrete operational* period proper. At the start of the pre-operational period, the baby's intelligence is still closely bound up in overt physical actions, such as hiding and retrieving an object, say. Understanding is rooted in physical *doing*. Gradually the child becomes more adept at internalising these actions, that is, at *symbolically* representing or *imagining* an object vanishing and reappearing, say, rather than actually hiding and retrieving it. But although the child can now mentally represent his or her actions and their physical consequences, consciousness and understanding are still limited and fragmentary, because the effects of one action are not related to the effects of another. For example, the act of hiding an object and the act of finding it again are represented as separate, unconnected things. For an adult mind, *hiding* an object is an intrinsically *reversible* operation: things that have been hidden can *necessarily* be unhidden, and vice versa. We understand that the act of hiding can be undone, to recreate the original situation. And because the possibility of undoing or reversing an action is an integral part of our understanding of that action, we can link the present situation (object hidden) with the previous or future situation (object present) and understand the causal connection between one situation and another. The pre-operational child does not represent actions as reversible in this way, and so cannot link one situation or action with another, or understand cause and effect, except on the basis of past experience, a practical demonstration. This is easier to understand if we look at some examples of children's reasoning.

Perhaps the most famous task Piaget used to demonstrate children's reasoning is the *conservation* task (Inhelder and Piaget, 1964). For example: the child is shown two identical glasses, each containing an identical amount of water, and confirms that the amount of liquid in each glass is the same. The child then watches as the contents of one glass are poured into another glass of a different shape: a taller and thinner glass, say. The child is then asked to say whether the amount of water in this new glass is the same as that in the original glass (Figure 4.2). Below the age of six or seven years, children will say that the amount of water in the new glass is *not* the same. They do not have 'reversible mental operations', and so cannot mentally undo the act of pouring the water from one glass to another, and so cannot understand the causal connection between the present situation and the original one. So they cannot understand that the amount of water *must* still be the same, because it has only been poured from one place to another *and could easily be poured back.* Unable to understand the links between how things were before and how they are now, the pre-operational child relies on perceptual appearances to make judgements. Do the amounts of water *look* the same?

Another classic task used by Piaget to demonstrate this same developmental limitation is the *transitivity* task (Inhelder and Piaget, 1958). Here, the child is shown two sticks: a yellow one and a green one. The green one is longer than the yellow. Then the yellow stick is removed, and the child is shown the green stick and a red one, the red stick being shorter than the green one (Figure 4.3). The child is then asked to say which is longer, the red stick or the yellow one? Up to about six or seven years of age, children will say that they can't tell: they have never seen the yellow and the red stick compared. Their problem, according to Piaget, is again the inability to mentally undo actions and so connect one situation with another. The pre-operational child cannot represent the relationship between the yellow and green sticks at the same time as the relationship between the green and red sticks, and so cannot understand the necessary connection between the yellow and red ones. With no direct perceptual comparison to hand, the pre-operational child cannot answer the question.

This inability to mentally reverse actions and understand connections is perhaps most clearly illustrated by Piaget's *class inclusion* task (Inhelder and Piaget, 1964). The child is shown a set of items such as those in Figure 4.4. Seven-year-old children know very well that dogs are animals, and can count up very well how many dogs there are in such a display, and how many animals. But if you ask them: 'are there more dogs or more animals?', children of six or seven will tell you that there are more dogs. Piaget's explanation is that this is because these children can only make one grouping at a time. Once they have assigned the dogs to the class 'dog', they cannot mentally undo that and include the dogs in the larger class 'animals'. Without reversible mental operations, the classes of animal and dog cannot exist simultaneously in the child's mind, and the relationship between them cannot be understood.

At around eight years, children develop reversible mental operations and so are able for the first time to understand how one thing is connected to another. At this age, they start to solve the conservation task, the transitivity task and the class inclusion task successfully, and most significantly, they can explain their answers. It is important to Piaget's theory that all these tasks come within the child's talents at about the same time: he argued that this was because the child has constructed a very general base for mentally reversing actions which is widely applicable. Reversible operations reflect the emergence of a very general logical structure in the mind. For the first time, understanding how events came about allows the child to deduce *necessary logical* relationships between things, rather than relying on perceptual appearances.

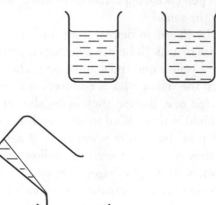

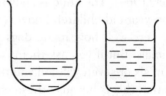

Figure 4.2 The conservation of liquid task, showing the initial state (top), transformation (centre) and key comparison

However, for the eight-year-old, these reversible operations are still very much tied to specific, concrete things (hence the description of this stage as 'concrete operations'). That is to say, logical necessity is understood only where the child can mentally reverse *specific* physical actions. The child cannot yet express the form of a logical relationship abstractly, nor separate it from its specific content. Thus there is as yet no understanding of logical necessity in the abstract. The ability to reason logically is still very limited, therefore: the child does not understand any principles of logic, and cannot reason in an abstract way or handle hypothetical ideas. These things come only in the final stage of development: the stage of *formal operations*, at around twelve years.

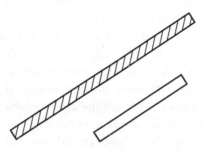

Figure 4.3   The transitivity task: first comparison (top) and second comparison (bottom)

Figure 4.4   The class inclusion task: are there more dogs or more animals?

Evaluating Piaget's theory

Piaget's theory raises a great many issues about the development of reasoning. Does the child's reasoning really pass through *distinct stages,* each reflecting a very general mental structure, and each qualitatively different from the other, as he suggests? Are these structures *logical?* Must each child really *construct* the mental processes supporting such reasoning for him or herself? We shall return to these questions in Chapter 5 and Chapter 7 respectively. Here, we shall focus specifically on two aspects of Piaget's theory: first, the claim that below the age of eight years or so, children do not understand logical necessity; and second, that this is because they are still in the process of constructing logical structures in the mind.

Piaget's own data tried to address both of these questions at the same time. His tasks provide really rather startling demonstrations of how different the conclusions young children reach are from those reached by adults. These demonstrations are very robust: if you do just what Piaget did, you will almost certainly get the same results. If one accepts that these tasks are measures of the ability to reason logically, then his data are a powerful demonstration that the young child does not do so. But can we accept his data at face value?

Success and failure as a criterion

A key difficulty with accepting Piaget's interpretation of his data is that he claims that *success* in a task reflects logical reasoning, while *failure* reflects the inability to reason logically. In other words, Piaget assumes that the main determinant of the child's success or failure in solving the logical problems posed by his tasks is the presence or absence of underlying logical competence.

Now, even a short reflection may lead us to question this assumption about the relationship between success in a task and underlying ability. Sometimes, of course, it is quite correct to assume that failure reflects incapacity. (Earlier today I failed to move a huge flowerpot because I am *unable* to lift such a heavy weight. I simply don't have the muscular power, it is not part of my *competence*). But sometimes failure reflects not so much your underlying competence as other factors, such as your understanding of what is required in the task. The instructions may be unclear, or you may be misled by some feature of the task and so fail to achieve something easily within your competence. (For example, I recently stacked all the dishes in entirely the wrong place in a friend's kitchen. This inept *performance* of what should have been an easy task happened because I forgot precisely what she had asked me to do, and misinterpreted the arrangement of dishes already in her cupboards).

For several decades a great deal of research on children's understanding of logical necessity focused on the question of whether failure in Piaget's tasks reflected a real lack of logical competence, as Piaget argued, or whether it reflected something else disrupting young children's performance and preventing them from using their competence. Many researchers, noting the apparent power of young children's reasoning in contexts that matter to them (such as the issue of *whether Jack broke the car*, quoted earlier) found it hard to accept that children were so inept in reasoning as Piaget supposed (Bryant, 1974; Donaldson, 1978).

A great many studies have shown that even children as young as three years old can succeed in drawing inferences about transitivity, conservation and class relationships in *some* contexts, even if they are unable to do so in traditional versions of Piagetian tasks (Donaldson, 1978 and Gelman, 1980 provide good reviews). Many researchers took this as evidence that Piaget's tests were too hard, and that even young children have far greater competence in logical reasoning than Piaget had claimed. Piaget's tasks were abstract and unfamiliar to children. These critics of Piaget's conclusions created more familiar, less abstract tasks which they felt gave children a fairer chance to show their skills, and found children much more successful (Bryant and Trabasso, 1971; Donaldson, 1978; Light, Buckingham and Robbins, 1979; McGarrigle and Donaldson, 1975; McGarrigle, Grieve and Hughes 1978). But other researchers and defenders of Piaget's work argued that children's success in these modified versions of Piaget's tasks was spurious: that the tasks had been so changed that success no longer reflected the use of logical competence at all (Moore and Frye, 1986; Tollefsrud-Anderson, Campbell, Starkey and Cooper, 1992) .

This debate is largely historic now, but it carries some key lessons for research at large. All efforts to establish a 'definitive' test where success would prove that children had a given logical competence and failure would show that they did not failed in a morass of claim and counter claim (Sophian, 1997). Success in any task need not mean that one possesses any specific competence, and failure need not mean that one lacks any specific competence. Success and failure may always occur for a great many different reasons, and so are not good measures of a child's abilities. The mere fact of success or failure in a task tells us little.

Looking for processes

The one indisputable conclusion of research showing children now succeeding, now failing in tasks involving conservation, transitivity or class inclusion is that *children's performance varies considerably between one version of a task and another*. Success in one version of a conservation task does not predict success in another. In fact, it is quite clear that children's success or failure in such tasks is very vulnerable to the specific details of the way the task is presented or the key question asked. This variation in children's performance across different versions of a task has two important implications.

First, whatever it is that determines their success or failure, *it cannot be logical competence alone*. Situational factors must also be playing a very significant role in determining how the child tackles a logical problem. Piaget's assumption that performance in his tasks reflects underlying competence per se is too simplistic.

In fact, of course, situational factors must *always* influence how and when any competence is displayed, since all competences must inevitably be displayed in some context. There will always be factors determining whether or not we realise that a given competence is relevant *here*, or whether we can see how to apply it. Understanding how competence is *produced* and *applied* is an essential feature of understanding what that competence is. One powerful fruit of the debate about success and failure in Piaget's tasks was the development of much more sophisticated models of what competence is and how it can be used (Gelman and Meck, 1992; Gelman and Brenneman, 1994; Greeno, Riley and Gelman, 1984).

Taking situational influences on the child's success or failure in logical tasks seriously led research to a far more *process* oriented approach to understanding the development of reasoning. By studying the details of when and where young children succeed or fail in tasks requiring any given type of logical reasoning, we can discover a lot about how they reason and what sort of information they do or do not attend to. This process oriented approach moves away from asking *whether* or not a child succeeds in any task to asking *why* or *how* he or she succeeds or fails. It leads to the construction of theoretical models of the range of processes involved in solving logical problems such as the conservation problem (Simon and Klahr, 1995) or class inclusion (Klahr and Wallace, 1976; Trabasso, Isen, Dolecki, McLanahan, Riley and Tucker, 1978). For example, Trabasso *et al.* (1978) produced a model of how a child's performance is affected by how the class inclusion data are encoded, how the key question is interpreted, the processes involved in quantifying the class and subclass involved and in the comparison and decision: a far more multivariate account of the child's reasoning than Piaget proposed. As we shall see in Chapters 5 and 6, this new approach has opened up a whole new understanding of the way we reason, and how such reasoning develops in childhood.

Is human reasoning logical?

Before looking in any detail at modern research into children's logical reasoning, it is worth pausing to query a rather basic issue. Piaget's theory
assumes that the child lacks, and is developing toward, logical structures in
the mind. Critics of Piaget who argued that young children possess logical
competences far beyond what Piaget allows them assumed that the child's
mind is already equipped with logical processes. The key point is that both
Piaget and his critics took it for granted that *logical reasoning reflects logical
processes in the mind.* That is to say, that being competent in drawing logical
inferences would involve the use of logical mental structures.

   In fact, the idea that logical reasoning necessarily reflects logical
processes in the mind is only a presumption. It is not necessarily true.
Many things are made by processes which do not in any way share a structure with the things they produce. For example, the flames that consume a
log in no way resemble the ashes that this combustion process produces
(Thornton, 1995). There is no a priori reason why logical *inferences* should
necessarily be produced by logical *processes* in the mind. And indeed,
studies of how adults produce logical inferences suggest that the mental
processes involved are not, in fact, specifically logical in structure
(Johnson-Laird, 1993).

   Let's think again about the nature of logic. As we saw at the start of this
chapter, the formal rules of logical inference have nothing to say about the
factual accuracy or otherwise of the premises on which they operate.
Applying logical rules gives you an answer which is logically valid, but may
be completely inaccurate. As Johnson-Laird and his colleagues have
pointed out (Legrenzi, Girotto and Johnson-Laird, 1993), human beings
reason and draw inferences in order to make practical decisions and understand the world around them. Mental processes which have no means of
assessing *factual accuracy,* such as would be the case for processes based on
the inferential rules of logic, do not seem very useful in that context. A
priori, then, it seems more likely that human reasoning processes are structured around information and meanings than around the rules of logical
inference.

Mental models and human reasoning

Johnson-Laird and his colleagues have produced a great deal of evidence
which suggests that human reasoning is in fact based on the construction
of mental models reflecting our understanding of the world (Johnson-Laird,
1993; Legrenzi, Girotto and Johnson-Laird, 1993). That is to say, when we
want to draw an inference or make a decision, we use the relevant informa-

tion available to build up a 'picture' of what the situation is, and then use that mental model to draw inferences and conclusions about the relationships between one thing and another. Using mental models in this way allows us to draw both logical and non-logical inferences. Johnson-Laird argues that there are no structures in the mind which reflect the structure of logic per se: all reasoning draws on mental models, even when what this psychological process yields is, from an observer's point of view, 'logical' reasoning.

Take the case of transitive inferences. Adults can solve such problems fairly well. But the evidence is that they do not use mental processes resembling logical inferences in doing so (Potts, 1974). Potts gave participants in his study (college students) information about adjacent pairs of items in six term series such as that depicted in Figure 4.5 (Jane has longer hair than Mary, Mary has longer hair than Sue, and so on). He then asked them to make transitive inferences, just as in Piaget's task, comparing pairs they had not seen together (for example, who has longer hair, Jane or Sue?). With a six term series, the closer together the pair to be compared are, the fewer the inferences needed to reach a conclusion. Comparing Jane and Sue needs only one transitive inference, to establish that since Jane has longer hair than Mary and Mary has longer hair than Sue, Jane must have longer hair than Sue. But comparing Jane and Betty, who are separated by three intervening girls, would need three transitive inferences: one to establish that Jane has longer hair than Sue, one to establish that Sue has longer hair than Betty, and finally one to infer that therefore Jane must have longer hair than Betty. Assuming that it takes time to make a transitive inference, we should expect it to take longer to compare faces far apart in the series (where more inferences are needed) than those close in the series, if the process of solving such puzzles relies on logical inferences. But Potts found that comparisons far apart in the series are made *faster* than comparisons close in the series! This result suggests that even adults cannot in fact be using logical inferences in solving transitivity tasks.

Pott's data suggest that adults actually solve transitivity problems by making a mental picture or model of the series as they learn it, and then by reading off the answer from this picture, rather than by using any process resembling logical deduction per se. For example, the fastest comparison of all is that where the two ends of the series are to be compared. This is the opposite of what one would predict, if logical inference were involved (it should be the slowest), but just what one should predict if people were answering by 'looking' at a mental 'picture': the ends of the series are easiest to find, and therefore easiest to compare, when one is looking at a picture. The most impressive result in Potts' data is that adults can make comparisons between items at the extreme ends of a series (which they have never

Figure 4.5 A six-term series: Jane, Mary, Sue, Kate, Betty and Louise

seen directly compared) faster than they can answer questions about adjacent pairs in the middle of the series, even though they have been directly shown those pairs. This is just what one would expect if someone were reading answers off a picture, but quite incompatible with the idea that the problem is being solved by logical inference.

Johnson-Laird has produced powerful evidence that adult inferences always depend on mental models rather than logical processes per se (Johnson-Laird, 1993). If this is so, then childhood development can hardly be a matter of constructing logical mental structures, as Piaget claimed.

Developmental change and mental models

If adult reasoning depends on the use of mental models, then the development of reasoning through childhood must reflect the growth of the child's ability to create and use mental models (Johnson-Laird, Oakhill and Bull, 1986). This conclusion opens up an entirely new perspective on the origins of reasoning in infancy, and on what it may be that prevents the young child from reasoning as effectively as older children or adults.

Mental models are *representations* of information. As we have seen in Chapter 2, there is good evidence that even very young babies can mentally represent things to some degree. For example, by the age of five months, babies can represent objects and their properties when the objects are no longer visible (Baillergeon, 1986; Baillergeon, Spelke and Wasserman, 1985). But the evidence suggests that infant representations are far simpler than those made by older individuals. As we saw earlier in this chapter, babies and young children cannot hold as much information in mind as can older children and adults, so the mental models they build are not so complex or detailed as those used by older people. Furthermore, the younger the child, the less experience of the world and the less knowledge and information. It may be that young children sometimes don't know enough about a situation to build an effective mental model to use in reasoning. Or it may be that young children's understanding is so bound up in a limited number of specific, concrete experiences that it cannot be easily generalised, and so is only useful in restricted circumstances. For example, eight- to ten-year-old children make models of mathematical problems which are very tightly tied to the circumstantial detail of the particular problems they have experienced (Bruner and Kenney, 1965). This means that these children's mental models cannot be generalised to be used in solving new problems with different details, even though the basic structure of the new problem is the same as before. As the child gains experience of a wider range of problems of that type, across a wider range of circumstantial details, the child is able to build up a 'composite' model combining all the different specific concrete experiences he or she has had with that type of problem. In such a composite model, the things which are constant across situations would gradually become clearer, where the things which are particular to a given example become less important. Thus through experience the child comes to extract the more general, abstract features of a problem, and so can more readily use the model in a flexible way across different and new contexts (Halford, 1993).

Piaget's emphasis on logical structures in the mind led him to pay comparatively little attention to what factual information children have, and how this information is acquired. But the thesis that reasoning depends on the construction and use of mental models emphasises that the acquisition of knowledge and the way that knowledge is structured in the mind are crucial to reasoning, as the brief survey above implies. How conceptual understanding develops, and the effects of different degrees of knowledge on reasoning is the main focus of current research on the origins of intelligence, as we shall see in Chapter 5.

Understanding logical necessity

If even very young children can build and use mental models to draw inferences to some extent, are they able to reason logically, after all? This question breaks down into two separate issues.

First, there is the question of whether or not young children can solve logical problems or draw logical inferences at a practical level. The general consensus is that even pre-school children can in fact construct logical arguments and draw logical conclusions to some degree (Hawkins, Pea, Glick and Scribner, 1984; Komatsu and Galotti, 1986; Miller, Seier and Nassau, 1995; Moshman, 1990), even if the range of situations in which they can do this is smaller than is the case for older children or adults.

But pre-school children do not understand the idea of logic, or have any insight into the properties of logical arguments. For example, they do not understand that some conclusions are *logically necessary*, where others are not (Komatsu and Galotti, 1986; Miller, Seir and Nassus, 1995; Osherson and Markman, 1975). The conclusion that a man cannot be fat and thin at the same time is logically necessary: he cannot be two contradictory things. The conclusion that he is not fat and a lawyer at the same time may be correct, given the facts, but is not logically necessary: there would be no logical inconsistency in a portly lawyer. Young children make no distinction between these two types of conclusion. Indeed, below the age of six years, children do not really even recognise logical inconsistencies of this type: for example, they do not say that there is anything inconsistent in saying that a character in a story is both tall and very short. (Ruffman, 1999).

In effect, then, it seems that the basic ability to draw logical conclusions in situations where the child has enough understanding to construct a useful mental model is present in very young children, but that the ability to explicitly *recognise* logical arguments as such is not. Some researchers believe, as Piaget did, that this latter kind of abstract understanding of logical reasoning develops only in adolescence (Smith, 1993), perhaps emerging from the child's reflections on his or her own reasoning, just as reflections on language develop in middle childhood (see Chapter 3).

However, even adults and adolescents seem to have only rather a tenuous grasp on logic at an abstract level. Like young children, adults and adolescents have difficulty telling the difference between conclusions that are logically necessary and conclusions which have some other basis, such as the balance of probability (Balacheff, 1988; Chazan, 1993; Lee and Wheeler, 1989; Martin and Harel, 1989). And adults often fail to use their understanding of logical necessity in situations where they ought to do so (Evans, 1989; Johnson-Laird and Byrne, 1991). Thus it seems that developing an abstract meta-level understanding of logical principles is not the norm. Even at a practical level, adolescents and adults are not very good at logical reasoning: we make mistakes, and, like young children, are more swayed by factual knowledge than by logical considerations in reasoning (Evans and Pollard, 1990; Evans, Barstow and Pollard, 1983; Evans, Newstead and Byrne, 1993; Oakhill and Johnson-Laird, 1985; Oakhill, Johnson-Laird and Garnham, 1989; Morris and Sloutsky, 1998). It seems that even in adult life, our ability to draw logical inferences varies from one context to another, and is bound up with the concrete specifics of the context, just as in childhood.

It seems that logical reasoning is not a natural feature of the human mind: it is a cultural artefact: a tool which people have invented, and which must be taught to successive generations, rather than developing of its own accord (Luria, 1976, 1977; Vygotsky, 1962). Support for this idea comes from studies of remote rural communities. Where there is no instruction on abstract reasoning , logical awareness does not develop in adults (Luria, 1976; Scribner and Cole, 1981; Cole and Scribner, 1974).

Literacy, formal schooling and the development of logical reasoning

There is an affinity between logic and language. Logical inference involves taking the meaning of certain words seriously: words such as *if, and, or, unless,* and so on. Learning to use these words in ordinary, everyday speech probably helps the child to begin making simple logical inferences in practical contexts, but it does not foster an explicit understanding of the strict force of such words. Everyday language is rather imprecise. Even adult speech is frequently not very grammatical, and we often mean something rather different from the literal force of our words. For example, if I say to you: 'could you lend me your coat?' you would assume that I actually mean: 'please give me your coat for a while', and would answer accordingly. But in fact, if one took what I had said literally, my question asked whether you were *able* to lend me the coat, not whether you were *willing* to do so. In everyday speech we rely heavily on our understanding of the specific context and social dynamics in interpreting meanings. Thus logical inferences based on everyday language are very much tied to, and embedded in the concrete specifics of the situation.

Everyday speech does not lead us to take individual words seriously, *but literacy does.* In learning to read, the child must pay careful attention to the literal words on the page, to the possibilities of alternative interpretations of meaning. And in learning to write, the child must become aware of the structure and rules of grammar. In other words, becoming literate lays the foundation for an analytic, reflective and abstract use of language. This is exactly what is needed for strict logical reasoning. Logic requires us to apply key words in a strictly literal way, without reference to their context. Once one can do that, one can reason logically regardless of the context or content of what one is reasoning about. And once one can reflect on this strict use of words, one is ready for an abstract understanding of logical necessity (Cole and Scribner, 1974; Donaldson, 1978; Scribner and Cole, 1981).

It is easy to see how being formally taught to read and write might lay the foundation for an awareness of logical necessity. But there is some evidence that literacy alone is not enough to evoke much understanding of logic. For example, Morris and Sloutsky (1998) found that only teenagers who had received very direct tuition in abstract ways of reasoning through an experimental teaching programme showed any real understanding of logical necessity. Teenagers going through the normal educational process showed far less awareness of logical necessity, though all were literate. The key thing fostering an explicit understanding of logical necessity in this study was not direct teaching on that subject, but a particular way of teaching algebra, which focused pupils on the abstract principles of algebra rather than starting by teaching from concrete examples (Morris and Sloutsky, 1998). Given the parallels between the formal rules and abstract principles of algebra and logic, it is easy to see how tuition in algebra could foster logical understanding. And given how hard most of us find it to understand and apply algebra, the mystery may be less a question of why human beings are so bad at understanding logical principles, and more a matter of how so many of us manage to grasp it at all!

In Summary

Overall, then, the research reviewed in this chapter shows that to understand the developing mind we must look in detail at the processes by which the mind works, rather than looking at what tasks children can or cannot successfully complete.

Memory is not like a box into which we put things: it is a process. What we can learn or remember depends on what we understand, and on how we structure or make sense of information. Developmental change in memory reflects developmental change in what children know, and in how they make sense of the world and their own mental processes, rather than change in the basic underlying processes of memory.

Likewise, studies of the process of reasoning show that inferences depend on our understanding of the world, on the mental models we can build rather than on abstract logical principles. The development of reasoning reflects the development of the child's conceptual understanding. More abstract, formal types of reasoning such as logic are cultural tools, induced by schooling.

EXERCISES

1   How could you test the theory that a four-year-old child is just as able as an adult to remember everyday events? What methodological problems would this pose?

2   What possible explanations might there be for a young child failing to recognise that someone cannot be tall and short at the same time? How could you test those explanations to see which apply?

SUGGESTED READING

For a review of research on memory development:
Schneider, W. and Bjorklund, D. (1998) 'Memory'. In: D. Kuhn and R. Siegler (eds), W. Damon (series ed.), *Handbook of Child Psychology*, vol. 2: *Cognition, Language and Perception* (New York: Wiley).

For an excellent overview of Piaget's theory (in the appendix) and a good survey of his early critics:
Donaldson, M. (1978) *Children's Minds* (Glasgow: Collins/Fontana).

For a flavour of modern experimental research on children's understanding of logical necessity:

Ruffman, T. (1999) 'Children's understanding of logical inconsistency'. *Child Development 70*, pp. 872–86.

For a collection of essays on reasoning, logic and mental models:

Johnson-Laird, P. and Shafir, E. (1993) *Reasoning and Decision Making* (Amsterdam: Elsevier Science).

Conceptual Development and Reasoning: a New View

5

Suppose I asked you to build a robot that would think and reason like a human being. Where would you begin? One thing is immediately obvious: the robot would have to have some way of taking in information from the world, making sense of it and using it to solve problems, reach insights and make new discoveries. Your difficulty would lie in working out effective ways to let it do these things, ways which were not fixed and static, but could grow and improve with experience. Our problem in studying children's minds is to understand how these problems are solved in human intelligence.

This comparison between a robot and a human mind raises a very important question: to what extent is human intelligence specifically *human*? Some theorists, most notably Piaget (1967, 1968) believed that all intelligence must necessarily rest on certain logical principles, and that therefore every intelligent being, whether human, animal, alien or robotic would necessarily function in more or less the same way. This view is no longer accepted by many people. In fact, the more common view now is that the overall structure and processes of human intelligence may turn out to be unique to our species. As we have seen in Chapter 4, the overwhelming evidence is that human intelligence is not based on any sort of abstract general principles so much as on the specific knowledge and understanding which our experience generates, and on the mental models we build of our world to reflect that understanding. And as we saw in Chapters 2 and 3, the roots and origins of our knowledge lie in our biological inheritance, in the ways our perceptual and memory systems are set up from birth to acquire and store information, and in the interaction between this biology and the specific activities and goals we pursue.

This insight into the origins and nature of mental processes raises a new question for an account of how intelligence develops. Piaget's view that intelligence reflects logic, which we all accept as 'clever', was comfortable in that the origins of our cleverness seemed obvious (we were logical). But the new view suggests that our intelligence has no such 'fancy' basis. How can the apparently ordinary psychological mechanisms of perception, memory and the accretion of knowledge lead the child to the powerful reasoning processes characteristic of the adult mind, and the rich phenomena of reasoning?

Perception, Memory and Reasoning

Some of the very basic functions we are born with – such as the ability to perceive the world around us, to recognise certain things as familiar, to learn new facts and new connections between things and to remember what we have learned – are shared to some extent with most other species, even if the specifics (such as whether one can see colour or infra-red, what shapes one can discriminate; what kinds of information one can remember, and how much; exactly how one learns) may vary between one species and another. Without very basic processes of this type, no animal could interact adaptively with its environment at all. In designing an intelligent biological system, the obvious place to start is to build on these very basic functions. And so it is in nature.

Even the apparently very simple mental processes of recognising similarities and recalling previous experiences and events provide some remarkably powerful tools for intelligence. For example, recognising that a given situation has generally been associated with food in the past, and that another has been associated with something bad happening allows even birds to learn to anticipate events and to take the correct action, securing the food or avoiding the disaster. Learning of this type gives even mice a primitive response to the balance of probability: a situation which is *always* associated with disaster is avoided absolutely, where one which is *sometimes* associated with disaster and *sometimes* with food is treated quite differently (we shall come back to the effect of such learning in children in Chapter 6). Recognising that there are similarities between one situation and another allows an animal to *generalise* behaviours to the new context, rather than having to learn afresh in each situation. And human beings take simple perceptual and memory functions a step further, to provide powerful general tools for reasoning and decision making.

Heuristic reasoning from perception and memory

Which kills more people: asthma or plane crashes? Statistically, the answer is asthma, but most people believe that plane crashes cause more fatalities.

This is an example of a systematic bias in human reasoning. Human reasoning shows many such biases: it often fails to correspond to the principles of probabilistic or logical analysis (Evans, 1989; Johnson-Laird and Byrne, 1991; Johnson-Laird, 1993; Johnson-Laird and Shafir, 1993; Kahneman, Slovic and Tversky, 1982; Kahneman and Tversyky, 1973; Tversky and Kahneman, 1973). Understanding how these systematic biases come about reveals the way we ordinarily draw inferences.

For example, the tendency to overestimate the frequency of plane crashes comes from the way we use our memory as a basis for inference. Other things being equal, it is easier to remember things that are common or frequent than to remember things that are rare or unusual. You can undoubtedly recall the school you went to more easily than you can recall a school you visited once for a sports match. This bias in memory toward easier recall of the common or familiar is so powerful that studies of how memory works have to take care to control for the familiarity of the items to be recalled to avoid biased results (Baddeley, 1976). And it seems that we use this memory bias in drawing inferences: since frequently experienced things are easier to recall, we infer that things that come easily to mind must be more frequent than things which are harder to remember. Kahneman and his associates called this the *availability heuristic* (Kahneman, Slovic and Tversky, 1982). Normally it works quite well, and provides us with a useful rule of thumb in estimating how common or likely something is. But memory is affected by other things besides how frequent or familiar things are. For example, something shocking or very vivid is very easy to bring to mind. These other influences on memorability can mislead us into believing that rare but vivid events (such as plane crashes) are far more common than they really are.

Another example of a heuristic inference process uses the way we perceive similarities as a basis for drawing inferences. In formal systems such as logic, categories are supposed to be defined by specific principles or criteria. That is to say, membership of a category such as 'dog' should be defined by possession of certain critical features, such as having fur, four legs and a tail and barking. But our perceptual systems do not ordinarily recognise category membership in that way: a bald three legged dog who has lost his tail and never barks is still recognisably a dog, albeit an unhappy one!

In fact, Rosch (1978) has shown that we normally recognise the members of a category by comparing them to our prototype or stereotype of what members of that category should be like. For example, for most people, a Labrador or a collie better fits the stereotype of a dog than, say, a dachshund or a chihuahua. In deciding whether some new individual is a dog, we compare it to that stereotype. The more the new individual resembles the stereotype, the more sure we are that it really is a dog (Figure 5.1). So, in a way, even *recognising* things involves a sort of inference: *if it looks like a typical elephant, it is an elephant.* Extending this simple perceptual process only slightly provides what Kahneman and his colleagues call the *representativeness* heuristic: if it looks like a member of the category X, assume that that is what it is.

Figure 5.1   Three dogs
Source: Thornton (1995).

As with the availability heuristic, the representativeness heuristic is normally a very useful and accurate basis for inference. But as with the availability heuristic, it can lead to biased reasoning in certain circumstances. Take the case of the room containing seventy doctors and thirty musicians. If one individual leaves the room, the objective statistical probability is that it is a doctor, since there are so many more of them than musicians. If adults are told nothing at all about that individual, they will use statistical probabilities to judge his or her profession. But if they are told anything at all about that individual (that he has long hair, say, or is wearing a psychedelic waistcoat) people ignore the statistical probabilities and use the representativeness heuristic, and since the information given here is more like our stereotype of a musician than of a doctor, most people would guess that it was a musician. Interestingly, adults will ignore the statistical probabilities and try to use the representativeness heuristic even where the information given about the individual in question is irrelevant to either stereotype (such as that he has blue eyes, or is six feet tall). The representativeness heuristic doesn't cue either profession here, so people infer that the individual is equally likely to be a doctor or a musician, despite the clear statistical probability that he is a doctor (Kahneman *et al.*, 1982).

Kahneman and his colleagues have identified quite a number of inference heuristics deriving from basic psychological processes in the same way as do the availability and the representativeness heuristics. Even highly educated adults, including those trained in formal logical or probabilistic reasoning use heuristics such as availability to draw inferences, and this is true even where more formal mathematical or logical procedures should be used (Block and Harper, 1991; Kahneman *et al.*, 1982; MacLeod, Williams and Berkian, 1991; Schneiderman and Kaplan, 1992). Heuristic reasoning extrapolating from memory and perception is characteristic of adult intelligence.

Is heuristic reasoning rational? Certainly, it can lead us into a variety of errors, and very probably contributes to some of the less attractive prejudices to which our species is prone. But it is important not to overestimate the extent to which such reasoning causes mistakes, nor to assume that logical or probabilistic reasoning would result in fewer errors of judgement. Heuristic reasoning is not illogical. Rather, it is quite different and independent from logic, working in a quite different way. Heuristic inferences provide a systematic basis for reasoning which in most contexts is functional and useful. It is 'rule of thumb' reasoning, which gives no guarantee of a necessarily correct answer as there would be, if we used a more formal logical basis for reaching a conclusion. But the rules of logical inference are concerned only with the legitimacy or otherwise of a deduction. Correctness is only a matter of whether the rules have been correctly followed, in such systems. So logical and probabilistic reasoning are only as good as the facts to which they are applied: there is no means within these systems of testing the truth or otherwise of those facts. Heuristic reasoning has the advantage of being rooted in our experience and understanding, and therefore is directly based in what we believe to be true. It draws very directly on the content of our knowledge, and since our knowledge tends to represent the way the world is in our experience, more or less, heuristic reasoning is generally effective and practical in everyday contexts.

The development of heuristic reasoning

Knowledge and understanding change dramatically as an infant passes through childhood. A three-year-old has not had the time or experience to build up stereotypes of doctors and musicians, and will have different vivid memories from an older child or adult. So even if very young children make judgements through heuristics such as availability or representativeness, they will probably come to different conclusions, and show different biases than their elders. But do they in fact make heuristic judgements in this way at all?

Kahneman and his associates argued that heuristic inferences are automatic and involuntary, a natural part of the way our memory and perceptual systems work and that these inference processes are hard to inhibit in favour of more sophisticated strategies. On this basis, we should find that even very young children use heuristics such as representativeness and availability, and indeed, we might expect them to do so to an even greater extent than adults (Fischbein, 1975; Ross, 1981). But this is not the case. Six-year-olds are very much less likely than older children to use either the representativeness heuristic (Jacobs and Potenza, 1991), the availability heuristic (Thornton, 1996) or other everyday inferential heuristics identified by Kahneman (Krouse, 1986). This is a surprising result, and worth considering further. Given how simple and natural these heuristics seem, what restricts the child's use of them?

If you ask college students *are there more mice or more ducks in cartoons**? and then ask them to recall as many as possible of each category, you find that those who say there are more mice subsequently recall more mice, and vice versa. This is the availability heuristic at work. Eight-year-olds behave in much the same way as adults, but younger children don't: they are very good at remembering ducks and mice from cartoons, but the judgements they make before doing so are not biased toward overestimating

---

* I have no idea what the correct answer is. What do you think? How did you come to that conclusion?

the more easily recalled category (Thornton, 1996). This is not a unique finding. If you read out a number of names, listing an equal number of male and female names but using very familiar names for one gender (Nelson Mandela, for example) and unfamiliar ones for the other (Jane Black, and so on) and ask adults whether there were more male or more female names, they will systematically overestimate the number of the gender represented by the familiar (and therefore more memorable) names (Kahneman, Slovic and Tversky, 1982). With children, of course, one cannot use politicians' and celebrities' names in this task, since these may or may not be familiar to young children. One substitutes the names of the child's school classmates for the familiar names. Again, eight-year-olds spontaneously show a bias toward overestimating the gender represented by familiar names, indicating the action of the availability heuristic, but younger children do not (Thornton, 1996).

Obviously, then, heuristic reasoning drawing on the properties of perception and memory is not automatic, as was initially supposed. Even such very basic everyday inferences processes must be *invoked* somehow. But do these data mean that young children *cannot* draw inferences in this way? Do the data mean that we have to learn how to use our basic psychological processes to draw inferences?

The youngest children tested for their ability to use heuristic inference processes so far are five- and six-year-olds (Thornton, 1996), so we do not yet know whether very young children can reason on this basis or not. But the evidence is that five- to six-year-old children *can* use heuristics such as availability, if something in the situation cues them to recall the things to be compared before making their judgements, or if they have a special reason to pay attention to the task in hand. For example, six-year-olds show no availability bias in judging which gender is more numerous on a list of names including their schoolmates as the familiar names, if asked to make the gender judgement *as an end in itself*. But 90 per cent of these children show a strong availability effect if they have a personal interest in the list of names: if the list tells which children will be included in those who will get a treat, for example (Thornton, 1996)!

The implication of these data is that, to understand the development of reasoning, we must focus on *how* skills are brought into play as much as on *what* skills the child has, even when the skills in question are apparently very simple, and very tightly tied to the child's basic perceptual and memory processes. It seems that young children do not automatically mobilise their memories or other mental processes in the service of reasoning as older children and adults do. We shall return to this issue in Chapter 6.

Knowledge and Reasoning

The inference heuristics identified by Kahneman and his associates are very general tools for reasoning. The same tools can be applied across all contexts and all sorts of information, even though the results they yield are highly dependent on the specific knowledge or information to which they are applied. But there is increasing evidence that knowledge itself can create new mental tools.

Studying the content of children's knowledge

How can we know what a child, or an adult for that matter, knows about a given topic? This methodological question becomes increasingly important, if we want to understand how changes in what an individual knows influence the development of reasoning.

One way to find out what knowledge an individual brings to a task is to analyse the task itself. For example, suppose we want to know what a child understands about what happens when scales balance. Here, there is a fairly circumscribed universe of factors that are potentially relevant, and it is possible to list all of them: balance is a function of the interaction between the amount of weight on each arm of the scale, and its position from the fulcrum. We can break the knowledge relevant to the task down into sub-elements: knowing about the effect of weight on balance, knowing about the effect of position on balance, knowing about the interaction of these factors. We can then build predictive models of how an intelligent system would behave if it had all, or only some elements of this knowledge. By comparing the predictions this model makes with the actual behaviour of children of different ages, we can *diagnose* what knowledge the child is using in the task. This type of *task analysis* has produced powerful insights into how children's understanding and behaviour changes, as we shall see below (Siegler, 1976).

But not all the knowledge we need to assess in understanding what children know can be explored through task analyses of this sort. Some kinds of knowledge, such as the child's conception of what it means to be alive or how biological systems work are very open ended: it would be very hard if not impossible to list all the elements which might make up an individual's understanding at any one moment, or to make diagnostic predictions a priori, in such a rich domain of knowledge. For example, young children may hold theories which are quite unexpected to an adult, as this question quoted by DeLoache, Miller and Pierroutsakis (1998) shows:

Tristan (three years): Why doesn't my blood come out when I open my mouth?

As DeLoache *et al.* point out, this question makes sense to a small child who knows that his body is full of liquid (blood) and that liquids pour out of holes in containers (such as his mouth), but it is hardly an idea which would have occurred to you or I to ask a young child about. Finding out how children think in rich, open ended domains such as their knowledge of biological processes needs a far more flexible approach than task analysis, involving the painstaking diagnosis of children's understanding of specific things from what they spontaneously say, the comparisons they make, the things they treat as the same or different, the things they accept as right or wrong. Whereas task analyses are driven by the structure of the task in which children's behaviour is to be studied, diagnoses of understanding in richer and more variable domains must be more directly driven by the child's own behaviour. An excellent example of this type of research can be found in Carey (1985).

Information and the construction of strategies

What a child knows can affect not only what conclusion he or she reaches in solving a given problem, but also how the child reasons in reaching it. The classic demonstration of this effect is a study by Siegler (1976, 1981) of children's behaviour in solving balance task problems.

Siegler used a balance scale such as is shown in the examples in Figure 5.2, where each arm has a number of pegs on which weights may be placed. The arms are supported by blocks, and the child is asked to say whether the scale will balance or not when the blocks are removed. Developmental changes in children's understanding of balance lead children of different ages to use different rules in solving such balance problems. Five-year-olds know little about balance, and use the simplest rule. They judge whether the scale will balance or not entirely on the basis of whether the amount of weight on each arm is the same. By contrast, most eight-year-olds know that the distance of a weight from the fulcrum is also relevant to balance, but they don't understand how the two factors interact. These children use a more complicated rule, starting out by looking to see if the weight on each arm is equal as a five-year-old would. If it is, then they look at the distance from the fulcrum of the weights, before making their prediction. But if the amount of weight is unequal, they ignore distance and judge solely on weight. By the age of fourteen, most children understand that both weight and distance must always be taken into account, but they do not understand how to do this when the amount of weight suggests that one arm will be heavier, but the distance from the fulcrum suggests that the other arm may be. These children simply guess at the answer in such cases, but can solve problems where weight and dis-

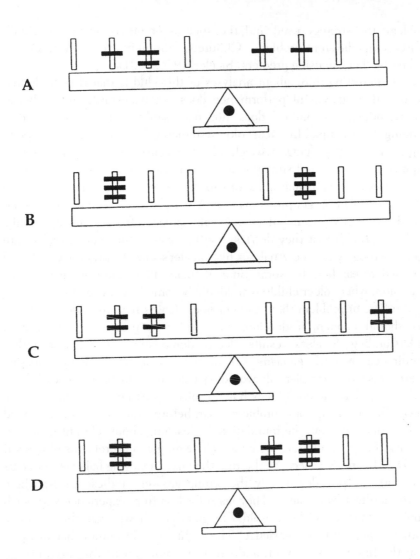

Figure 5.2 Balance scales
Source: Siegler (1976).

tance can be handled separately. Few adults in Siegler's studies progress beyond this point to the most sophisticated rule, which is based on an understanding of how to take the cross-product of weight and distance from the fulcrum into account (Siegler, 1981). Three-year-olds in Siegler's studies knew too little to use any rule at all.

The power of this kind of analysis becomes apparent if you look at the pattern of success and failure one would predict for each type of rule, across different types of balance problem, Differences in what the child knows at different ages affect the factors taken into account in solving the problem, the strategy used and the success or otherwise of the child's efforts across different problems. Children of different ages perform exactly as the rule they are using predicts (Siegler, 1976, 1981).

One interesting thing about analyses of this kind is that they underline the fact that successful performance does not necessarily reflect better understanding, and failure does not necessarily reflect poorer understanding. For example, five-year- olds systematically get problems of type C (Figure 5.2) right, judging by weight alone, because they do not realise that distance is relevant and simply ignore it. In effect, they systematically get the right answer with such questions for the wrong reasons. Fourteen-year-olds are less likely to get problems of type C right, because they understand that distance is relevant but cannot calculate its effect. Knowing (unlike the five-year-old) that they don't know the answer, they guess, and so are right or wrong by chance. Analyses like Siegler's solved a mystery which had intrigued researchers for some time: in many tasks there is an apparent regression, where older children suddenly become less successful in solving a given type of problem than younger ones. It was hard to understand why this should happen, if development involves a progressive increase in understanding. Siegler's results clearly demonstrate how better understanding can result in *knowing that you don't know*, and hence in guessing where a discarded simpler rule would have accidentally been successful.

Knowing that you don't know how to solve a problem may make you less successful in solving some problems than before. But recognising the need for new discovery lays the foundation for learning about relevant factors in the task. Five-year-olds are systematically wrong about problems of types B and D in Figure 5.2, because the rule they use in solving balance problems systematically provides exactly the wrong answer in these cases, where weight is offset by distance. They learn far less from experience with such problems than do eight-year-olds. Siegler has shown that this is not a matter of age, but of knowledge. The eight-year-old knows that distance from the fulcrum is relevant, and can learn more about that from experience. The five-year-old does not suspect distance to be relevant, pays no attention to it and so learns nothing about it from experience. But five-year-olds can be taught to attend to distance as a relevant factor, and will then learn as much as an eight-year-old. Equally, eight-year-olds can be taught the cross product rule, and so perform better than the average adult (Siegler, 1976). It is information and not age which determines the child's performance.

This 'information processing' approach has been applied to understanding developmental change in a great many tasks, including tasks previously supposed to reflect changes in logical skill rather than changes in knowledge (Klahr, 1984; Klahr and Wallace, 1976; Klahr and MacWhinney,

1998; Johnson and Morton, 1991; Munakata, 1998; Siegler, 1996; Siegler and Chen, 1998; Siegler and Jenkins, 1989; Siegler and Shrager, 1984). In each case, developmental change in children's problem solving has been predicted on the basis of changes in the child's understanding of what is relevant to the task, and what strategy for solving it he or she adopts as a consequence. The detail of the strategy or 'rule' used in tackling the problem predicts which specific problems children of different ages will complete successfully and which they will fail, and what they will learn from experience with the task. In many cases, researchers have built computer models which use different strategies reflecting different levels of information, and so have created computer simulations of children's performance at different ages (Klahr and Wallace, 1976; Klahr and MacWhinney, 1998; Siegler and Jenkins, 1989). Such programs are impressive demonstrations of the sheer power of information in shaping how we reason and learn.

Conceptual change and mental tools

Information processing approaches to cognitive development emphasise the way in which knowledge changes the strategies children use in problem solving. Other research is showing that changes in the child's knowledge about some topic can also create powerful new ways of reasoning. For example, an increasing understanding of some topic or phenomenon can create bases for drawing inferences which are not available to the less knowledgeable child (Carey, 1985).

Carey's study of how children understand the concept of animacy is the classic demonstration of how increasing causal understanding can create qualitative change in how children reason about a particular topic. As we have seen in Chapter 2, babies are born predisposed to quickly learn to distinguish between animate creatures and inanimate objects, on the basis of the way these things move: animate objects can move themselves and are goal directed, whereas inanimate ones cannot propel themselves and have no goals (Slater, 1997). It seems that our perceptual systems are pre-set to make this distinction, and to identify human beings as special and different from inanimate objects (Slater, 1997). By the age of three years, many of the child's judgements about whether something is alive or not are very like the judgements made by an adult. They know, for example, that dogs are alive and dolls are not. But this apparent competence hides some radical differences in the way younger and older children conceptualise the notion of 'being alive', and how they reason about it. The differences emerge if you ask younger and older children whether trees are alive, for example, or whether lizards eat. The young child will probably say that trees are not alive, and be very unsure whether lizards eat or not, whereas the older child has no difficulty with such questions.

Despite their inborn predisposition to orient to animate entities, children below about seven years of age generally have little or no real biological knowledge. They have no real idea what a biological organism actually is, or what is inside it. They do not understand biological processes such as reproduction or death. They know that they must eat and defecate, but do not understand the purpose of digestion or the nature or function of the digestive organs. They know that wounds bleed, but do not understand the purpose of blood nor the role of the heart: at this age hearts are for loving, not pumping oxygen and other vital substances around the body (Carey, 1985).

Since these young children don't understand what a biological organism really is, they have no conception of any characteristics which might be common across all organisms. Thus they have no basis for inferring whether or not something is a living organism, or will do the things a living organism does, other than its similarity to the things they already know are alive. They have no basis for reasoning except Kahneman's representative-ness heuristic: the more something looks and behaves like the prototypical animate creature (which for us is a human being) the more likely it is to be judged to be alive (Carey, 1985). Monkeys and even dogs look and behave somewhat like people and are therefore confidently judged to be alive, and to do the things that people do, such as having babies. But daffodils and shrubs do not look or behave like people, and will be judged to be inani-mate, and not to reproduce.

By the age of ten years or so children have typically learned quite a lot about biology. They know, for example, that respiration supplies the blood with oxygen, which must then be pumped around the body by the heart to feed the tissues, and subsequently removes waste products. They under-stand the purpose of digestion and the relationship between functions such as eating and defecating, and so on. Crucially, they understand that *all* living organisms must feed, eliminate, breathe, reproduce and die, because that is what defines life.

This insight into what defines life radically changes how the child under-stands and reasons about animacy. Now, the child has a *principled*, rather than a *perceptual* basis for drawing an inference as to whether or not some entity is alive, or whether some organism reproduces, say. That is to say, the ten-year-old understands that membership of the category 'alive' is defined by the presence of certain properties (reproduction, elimination, and so on), rather than by what the entity looks like or how it behaves, and can reason on the basis of category membership. Confronted by a new entity, the ten-year-old can decide whether or not it is alive by asking whether it has those defining properties, no matter what it looks like, so that plants and insects can be recognised as alive despite looking entirely different from people. Conversely, knowing that a cactus is alive, the ten-year-old can infer that it must reproduce, even if the means of reproduction is not understood.

This change from reasoning based on simple perceptual similarities to reasoning based on category definitions represents a radical developmental change. It restructures what the child sees as important about any category. For the young child relying on simple perception based reasoning, for example, a critical feature of the concept 'baby' is being very small, because that's what the archetypal baby looks like, relative to adults. But the older child who has enough biological knowledge to use category based reasoning understands the principle that babies are in fact defined as newborn off-spring. Suddenly size, which was the key element in their understanding of the concept, becomes almost irrelevant.* Overall, the shift to category based reasoning through the growth of causal understanding creates a general restructuring of the child's conceptual understanding: elements which were core features of the child's understanding become peripheral, and vice versa. And since category based reasoning rests on principled understanding rather than on simple perceptual inferences, it provides the child with a new and more powerful basis for reasoning, better suited to formal, analytical thinking.

It is worth noting that Carey's work explains the same shift from rea-soning embedded in concrete experience to more abstract formal reasoning that Piaget sought to explain (Chapter 4), but in a very different way. Carey's work shows how the important developmental change Piaget observed can derive from changes in factual understanding, rather than changes in the logical tools available to the child. In fact, Carey's work shows how new mental tools can derive from knowledge, rather than new knowledge arising from the construction of new mental tools as Piaget argued.

Furthermore, Carey's work explains why children's reasoning can be so variable from one context to another. The same change from similarity based reasoning to category based reasoning occurs as the child acquires

---

* This developmental change explains the anecdote in Chapter 1: Simon cannot understand that the larger dog is younger, because his lack of biological knowledge confines him to simi-larity-based reasoning, and he is unshakeably convinced that smallness is critical to age. Mary cannot persuade him otherwise because he lacks the biological knowledge to understand what she is saying. She herself has realised that size isn't relevant to age, but has not yet gathered enough specific knowledge about selective breeding to understand the concept of sub-species within a species.

more causal knowledge, across all topics and domains. But since the development of category based reasoning about a given topic depends on the child acquiring a certain level of causal understanding in that specific area, there is no reason to suppose that category based reasoning would develop at the same time across different topics. A child might know a great deal about one topic, and be able to reason in a category based way in that area, while knowing very little about another area, and be confined to similarity based reasoning on that subject. (Indeed, the same is true for adults: one may, like me, be capable of category based reasoning in many esoteric areas, but reduced to similarity based reasoning when confronted by a recalcitrant car engine).

Exactly what the young child knows about living things and biology at any particular age is still not very clear (Coley, 2000). Even four-year-old children may recognise some similarities between plants and animals: that they grow and change, and can die, for example. And there is no reason to suppose that every child would know the same things, or make the same discoveries at the same age. The crucial insight of Carey's work is not about what children know at any given age: rather, it is that *what* you know determines *how* you reason.

Even babies in their first year have been shown to use category based reasoning in some simple contexts (Smith, 1989). Asked to say whether a shark breathes like a very similar looking dolphin or a very different looking fish, three-year-olds can ignore what the creatures look like and use category information to draw the right inference, if the shark is labelled as a fish (Gelman and Markman, 1986, 1987). And even college students resort to similarity based reasoning in areas (such as physics) where they lack causal understanding (Chi, Feltovich and Glaser, 1981). The switch from similarity based reasoning to category based reasoning is not related to age, but to the level of causal understanding the individual has about the topic in question.

Novices, Experts and Domain Specific Knowledge

Carey's (1985) work demonstrates that changes in knowledge and causal understanding about a specific topic or area ('domain') have fundamental effects on the character and form of reasoning in that domain. Such 'domain specific knowledge' determines not just the conclusions drawn but how concepts are structured, the extent to which reasoning in that domain can be principled or abstract, the very way inferences in that area are drawn. Domain specific knowledge creates the very tools we need for reasoning.

Can change in domain specific knowledge explain all the phenomena of childhood cognitive change and development? A number of researchers have argued that it can (Carey, 1985; Chi and Ceci, 1987; Wiser and Carey, 1983). Certainly, it is generally accepted now that the acquisition of domain specific knowledge is a critical factor in the development of intellect (Kuhn, 2000).

Research on adult novices and experts support the claim that domain specific knowledge is critical to skilled intelligent functioning. There is a tendency to assume that expertise reflects some sort of general ability, so that an expert chess player or a physicist is deemed, in the popular mind, to be 'super intelligent' where individuals with poor skills in those areas are popularly viewed as less able. But in fact, expertise in one area does not indicate general ability so much as rich and highly structured knowledge. Being an expert scientist does not make one more able than the average at managing the family budget, say, or repairing the family car (as our stereotype of the 'mad professor' suggests). An inability to play brilliant chess does not mean that one will be unable to manage the intricacies of playing the stock market or running an international business. Expertise reflects not so much general mental power as specific knowledge in the particular domain of that expertise.

Experts and novices in certain domains represent problems and their solutions in an entirely different way (Chi, Feltovich and Glaser, 1981; Chi, Glaser and Rees, 1982; Larkin, 1983). The difference is very much like the difference Carey (1985) noted in children's biological knowledge: novices lack understanding of how one thing relates to another, and so structure elements of the problem in terms of similarities rather than organising their knowledge around principles guided by causal understanding. The consequence of these differences in knowledge is that experts and novices approach a problem in that domain in quite different ways, guided by quite different processes. They see different patterns in the information on that topic, and reason quite differently as a consequence. Every aspect of reasoning is affected, from what analogies can be drawn to how strategies for solving a problem are identified and how plans are constructed.

It is worth emphasising that it is the content of knowledge itself which creates new conceptual structures as expertise develops. For example, knowing that babies are defined as newborn makes it impossible to retain size as a critical defining feature of babyhood. The gradual accretion of knowledge, and connections between one piece of information and another itself generates the restructuring of the mind and of the bases for inference.

Expertise not only leads to different and better solutions and strategies, it also makes problem solving easier: the expert has a vast store of past experience to draw on, and can often recognise a problem as familiar, and recall the best means of solution where a novice meeting that same problem for the first time must work out the solution from scratch. The classic example comes from studies of chess (De Groot, 1965). Where novices see each piece on the chessboard as a separate individual, and must plan for each separately, experts recognise patterns among the pieces and can plan for the movements of a number of pieces simultaneously as part of that pattern. Many of these patterns will be familiar so that the expert need not work out what to do or what the opponent is likely to do as the novice must, but can simply remember what worked best last time. Thus the expert has a far simpler problem to solve, and far less to try to bear in mind or calculate than the novice.

Chi (1978) has shown that expertise depends not on age but on knowledge. For instance, child chess players may have more knowledge and behave more expertly than adult novices to the game. In situations where adults lack relevant knowledge, we behave very much as children do, trying things out by trial and error, using primitive concepts and processes (Brown and DeLoache, 1978). There is a powerful sense in which changing knowledge through childhood moves the child from a *universal novicehood* in infancy to progressive expertise across a vast range of separate domains (Brown and DeLoache, 1978; Carey, 1985; Chi and Ceci, 1987; Wellman and Gelman, 1997).

Knowledge and analogy

Whether within or across domains, one of the most powerful tools of reasoning is the ability to draw analogies, and so to transfer skills and understanding from one domain to another, or from one context within a domain to another. This ability, too, reflects the richness and structure of our knowledge.

Children are notoriously bad at drawing analogies. Even at the age of ten years, children often fail to draw analogies which seem perfectly obvious to an adult mind (Inhelder and Piaget, 1958). This fact is the bane of many a teacher's life: one may produce a classroom of children who are adept at solving some mathematical problem in a given format, but who utterly fail to recognise the very same problem, or to generalise their skills, if the format changes even slightly (Bruner and Kenney, 1965; Werthheimer, 1945). The same is true, of course, for student psychologists struggling to learn statistics: what turns out to be just the same problem one has practised a dozen times may seem bafflingly unfamiliar if presented in even a slightly different format.

Inhelder and Piaget (1958) argued that the young child's difficulties with analogies come from the fact that they lack the kind of mental structures required to perform abstract comparisons between two different-seeming problems. They argued that such comparisons required the ability to reason in an abstract, formal way, disregarding the specific content of both situations. Abstract formal reasoning is hard, and develops late in childhood or early in adolescence (Inhelder and Piaget, 1958; Piaget, 1968; Smith, 1993), to the extent that it develops at all (Kahneman *et al.*, 1982). Indeed, it can be the case that a child's representation of a problem is so embedded in the peripheral concrete details of the particular examples he or she has experienced so far that recognising what is essential to the problem and what is not is impossible, and transferring the skill to a new situation where some aspect of the peripheral detail is different is impossible (Bruner and Kenney, 1965). However, the consensus of research is that even in adults, the ability to draw analogies depends not on the ability to reason in an abstract and formal way, but on whether or not one has rich enough knowledge of the two situations compared to perceive parallels and connections (Brown and DeLoache, 1978; Johnson-Laird, 1983, 1993).

To recognise a useful analogy between a familiar and an unfamiliar situation, one has to be able to map the structure of one situation onto the other (Gentner, 1983). That is to say, one has to be able to recognise that there is something useful in common between the two situations. This can be more complex than you may suppose. Sometimes recognising commonalities between two situations is a matter of recognising that the *elements* of the problem look very similar: both involve dealing with a mother infuriated by a broken item, say. Sometimes the elements of the problem may look entirely different, and the commonality between situations lies in the *structure of the relationships* between these elements: both involve mechanisms for steering vessels, for example.

Young children may fail to solve analogies simply because they don't have enough knowledge of one or both situations to recognise that there is an analogy between either the elements or the relationship between them. For example, very few children under ten years of age can solve the analogies Piaget posed them, which include examples such as:

'A bicycle is to handlebars as a ship is to . . . ?'

Children know too little about ships to work out the answer 'rudder'. There is no perceptual similarity between the elements: bicycles do not look like ships, nor handlebars like rudders. Equally, the relationship between the way handlebars and rudders function is esoteric: they function in quite different ways. Thus Piaget's analogy tasks tested not so much the ability to reason by analogy as the depth of the child's knowledge.

When the child has enough knowledge of the two situations to be compared to map the elements and the structural relationship onto one another, even very young children can solve analogies (Goswami and Brown, 1989). For example, three-year-olds can readily solve analogies such as:

'Chocolate is to melted chocolate as snow is to . . . ?'

Here the structural relationship between the elements is considerably more straightforward than that used in Piaget's analogy tasks.

Overall, the evidence we now have strongly suggests that the young child's ability to draw analogies is limited only by how much knowledge he or she has of the situations compared. This conclusion is confirmed by studies of the detailed processes involved in drawing analogies. Sternberg (1977a, 1977b) identified five separate steps in this process: *encoding* the elements of the situation; *inferring* the relations between them; *mapping* links between the elements of the two situations; *applying* the relationship inferred in the given situation to the new one and *justifying* the resulting analogy. Goswami (1992) has shown that three-year-old children can be taught and can use all these elements of analogical reasoning. There is some evidence that the basic ability to draw analogies is present from birth (Goswami, 1995).

As we have seen earlier in this chapter, being able to use a given cognitive process does not necessarily mean that the young child will actually use it. The evidence suggests that very young children do spontaneously draw analogies in solving problems (Gholson, Dattel, Morgan and Eymard, 1989; Holyoak, Junn and Billman, 1984). For example, Holyoak *et al.* asked four-year-olds to solve a problem which involved moving gumballs from a bowl in easy reach to another which was out of reach, without getting out of the chair. A walking stick, a big sheet of card and various other things were available to solve the problem. Before tackling this task, the child was told a story which involved someone solving an analogous type of problem: for example, a genie who moved jewels from one bottle to another either by using his magic staff to move the far away bottle closer, or by rolling his magic carpet into a tube and pouring the jewels down it to the other bottle (Table 5.1). Four-year-old children spontaneously used the analogies in the stories to solve their problems, even when the elements of the specific story they heard were less obviously similar to the analogous problem (a character from Sesame Street, a popular TV programme of the time, 'Miss Piggy', transferring jewels to a safe, for example). In still simpler tasks, even children as young as two years spontaneously solve problems by analogy (Crisafi and Brown, 1986).

Table 5.1 Story/task analogy

	Story analogues	Ball problem
Initial state		
Goal	Genie wishes to transfer jewels from one bottle to another.	Child wishes to transfer balls from one bowl to another.
Resources	Magic staff/magic carpet.	Walking cane/sheet of paper.
Constraint	Must not drop or lose jewels.	Must not drop or lose any balls.
Solution plan 1	Genie (a) uses magic staff to pull goal bottle closer to initial bottle; (b) drops jewels into goal bottle.	Child (a) uses cane to pull goal bowl closer to initial bowl; (b) drops balls into goal bowl.
Solution plan 2	Genie (a) rolls magic carpet to form a long hollow tube; (b) places tube so it extends from initial bottle to goal bottle; (c) rolls jewels through tube to goal bottle.	Child (a) rolls sheet of paper to form long hollow tube; (b) places tube so it extends from Initial bowl to goal bowl: (c) rolls balls through tube to goal bottle.
Outcome	Jewels are transferred safely.	Balls are transferred safely.

Source: Holyoak *et al.* (1984) pp. 2042–55.

Richer knowledge across a broader range of topics will expand the range of analogies the child can draw and allow an ever wider generalisation of skills. Older children will often be able to detect analogies still invisible to the less well informed younger child, and so can transfer skill without having to work through the problem from first principles, as the young child must. The impact of a rich capacity for analogy on the power of the child's reasoning is explosive. Perhaps analogy is a key vehicle through which skills begin to become general, rather than specifically tied to the content of the domain in which they were constructed.

In Summary

Basic psychological processes such as the way we perceive one thing as similar to another, or the way our memories work provide surprisingly powerful general tools for human reasoning. Such processes allow us to draw heuristic inferences from what we know about the world and the way things work. This way of reasoning is quite different from logical reasoning.

Inferences of this type are typical of how adults make everyday judgements. Since heuristic inference processes involve such small extrapolations from how perception and memory work, it seems likely that very young children can draw inferences in this way, though the evidence suggests that even six-year-olds may need prompting or a personally relevant motive to do so. But even when adult and young child use the same everyday inference process in reaching a conclusion, we may expect them to reach different conclusions, since the knowledge and experience on which these inference processes depend is likely to be very different for a child of three, say and an adult of thirty-five.

But very general tools such as heuristic inference mechanisms cannot account for the rich character of human reasoning, nor explain the complex patterns of developmental change we see in children's thinking. There are strong grounds for supposing that the specific knowledge a child has on some topic or domain plays a far more critical role in determining how the child will view problems in that domain, how he or she will construct strategies for solving those problems. The particular knowledge that we have about some topic determines the way our concepts in that area are structured, and hence what kind of inferences we can draw: whether we can reason in a principled way, or whether we are limited to judging by surface appearances. Changes in children's knowledge affect not just the conclusions they come to, but the means by which they do it.

So great is the power of domain specific knowledge in creating expertise that many researchers believe that change in such knowledge is the basis for all the phenomena of intellectual development which we see through childhood. The infant is a universal novice, who gradually acquires the information within a range of specific domains of knowledge, progressively achieving a greater expertise in more and more areas. The richer the knowledge a child has across a variety of domains, the greater his or her ability to draw analogies between one type of problem and another and so to transfer skills, creating a more general basis for ability.

Without doubt, the effects of changes in knowledge we have reviewed in this chapter play a vital role in the development of children's minds. But this research still leaves a number of questions open. For example, how do children acquire all that knowledge? Why do they sometimes fail to use skills they could use? Exactly what processes allow them to put knowledge to practical use in solving problems? We shall return to these questions in the next two chapters.

EXERCISES

1   Keep a diary of what you understand and what you don't understand as you master a new skill: learning to choose which statistical test to use in analysing data in a lab class, for example. How does your understanding change as you become more expert? Do other students share the same misunderstandings and insights, or are their specific experiences different? How could you devise a way of testing that?

2   What are the relative strengths and weaknesses of diagnosing what someone knows starting from a task analysis and using more open-ended diagnostic techniques?

SUGGESTED READING

For a flavour of experimental analyses of children's knowledge:
   Carey, S. (1985) *Conceptual Change in Childhood* (Cambridge, MA and London: MIT Press).
   Siegler, R. (1976) 'Three aspects of cognitive development'. *Cognitive Psychology* 8, pp. 481–520.

For essays on the role of knowledge in cognitive development:
   Carey, S. and Gelman, R. (eds) (1991) *The Epigenesis of Mind: Essays on Biology and Cognition* (Hillsdale, NJ: Erlbaum).

For essays on human heuristic reasoning:
   Kahneman, D., Slovic, P. and Tversky, A. (eds) (1982) *Judgment under Uncertainty: Heuristics and Biases* (Cambridge: Cambridge University Press).

Planning and Problem Solving

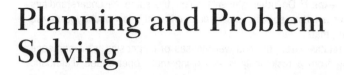

Earlier chapters of this book have looked at the broad characteristics of cognitive development, what it is that changes as children's minds grow. This chapter looks at how we actually *use* our minds to solve problems, and how that changes with development. In almost every test of problem solving skill, younger children perform more poorly than older children or adults. The range of problems they can solve is limited to the simpler tasks. In part, of course, the younger child's limitations reflect the level of conceptual development relevant to the task which they have achieved, so all the factors reviewed in earlier chapters contribute to the child's weaker problem solving. But conceptual development, the growth of knowledge alone does not wholly explain these developmental effects.

Planning in Problem Solving

In addressing any problem, or even everyday tasks such as how to get to a lecture on time, we must, in effect, create some sort of plan: that is to say, we must evaluate our current situation, the goal we want to achieve, and construct a sequence of actions which will move us from the former to the latter.

In almost every situation, the younger the child, the poorer the planning he or she will produce (Brown and DeLoache, 1978; Fabricius, 1988; Klahr and Robinson, 1981; Willatts, 1997). The older the child, the more complex the plans he or she can create, the more factors that can be taken into account, the greater number of steps the plan is likely to have. Complex plans with many steps obviously place a greater demand (M demand*) on

---

* M demand is the amount of processing capacity a task requires. This concept is discussed in detail in the section on memory development in Chapter 4.

processing than shorter, simpler plans, so it is tempting to suggest that the younger child's poor planning reflects a generally lower capacity for processing information. However, this is far too simple: the M demand the child can apparently manage varies from one planning situation to another, being greater in familiar situations and lower in novel ones (Brown and DeLoache, 1978).

Strategies in planning

How do we create plans? Researchers studying adults have identified a number of different strategies for planning. The simplest of these is *trial and error*. Suppose you want to find a way to fasten something securely to the roof of your car, say, but had no proper equipment. You might search the house, trying out different items you found there (a very long belt, say, or a piece of rope, or something stretchy) until you found something that worked. A more sophisticated way to plan is to *analyse subgoals*: to work out a series of steps which will provide the *means* of achieving your *ends* or eventual goal.

Even very young children use trial and error to solve problems, for example in swiping at cot toys to make a hooter sound or pull a cord. In fact, so simple is trial and error as a plan that it is hard to imagine any goal directed creature that could *not* 'plan' in this way. Trial and error is what any creature must do, to achieve a goal for which it has no more conceptual basis for planning. But trial and error is not a primitive strategy which falls out of use with development: we all use trial and error all the time, and even science and technology progress on this basis from time to time. The best known example is Edison, who tried out hundreds of possible substances while looking for a filament for his invention, the light bulb, before happening on an effective substance.

Piaget (1953) argued that trial and error is the only planning strategy available to the infant, and that in early infancy trial and error is very basic, very much rooted in physical actions which the child must try out and evaluate on the basis of what results they produce, rather than having any advance expectations or anticipation of what will work. And indeed, it is the case that the character of trial and error approaches to problem solving tends to change developmentally. Edison, for example, worked systematically through a coherent series of possibilities, narrowing down on an effective solution in his search for an effective filament. Twelve-year-olds tend to show the same sort of structured and systematic approach to trial and error problem solving, whereas two- or three-year-olds will try out different possible solutions in no particular order, perhaps repeating themselves. Equally, older children will try out more sophisticated or more relevant possibilities, and will try a a broader range of things than will occur to the younger child. As a consequence of their more systematic and more sophisticated approach, older children are more likely to be successful even by trial and error than younger ones.

Was Piaget right in saying that infants cannot use more sophisticated strategies than a rather random physical trial and error in planning? Certainly it is true that young babies are surprisingly poor at solving problems such as retrieving things that have been hidden (Willatts,* 1997, and see Chapter 2 of this book). And in fact, deliberate actions to retrieve a toy seem not to develop until around seven months (Willatts, 1984, 1999). For instance, Willatts (1999) made very detailed records of babies' behaviour in a situation where a cloth is placed within the baby's reach. Sometimes an attractive toy was placed on the far end of the cloth, outside the baby's reach, and sometimes there was no toy. Six-month-old babies would reach out for the cloth in either situation and would play with it. If there was a toy on the cloth, it would often be accidentally pulled within the infant's reach by this playing with the cloth, and then the baby might well pick it up and play with that. However, there was no sign that these infants had pulled on the cloth as a means of retrieving the toy: their behaviour towards the cloth was exactly the same, whether or not there was a toy on it. But by the age of seven months babies behaved much more as if they had made a means–ends analysis of the situation: they were much more likely to pull on the cloth if there was a toy on it, and would simply pull it rather than playing with it in an apparently deliberate effort to retrieve the toy.

On the one hand, the fact that seven-month-old babies can make simple means–ends analyses in this way is very impressive. On the other hand, the fact that younger infants do not do so poses a puzzle: why is this form of planning not found in younger babies? A number of hypotheses have been explored, including the possibility that younger babies are not interested in retrieving the out of reach object (Baillargeon, Graber, de Vos and Black; 1990; Willatts, 1997), or lack the motor coordination to retrieve the toy (Willatts, 1984), or that during the period when the ability to coordinate hand and eye to reach out in a focused way is developing (at around seven months) babies don't have the mental capacity to concentrate on reaching *and* hold even a simple means–ends analysis in mind at the same time (Bushnell, 1985). But the data do not fit any of these hypotheses (Baillargeon *et al.*, 1990; Willatts, 1997).

A study by Baillargeon *et al.* (1990) shows that young babies understand in principle that a toy bear under a cover can only be retrieved if the cover

---

* The studies reviewed here are described in considerably more detail in Willatts (1997), which is set as recommended reading at the end of this chapter.

is removed: if the bear and its cover are hidden behind a screen, five-month-old babies are surprised if a hand goes behind the screen and retrieves the bear without first removing the cover. In other words, they have a rudimentary understanding of what has to happen, to retrieve an item from under something else. But this does not mean that they understand how to make it happen themselves (Willatts, 1997). In other words, a lack of understanding of what specific *actions* are required to retrieve a toy may be the critical factor preventing the young baby from making an effective means–ends plan in this sort of situation. How could a baby possibly understand that a cover must be removed to retrieve a toy, and still not know how to do it? Willatts draws a parallel between the baby's problem and a similar situation more familiar to an adult: one may know that a dishwasher can only be repaired if the front panel is taken off and a faulty mechanism replaced, but still have no idea how to do that, even though one is able to say whether the repairman has done it properly or not (Willatts, 1997).

Our surprise at the young infant's poor ability in means–ends analysis may come from our tendency not to recognise just what a big task the newborn baby faces in learning to control a brand new body, in learning to direct his or her actions and to understand what the effects of those actions are. It may be that experiences of *accidentally* retrieving a toy by pulling on a cloth, say, as in Willatts' study (Willatts, 1999, 1997) are just the kinds of experience which lead infants to discover more about actions and their effects. The conclusion that the ability to plan how to retrieve a toy depends on learning about the effects of very specific actions is supported by the fact that an infant's success in making such retrievals depends very much on the type of obstacle which must be overcome, and what specific action is required to do that, just as one would predict if learning specific actions and their effects were the critical constraint on planning (Willatts, 1984, 1997).

The means–ends analysis involved in deliberately retrieving a toy from the far end of a cloth is very simple. In most contexts, means–ends analysis involves identifying a series of *subgoals* which step by step move one from the initial state of affairs to the desired or 'goal state'. For example, to cook a stew you must first acquire the ingredients, so that your first subgoal may have to be going shopping, rather than directly starting to cook. In very simple situations, infants might not need to have any direct representation of a subgoal at all (Willatts, 1997), but rather, might deploy actions as more or less direct means of achieving the goal in a single step. Knowing what all the individual actions relevant to solving a problem are, and being able to execute them in one step solutions to a problem is not enough to mean that a baby can string different actions together to solve more complicated problems. The ability to plan what to do when two steps are needed to solve the problem, in other words where a subgoal is necessary seems to develop only at around nine months (Willatts and Rosie, 1996).

The ability to plan the sequence in which subgoals must be achieved continues to develop through infancy and childhood. For example, in another version of Willatts' task, a toy is placed on the far end of a cloth as before, and a screen is put on the cloth between the infant and the toy. Here, the baby must plan whether to remove the screen first or pull the cloth. If the cloth is pulled first, the screen will dislodge the toy out of the child's reach! Up to the age of twelve months, babies have enormous difficulty with this task. Even at eighteen months, only a third of infants removed the barrier first on half the trials in this task. Only by the age of two or three years can children solve this problem easily (Willatts, 1989). Even four-year-olds can have difficulty in creating effective sequences of subgoals. For example, asked to plan a route to collect baby animals from various locations and return them to their mothers, four-year-olds will zigzag back and forth rather than planning an efficient, direct route (Fabricius, 1988). These children often go back and amend inefficiencies in their plan, suggesting that their problem was in devising the plan rather than any lack of intent to plan a direct route. By the age of five years, children were much more efficient in planning in this task (Fabricius, 1988).

There are a great many studies which show that young children have difficulties in planning sequences of steps in problem solving. But it is important to consider these studies critically. Some of the problem is less a matter of weak planning abilities and more a reflection of the peculiarities of the task. A classic demonstration of children's problems in many tests of their planning skills comes from work by Klahr and Robinson (1981), using the 'Tower of Hanoi' problem. In the traditional version of this task, three disks must be moved from pole A to pole C (Figure 6.1), subject to the rules that only one disk can move at a time and must come to rest on a pole at the end of each move, and that no disc can rest on a disk smaller than itself (if you are not familiar with this problem, try it for yourself, for example using three marks on paper to represent the poles and three coins of different sizes for the disks). Even six-year-old children normally do very badly in this task, which has traditionally been taken as evidence of poor means–ends planning. However, the evidence suggests that children readily forget the rules and lose track of the goal in traditional versions of the task. Klahr and Robinson made the task simpler in two ways: first, by replacing the disks with 'monkey cans', a big 'daddy' can, a medium sized 'mummy' can and a small 'baby' can. These cans had to be balanced on the poles, and were so devised that it was only possible to put a larger can over a smaller one. This reverses the usual rule for the task, but takes away the child's need to remember the rule because breaking the rule is not physically possible. Furthermore, the child is given a physical model of the goal state to be achieved, which is left in view all the time, and asked to make his or her cans match that. So there is no need to remember the goal. Children were much more sucessful in this task than in the classic version of the game. But there was still a developmental change in the success of planning: 60–70 per cent of three- and four-year-olds could successfully make two step plans in the task, as could all the older children. Sixty-five per cent of five-year-olds and nearly all six-year-olds could make effective four move plans, though very few four-year-olds could do this. More than half of the six-year-olds in the study made perfect plans even when six moves were required.

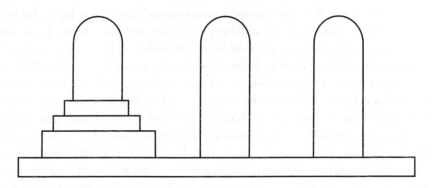

Figure 6.1   The Tower of Hanoi problem

Plans, subgoals and knowledge

Why are younger children less effective in identifying sequences of subgoals than their elders? To answer this question, we have to look at what it is that affects our ability to plan in adult life. As we have already noted here and in Chapter 5, how much we know about a problem can make an enormous difference to how we approach solving it, including how successfully we can plan a way of tackling it (Brown and Deloache, 1978). Effective planning is really only possible when we understand which factors are relevant to the problem and which are not, what strategies we might try and how effective these different strategies are; in other words, in situations where you have rich knowledge or expertise. In a new task, or one which you don't understand much about, you may be unsure what is relevant and what is not. Like the babies in Willatts' studies, you may not know of any strategies for dealing with the problem, or may only know of a relatively weak strategy. Or perhaps several alternative strategies occur to you, but it is unclear how effective any of them will be, or which is the best. Planning in such a situation will be difficult, and may well be weak or even impossible, and even an able adult might well be reduced to mere trial and error (Brown and DeLoache, 1978). And it is worth noting that the 'M demand' of a task may be far smaller in a familiar task where one has the knowledge and experience to summon a successful strategy out of memory than the M demand of that same task when one must cast about and find a strategy from scratch.

Brown and DeLoache suggest that the young child's difficulties in planning stem primarily from their relative lack of relevant knowledge and experience rather than their age per se. In certain familiar situations, even very young children can compose effective plans. However, in most tasks, the younger the child the less relevant knowledge and experience he or she will bring to the situation. Young children may often be trying to work out the steps necessary to solve a problem where an older child or adult is merely remembering how they solved the same type of problem last time. Where young children have very little knowledge at all they will have no insight into what actions are likely to be effective, and no real basis for interpreting feedback from the task either. Things either work, or they don't. The child's behaviour is gradually shaped toward the more successful actions, without the child understanding why these work best. This 'data-driven' approach (Karmiloff-Smith, 1992) is very much a trial and error process, but can nevertheless generate effective solutions to problems, as we shall see later in this chapter.

As the child gets a better grasp on the problem, he or she will begin to develop theories about how one element of the problem is connected to another, or why certain strategies work and others don't (Brown and DeLoache, 1978; Karmiloff-Smith, 1992). Developing such a theory is a great step forward in that it gives the child a basis for interpreting and understanding feedback from the task, and for anticipating and planning the next move. Now the child can move away from trial and error to a more systematic approach.

However, planning can still be limited by the adequacy of the child's theory about the task. A faulty theory can sometimes lead a child to a systematically wrong strategy (Siegler, 1976; 1981). The errors this produces can undermine the child's *commitment* to planning: having the wrong theory can mean that the child has no idea why some of his or her responses are wrong. The feedback from the task is simply baffling. Unable to understand why predictions have failed, the child's incentive for actually trying to make consistent predictions is reduced. Guessing at random may look as good an option as trying to plan effectively, where partial knowledge makes planning only partially effective.

Thus developmental changes in knowledge of the specific task in hand play a vital role in determining whether or not the child can plan a useful strategy in a systematic way, or is forced to rely on trial and error. Understanding determines the extent to which the child is confronted by a welter of seemingly unconnected elements, taxing M space, as opposed to a meaningful pattern, imposing less M demand. Levels of knowledge determine how effective the plans children generate are, and whether or not the child can interpret failures or understand the limits of certain strategies. In other words, levels of understanding affect the child's ability to reflect on his or her own plans, to understand why, when and where these plans have or have not worked successfully.

A More Detailed Look at the Development of Problem Solving

For a number of decades, the main focus of research into children's intellectual development has been on trying to understand what conceptual understanding or reasoning processes characterise a baby or child of a given age, and how these things change over time. This emphasis reflected the realisation of just how important such conceptual structures or knowledge are, in generating the child's thinking and behaviour: for example, in supporting the ability to plan, as we have just seen, or the functioning of our memories, or the types of reasoning we can produce or understand (Chapter 5). But this emphasis on what the child's mind is like led research away from detailed studies of knowledge in action, and of the direct processes through which children learn and make new discoveries. Recent work using new and more detailed methods for studying learning processes in problem solving more directly has led to important new insights about the way our minds work and grow.

Microgenetic methods for studying the development of problem solving

Often, in exploring the general character of intellectual development, we collect data about a number of children and look for the patterns across children that characterise a given age group. We look for how many digits five-year-olds or eight-year-olds can typically hold in mind (Case, 1985), or what an average eight-year-old knows about biology (Carey, 1985), or the typical skills of a seven-month-old baby in retrieving a toy (Willatts, 1997). The answers to such questions give us a global picture of what it is that changes during development, and how progress proceeds through childhood. But it is only by studying the specific problem solving processes used by an individual child that we can see how skills and knowledge come together to produce an actual strategy, or new learning in a task.

Studying the detailed processing of an individual problem solver poses some problems. Early efforts to do this tried to get problem solvers to introspect on what they were doing: to solve some problem and to comment on how they were thinking as they went along (Ericson and Simon, 1993). But this method has very serious drawbacks. First, there is good evidence that what people *say* they are doing when solving a problem and what they are *actually* doing are not necessarily the same thing at all. Much of the processing we do in problem solving may be unconscious, hard to notice in oneself. For example, I have no real advance awareness of exactly what words I will write next as I complete this sentence, still less of how I choose them. If you ask me to explain it to you, I would produce a plausible sounding rationalisation of what I probably did, rather than reporting the actual psychological processes per se. The classic example of the point comes from Piaget's report of a number of philosophers: asked to crawl across the floor, all were able to do it, but none could accurately describe how they had done so. There is clear evidence that children introduce new strategies into their problem solving before they report the new strategy (Siegler and Stern, 1998), as one would expect if its emergence, and the processes associated with that emergence were not conscious. And indeed, the youngest children have great difficulty in telling us anything about their thinking at all: three- to five-year-olds seem not to have much ability to reflect on their own thought processes, nor even to really understand what such processes are (Flavell, Green and Flavell, 1995).

Rather than asking children to tell us about their problem solving processes, then, researchers have developed *microgenetic* techniques for more direct scrutiny of precisely what a child (or an adult, for that matter) does while engaging a task. Of course, such analyses also look at what the child says while tackling the problem: but such speech is left to be task directed, rather than directly elicited as a reflection on mental processes per se.

A microgenetic study of children's problem solving has several key characteristics (Siegler and Crowley, 1991). First, a very detailed recording is made of precisely how a problem solving session goes for an individual child. Often the session is video taped, and every aspect of the child's interaction with the task is carefully noted. The focus is on recording problem solving during a period of change or new discovery, and repeated recordings will be made of the child's problem solving during that period, the more the better. Thus the child's problem solving is studied not on just one attempt to solve a problem at one time, but over many trials, over a period of time. The main interest is not in whether the child can complete a given task successfully or not, but on the processes by which performance is produced. All of the data for an individual child will then be analysed to try to infer what specific goals and representations of the problem directed the child's behaviour at any one time, the processes through which these were brought to bear on the task, and how changes in strategy emerge. Such analyses provide rich insights into how reasoning operates and develops, as the rest of this chapter shows (Kuhn, 1995; Siegler, 2000; Siegler and Crowley, 1991).

Strategy choice and developmental change

One insight from microgenetic analyses of children's problem solving is that our traditional model of how development progresses may be fundamentally wrong. This traditional view was based on studies which looked at children's success or failure in a task at a given age, inferring what skills and strategies the child must have used from the situations in which he or she succeeds or fails (Piaget, 1954; Inhelder and Piaget, 1958, 1964; and see Chapter 4). This methodology produces 'snapshots', like still photographs of the child's abilities. Such data seem to support Piaget's theory that developmental change is fundamentally a matter of the growth of more adequate and sophisticated strategies or ways of thinking out of weaker or less adequate ones, with new and powerful strategies replacing older ones as they develop. Figure 6.2 shows a schematic representation of this model of the nature of intellectual development, with each strategy merging into and being overwritten by the one a stage ahead.

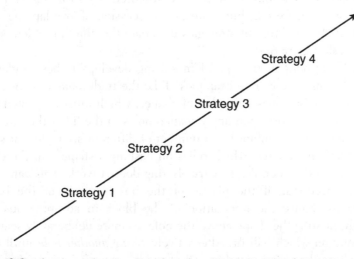

Figure 6.2 A schematic representation of traditional models of strategy development

Microgenetic studies completely undermine the traditional view of development represented in Figure 6.2. By looking at problem solving for longer periods of time, by focusing in detail on what is actually happening rather than on whether the child is successful or not, we see a completely different picture. Older and weaker strategies are not, in fact, superseded and replaced by new ones (Kuhn, 1995; Schauble, 1996; Siegler and Chen, 1998; Siegler and Jenkins, 1989; Siegler and Shipley, 1995; Siegler, 2000). At any one time children (and for that matter, adults) normally have a range of different strategies for solving any particular problem. Simpler, less adequate strategies co-exist alongside more sophisticated ones, and continue to be used long after the more sophisticated strategy has come into the child's repertoire. Children (or adults) may use a variety of different strategies during the course of even quite a short period of problem solving, moving between more and less sophisticated strategies and back again (Siegler, 1996; Siegler and Jenkins, 1989). Furthermore, new and more powerful strategies do not necessarily grow out of older and less sophisticated ones: rather, they may develop entirely separately from the older strategy, and operate on a quite different and unconnected principle (Siegler and Jenkins, 1989). What research must explain is not the transformation of poor strategies into good ones, but the origin of a plethora of different and unconnected strategies. Developmental change in reasoning is less a matter of the construction of better tools for reasoning, and more a matter of progressive change in which the child selects from a range of possible strategies, until there is a systematic tendency to choose the most sophisticated strategy for the context (Siegler, 1996). These findings suggest that the development of reasoning should be represented not so much as a linear process, as in Figure 6.2, but more as a succession of 'overlapping waves' (Siegler, 2000), as different strategies dominate the child's problem solving in some task (Figure 6.3).

Siegler's account of how problem solving develops is best understood through looking at concrete examples. Take the traditional 'post box' game for infants: the baby has a number of shapes, which must be posted into a box via a series of correspondingly shaped holes in the lid of the box. From a very young age, the infant has a number of different strategies for solving this problem: *brute force*, which relies on bashing a shape into the chosen hole harder and harder, if a first try offering doesn't work. This can be surprisingly successful, if the plastic of the box is weak, or the bashing happens to change the orientation of the block in advantageous ways. Secondly, *twisting* the shape above the hole, to more deliberately search for an orientation which will fit. Alternatively, *trying another hole* until one is found where the shape matches. All of these strategies may appear in the baby's problem solving in a single session. It is hard to see one strategy as a

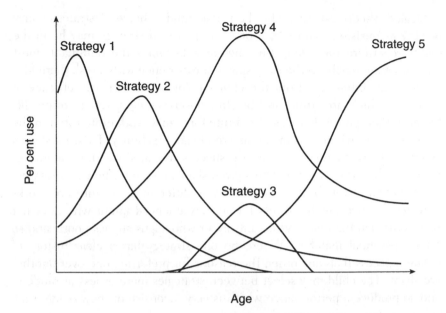

Figure 6.3 The 'overlapping waves' model of development
Source: Siegler (2000), pp. 26–36.

primitive version of a better one, here: each strategy draws on a quite different approach, and looks more like a separate and different kind of strategy, even if an observer might want to rank order them for sophistication. The same variety of seemingly unconnected strategies can be identified in individual's problem solving in all tasks so far studied (Siegler, 1996), both in children and in adults.

How does the child choose which strategy to select at any one moment? Each of the strategies in the child's repertoire (such as the three for the post box game noted above), will have a 'history', in the child's experience. That is to say, each will have been used in the past, in analogous situations, with greater or lesser success. Siegler and Jenkins (1989) suggest that the child selects whichever strategy currently has the greatest historic association with success and the least association with failure. So, for example, a child who has had great success with brute force in similar situations in the past, but relatively little success with either twisting the shapes or trying other holes will select a brute force strategy first in the post box game. But each experience with the task provides more feedback. If the brute force strategy doesn't work very well this time, its association with success may decline until one of the other strategies has a better 'track record', and the child will then swap to this second strategy. These associative processes controlling strategy selection need not be conscious (Siegler and Chen, 1998).

Siegler's theory explains why the young child's choice of strategies may be very inconsistent, and why a new and powerful strategy may be in the child's repertoire for a long time before it becomes the dominant, most often used approach. In the early stages of experience with a task there may be no clear difference, from the child's point of view, in the efficacy of strategies which are, from an objective observer's perspective, quite different in their power. For example, brute force may work quite often in the 'post box' task, where the materials are cheap and flimsy. Twisting shapes about to find a fit may not improve success much, since the majority of holes simply won't accommodate a given shape, no matter how it is rotated. Even the objectively best strategy of trying different holes until one works may not produce much success for an inexperienced infant who does not search through the holes systematically, or who aligns shapes poorly and so misses potential matches. Where no one strategy has a clear history of greater success than any other, the reasons for preferring one over another are slight. The child may select between strategies more or less at random, and so produce a performance which is very inconsistent, now using weak strategies, now more powerful ones.

Practice with a task gives the child considerably more feedback about the efficacy and properties of each strategy, until one or more strategies emerge as clearly more successful than the others. Now these more successful strategies will be systematically selected in preference to other, less successful ones, so that the child's performance will become more consistent, and more rooted in sophisticated approaches. This developmental process can take a surprising amount of time: older, weaker strategies may be used for a long time after newer and more powerful ones are available (Kuhn, 1995; Schauble, 1996; Siegler, 1994), particularly where the older strategy is already fairly successful, or where the newer one is much harder to use (Bjorklund, Miller, Coyle and Slawinski, 1997). But where the advantages of a new strategy are obvious, it may become the child's normal approach fairly quickly (Alibali, 1999).

The very same processes which account for developmental change in children's strategies in Siegler's theory also account for problem solving and cognitive change in adults (Shrager and Siegler, 1998; Siegler and Shipley, 1995). Development is, according to this theory, very importantly the product of learning from feedback through interactions with a task. Such feedback driven learning processes have received comparatively little attention in developmental psychology for a number of decades, despite their power and ubiquity (for example, similar associative processes of learning occur in all animals, and play a critical role in shaping the rich patterns of adaptive behaviour across the species). This neglect stemmed from the fact that early research into associative learning portrayed such processes as far simpler than they really are, with little connection to, or contribution to make in the development of complex conceptual structures. It is only in the last decade or so that we have begun to see that learning processes are in fact an integral tool of development, with a critical role to play in the construction of new undestanding and knowledge (Kuhn, 1995; Siegler, 2000).

Learning from feedback contributes to development in four distinct ways (Siegler, 2000). It refines and improves the efficiency with which children use each strategy in their repertoires. For example, children solving multiplication problems by retrieving the answer to a given problem from memory (as opposed to working it out) become markedly more efficient in using this strategy over the course of a week, reducing their errors from 23 per cent to 2 per cent (Lemaire and Siegler, 1995). And learning from feedback allows the child to learn not just which strategies work best in general terms, and so to begin systematically preferring these, as we have seen, but also to identify when and where it is worth using a more complex and powerful strategy, and when and where an older, easier strategy will work perfectly well. For example, in Lemaire and Siegler's study, children became much more selective in when they would rely on recall to answer multiplication questions and when they would use more complex strategies to work out an answer, progressively reserving the latter for situations where recall was less likely to succeed. Each of these three effects of learning serves to refine the efficiency with which a strategy which is already in the child's repertoire is deployed and used. But learning processes also contribute in important ways to the genesis of new strategies.

The genesis of new strategies

In some senses, we have known for a long time that new strategies can be invented through the feedback we get from a task. Every time we try to solve a problem to which we do not know the solution, we in effect expose ourselves to such feedback, and, through a more or less trial and error process, allow it to shape our behaviour towards a successful strategy. Such 'data driven' processes play a powerful role in new discovery, for example, in the infant's discovery that pulling on a cloth can bring a toy nearer, in Willatt's studies of infant problem solving (Willatts, 1997). But the enormous power of such feedback driven learning in creating new understanding has not really been recognised until very recently. This was because it was widely believed that children can only develop new understanding on the basis of existing conceptual structures or knowledge, so that feedback from a task will be powerless to create new understanding unless it makes sense within the child's existing mental structures. From this point of view, all important conceptual change must be constrained by the child's existing conceptual understanding, and must derive from that understanding rather than from crude feedback from experience in any task (e.g. Karmiloff-Smith, 1992).

There is a great deal of evidence to suggest that learning is indeed constrained by what we already know (Moore, 1996). For example, five-year-old children learn very little by comparison with eight-year-olds from experience in a balance scale task, because unlike the eight-year-old, the five-year-old doesn't understand that weight is not the only factor affecting whether things will balance: the position of a weight relative to the fulcrum matters too (Siegler, 1976, 1981; see Chapter 5). The five-year-old does not pay attention to the position of the weights and so learns nothing about this factor, while the eight-year-old does. But conceptual constraints on learning such as this tell only half the story. For it is entirely possible for the simple feedback of success and failure to generate new strategies which we not only do not understand, but of which we are not even aware (Siegler and Stern, 1998; Thornton, 1999). And indeed, if this were not the case, it is hard to see how any genuinely novel discovery could be possible (Sophian, 1997; Thornton, 1999).

New strategies from existing conceptual structures

Even those theorists who most strongly urge that real developmental change must come from within the child's own conceptual structures concede the point that behaviour, at least, can be shaped by learning processes in some task. Thus Piaget, for example, believed that all real developmental change in understanding comes from reflection on the effects of one's actions in the world. But action must preceed thought, and action can be structured by feedback from the world (Piaget, 1967, 1968). Many theorists agree that development derives importantly from processes which come to explicitly represent structures which are implicit in patterns of behaviour. Patterns which have themselves been shaped by 'data driven' processes: in other words, by feedback from interaction with some task (Bremner, 1997; Gelman, 1982; Karmiloff-Smith, 1992; Wynn, 1992).

Processes which explicitly represent what is already implicit in a child's behaviour undoubtedly make a powerful contribution to development in a number of ways. Such processes can bring new elements of a task into clearer focus, so that the child can recognise their relevance and use these factors in guiding new problem solving (Karmiloff-Smith, 1992). And they can allow the identification of recurring patterns in behaviour, so that these patterns can be 'chunked' into coherent units and so deployed more economically and effectively (Klahr and Wallace, 1976; Klahr and MacWhinney, 1998). Or they may allow the child to eliminate redundant elements of an old procedure and so discover a new and more efficient strategy (Siegler and Jenkins, 1989).

Figure 6.4 Map route
Source: Karmiloff-Smith (1979).

For example, Karmiloff-Smith's (1979) classic study asked children to make notes on the route to be followed by a toy ambulance. The ambulance travelled down a 'road' drawn on a roll of paper, passing a variety of bifurcating turns (Figure 6.4). Some turnings had useful landmarks (such as trees) and others did not. Children saw the route a bit at a time, and so had to find a way of noting which turning to take at each junction. Children used a variety of strategies in this task, from redrawing the whole route to noting landmarks to simply recording 'turn left / turn right', and so on. Sometimes the strategy a child began with could not cope with all of the turns, and children reacted by modifying the strategy to cope better. But children *also* modified strategies (such as recording left or right turnings) which could successfully cope with all of the turnings. For example, Figure 6.5 shows an initial version of a child recording whether to turn left or right (A), and a subsequently modified version (B), in which the child has added redundant information. This change in strategy has no obvious objective utility, and is not driven by any aspect of the task per se, nor by a pursuit of success (since the original strategy is perfectly adequate). Karmiloff-Smith (1992) argues that such modifications occur as a result of the child's reflections on his or her strategy: the child observes and notes the properties of the successful strategy, and then makes these more explicit, perhaps becoming explicitly aware of *why* a strategy works, and what elements it draws on for the first time through such reflections.

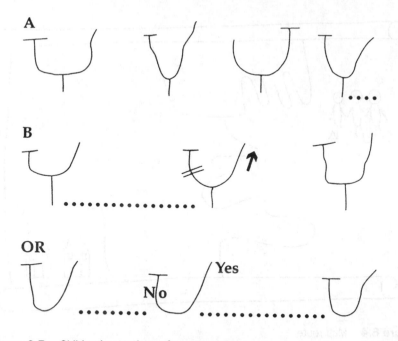

Figure 6.5   Children's notations of map routes
Source: Karmiloff-Smith (1992).

A further example comes from studies of how children learn to add (Siegler and Jenkins, 1989). Four-year-old children typically add two numbers together in a rather laborious way. Asked to add five and three, for example, they first count out the five on one hand, then separately count out three on the other hand (Figure 6.6) before then counting all of the fingers together to make eight. Implicit in this strategy is that one can *directly count on* from the first sum, for example, counting out the first five on one hand, and then carrying on 'six, seven, eight' on the other, without counting the three extra fingers separately (Figure 6.6). This intermediary strategy then paves the way for a further refinement: not counting out the first five either, but starting 'five . . . six, seven, eight' (Figure 6.6). Thus a sequence of small steps, each making explicit something which was implicit in the previous strategy, has created a new and more streamlined strategy for adding (Siegler and Jenkins, 1989).

Similar analyses have shown how new strategies grow out of old ones across a variety of different tasks (Klahr and MacWhinney, 1998; Siegler, 1996). In fact, there have been a number of computer simulations of how one strategy can evolve from another through the action of processes which monitor ongoing problem solving looking for patterns (Klahr and MacWhinney, 1998; Shrager and Siegler, 1998; Siegler and Shipley, 1995).

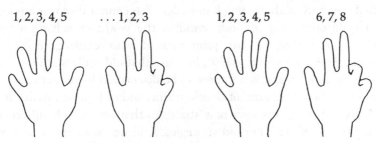

First strategy: counting everything out.

Intermediate strategy: counting out the first number and then counting on.

Final strategy: counting on from the first number.

Figure 6.6 Counting strategies
Source: Thornton (1995).

But powerful as such self-reflective processes are in the construction of new strategies, they cannot really account for all the rich phenomena we see in childhood development, nor even for the process of new, creative discovery in adult problem solving. The difficulty is this: the only thing that one can discover from this kind of self-reflective process is, by definition *something that is already implicit in your existing strategy or understanding.* This means that all new strategies and discoveries constructed in this way must inevitably build on and resemble existing strategies, and share a conceptual structure with existing knowledge. You cannot discover a new, qualitatively different way of understanding the world or solving a problem simply by reflecting on the properties of your existing understanding (Sophian, 1997; Thornton, 1999), because that old understanding does not contain the new idea: it is not there to be discovered by reflection.

And yet, the key feature of development, and of human intelligence as a whole, is that we *do* discover new strategies that are entirely different from and unconnected with our old strategies. And we do discover new ways of understanding the world which are qualitatively different from our previous ideas, even revolutionarily different (Brown, 1990; Gelman and Brenneman, 1994; Kuhn, 1962; Siegler, 1997). The obvious implication is that somehow, our interactions with the world, the learning processes involved in shaping our behaviour as we solve problems must import the seeds of these new ideas and strategies (Sophian, 1997). How could this be, if learning from feedback is itself constrained by our existing conceptual understanding?

Conceptual change from problem solving processes

As Piaget pointed out, it is very hard to see how the mind could come to discover something for which it has no pre-existing structure or representation. How can we discover what we lack the mental apparatus to understand? But this problem may look harder than it is: for the structure of our conceptual understanding is not the only source of structure which influences our behaviour (Lewis, 2000; Sophian, 1997; Thelen and Smith, 1994; Thornton, 1999). There is also structure in the world, in the mechanics of our bodies and in the physical and social worlds with which we interact. These multiple sources of structure come together to shape problem solving behaviour in ways which can implicitly incorporate ideas and patterns of action which need have no initial representation in our minds at all. This new behaviour is then available for review by self-reflective processses, which now have something new to discover.

One key characteristic of problem solving is that it is *goal directed*. As we have seen earlier in this chapter, solving a problem involves finding a means of changing an initial state of affairs into a new one. This eventual goal may not be reachable in one step: it may be necessary to work through a series of subgoals along the way. The exact nature of these subgoals may be influenced by many factors, from our understanding of the social dynamics of the problem to be solved to the physical details of the problem or the limitations on the tools available to deal with it. The complex patterns of subgoals we adopt during problem solving may change and redirect our problem solving in unexpected directions, and so lead us to novel strategies (Sophian, 1997).

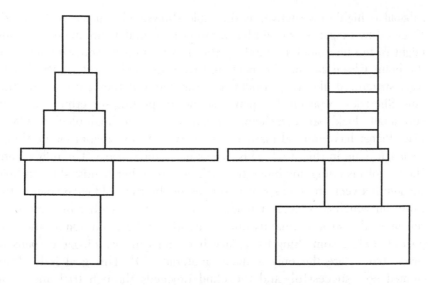

Figure 6.7   Building a counterbalance bridge

An example of such processes at work comes from a microgenetic study of children's efforts to build a bridge between two towers either side of a 'river', using wooden blocks as shown in Figure 6.7 (Thornton, 1999). None of the blocks provided is long enough to span the river, so the child must construct a counterbalanced bridge to solve the problem. Few children solve this problem immediately, even at the age of nine years. But the majority of seven- and nine-year-olds do solve it, by building bridges where counterbalance is either implicit or explicit. But five-year-olds have enormous difficulty with this task. They do not know enough about balance to understand how to construct any sort of counterbalance. Only one five year old in Thornton's study discovered how to build a counterbalanced bridge and so solved this problem, and it is clear from her problem solving that she did so entirely on the basis of feedback from the task.

Tablee 6.1 summarises how this child went about exploring this problem. This analysis shows how the child's goals gradually evolved through the course of problem solving as a result of feedback from the task. At first her goal is simple: find a block long enough to span the river (A). When none can be found, she adopts the subgoal of *making* a block long enough to do the job, by using two blocks to create a long enough span (B). This in turn leads to a new problem: the two blocks will not stay in place, they fall into the river. She adopts a new subgoal of fastening them together to solve this problem (C). This subgoal is doomed, since no means of actually fastening the blocks together has been provided. Nonetheless, this subgoal is highly instructive, as the table shows. Like many five-year-olds observed by Piaget, this child has a rather poor understanding of how one might fasten one block to another. She tries to do it by squeezing hard on the point where the blocks meet mid river, as might work, if the blocks were structured like 'Lego' bricks, for example: but they are not, and this fails. She tries to fasten the spans together by putting something (another, very small block) between them, as might work if the small block had been glue (Piaget has reported many children trying to use inappropriate things as 'magic' glue in this way). This makes everything worse. The only means she has of fastening any block to anything else is her hands: she can hold the join between the two spans mid river, or she can hold each span to the tower on which it rests. But holding the assembly together by hand does not meet the social demands of the situation. The child adopts the new goal of finding something to replace her hands in fastening the spans in place: blocks are the only available materials (D). This goal is far from immediately successful, and the child proceeds through trial and error, showing no sign of conceptual understanding of the solution she is now working towards. Indeed, her early efforts are so unsuccessful that she several times abandons this goal and goes back to looking for one block long enough to span the river (E, F). However, eventually, feedback from the physics of the task shapes her towards discovering that bigger blocks make better substitutes for her hand pressure than smaller ones (though she may not yet realise that it is their weight which is relevant), until she has constructed a counterbalanced bridge.

Step by step, then, this child's goal driven behaviour gradually exposed her to new feedback from the physics of the task in hand, which then gradually restructured her behaviour until an entirely new and qualitatively different strategy had been formed. This new strategy was not inherent in the child's initial understanding, but is now available to be reviewed and reflected on, and in time, explicitly understood. Note that it is not just the child's actions that have changed: her attention has also been directed to the relevance of the size of blocks best used as substitute hands. She ends the task far better placed to attend to, and so learn about factors relevant to counterbalance. And this qualitative change has been achieved without the need for the child to have any anticipation of the eventual outcome of her problem solving. Each small change in her goals on the way to forming this new strategy made sense to the child, from the persepective she had at the time (Table 6.1). The crucial factor in the construction of this new strategy was the structure of the physics inherent in the task itself, which constrains both the goals and the actions the child adopts, without the child needing to understand what those physical forces are. Gravity will cause her simple two span bridges to fall in at step C, whether the child understands gravity or not. And the principles of balance and counterbalance will apply at steps G, H and I , whether the child understands them or not.

The process described by Thornton (1999) is not new: at some level we have always known that the characteristics of tasks shape our problem solving. What has been underestimated is the power of such apparently simple learning processes in creating the conditions for changes in the structure of our behaviour and the factors we attend to in problem solving, and so to open the gateway to fundamental conceptual development.

If simple learning processes have such power in shaping new ideas, why did only one five-year-old in Thornton's study discover how to build a counterbalanced bridge? Of course, the answer must in part lie in the children themselves: the successful five-year-old was very persistent in trying to meet each of her subgoals, but did not persevere endlessly on any one effort. Other five-year-olds either gave up on fruitful strategies too quickly, without exploring them much, or persisted with unfruitful strategies to the exclusion of trying anything else. Getting the right balance between trying new things out and sticking with a strategy is a crucial factor in the development of new strategies (Siegler, 2000).

But analysis of the other five-year-olds' problem solving in this task shows that very fine grain details of a child's strategy can greatly alter the feedback the child gets from the task, and so determine the likelihood of making a new discovery. For example, two other five-year-olds tried to hold spans in place atop their towers, as the child in Table 6.1 did, and so could have received the same useful feedback from the task that she received. But in both cases, the towers these children had built were so unstable that they collapsed. Thus these children received very different feedback, which discouraged them from exploring the avenue so fruitful to the successful child. In both this task and other types of problem solving, some strategies will be more effective in leading to new discoveries than others (Thornton, 1999), and some versions of a task will be richer in feedback likely to trigger strategy change than others.

In Summary

What a child knows, and the way his or her knowledge is structured have an enormous effect on planning, problem solving and learning.

Planning – the process of identifying goals and actions which will achieve those goals – is, in many ways, a critical control process in problem solving. The ability to plan effectively depends on understanding the nature of the problem, the nature of the solution, and the possible steps which might transform one into the other. The younger the child,

Table 6.1 One child's path to new discovery

Sequence of construction	Goal	Feedback available	Comment
A: Measures single blocks against the gap between towers	Find long enough span	There isn't one	Always chose one of the four longest blocks, two or three repetitions with each
B: Measures two span blocks against the river	Make long enough span	Two blocks will reach	Still aiming at a support bridge
C: Juxtaposes two span blocks, varying the point of contact (end on/overlapping at centre – left over right over left); and varying the means of securing the join (squeezing join together very hard/inserting another small block at centre join between spans (apparently as a 'fastener') before release; holding in place by hand)	Fasten two span lengths together	The point of join makes no difference; squeezing does not create a join; inserting a block does not create a join; this assembly is less stable, centre of bridge dips more strongly, ends of bridge lift away from towers more strongly; hands can enforce join; hand pressure maintains spans on towers	Focus is plainly on fastening things together to allow a support bridge: no balance related procedures and insertion of 'fastener' block at central join confirms no recognition of need to bring bridge pieces into balance; proprioceptive feedback could cue the new goal of fastening bridge ends to towers; and also the idea that pressure (e.g. of hands) can fasten the spans to the tower
D: Moves small 'fastener' block from central join; after maintaining assembly by hand pressure, replaces one hand with small block at tower end of span; repeats with numerous different small blocks, using one block at a time	Use blocks to substitute for hand pressure in fastening span to tower	Blocks fail as fasteners	Still no recognition of weight as relevant here; successive blocks tried as 'fasteners' are all small and light (e.g. semicircle; triangle; small square; small pillar); only one is ever used at a time, so successive tries do not add weight – and often reduce it

	Reversion to original goal	This is still not achievable	
E: Returns to seeking one span long enough to cross the river in a simple support bridge	Reversion to original goal	This is still not achievable	This reversion confirms that the child did not recognise how promising her previous strategy was, and could not interpret the reason for its failure (i.e. inadequate weight on rear of span)
F: Alternates between Phases D and E, as above	Alternating between D and E, as above	As for D and E above	The child faces two sets of negative feedback, but has prior experience of successful support bridges; the only positive feedback so far is that pressure (hands) can support spans
G: As Phase D, but widens the range of blocks tried as 'fasteners' – including some larger (heavier) ones	Use blocks to substitute for hand pressure in fastening span to tower	Larger blocks work better	This grew gradually from previous alternating strategies – during which search slowly widened both when looking for a single span and when looking for an effective 'fastener'
H: As Phase D, but focusing on finding large blocks to place on towers, and now using more than one block to secure each span	Press spans in place with larger/heavier blocks	Larger/heavier blocks are more successful but often overbalance on unstable towers	The child's actions are now creating a counter-balance bridge, though it is unclear that the role of weight per se is explicitly recognised; the feedback from her actions is capable of revealing the role of weight and balance
I: Adjusts towers creating broader and more stable structures able to support more blocks; adds spans and fixes in place with stable piles of large blocks; successfully completes counterbalanced bridge	Create stable towers to support more blocks; fasten spans in place with big/heavy blocks	Problem solved	The child's actions now swiftly create an effective counterbalance bridge; it remains unclear to what extent the role of weight or balance is explicitly recognised

Source: Thornton (1999) pp. 588–603.

the less such knowledge has been developed, and the less powerful is the ability to plan.

However, successful problem solving need not depend on conscious processes of planning at all. The strategies the child uses in any task, the way these strategies are shaped and deployed, indeed, the very process by which fundamentally new strategies are discovered need not involve conscious understanding, nor any sort of plan. Children's actions are shaped, not just by their minds, but by structures in the world. Simple learning processes can, in interaction with such world structures, create complex patterns in the child's behaviour: patterns which the child need not understand or recognise to acquire, but which, once learned, can be reflected on to allow more conscious discovery and understanding to develop.

EXERCISES

1   Ask a friend to complete a puzzle such as the 'Tower of Hanoi'. How hard is it to record everything he or she does in such a task? What are the difficulties in making a microgenetic study of how people solve such problems?

2   Compare the traditional 'linear' model of cognitive develpment shown in Figure 6.2 with the 'overlapping waves' model shown in Figure 6.3. Which fits the evidence better? Why?

SUGGESTED READING

For a study of the development of planning in infancy:
  Willatts, P. (1997) 'Beyond the couch potato infant: how infants use their knowledge to regulate action, solve problems and achieve goals'. In: G. Bremner, A. Slater and G. Butterworth, *Infant Development: Recent Advances* (Hillsdale, NJ: Psychology Press, Erlbaum).

For an account of Siegler's theory and research:
  Siegler, R. (1996) *Emerging Minds: The Process of Change in Children's Thinking* (New York: Oxford University Press).

For an excellent review of why children's performance in some tasks must be a key source of conceptual development:
  Sophian, C. (1997) 'Beyond competence: the significance of performance for conceptual development'. *Cognitive Development 12*, pp. 281–303.

What Drives Development?

Human intelligence is a complex, multi-faceted thing. In the earlier chapters of this book, we have looked at what intelligence is actually like, what it is that changes as the child develops and grows. But this research leaves a very fundamental question open: *why* does intelligence develop? Why is it that all normal babies eventually develop the characteristic patterns of adult intelligence and powers of reasoning? Does the human mind grow the way a robust plant, a weed does, say, through the unfolding of a genetic predisposition, or does it have to be cultivated, nurtured and *grown* the way some tender hothouse plant must be? Answering this question will obviously bring us a deeper understanding of the nature of the human mind. But it also bears on very practical issues, to do with the way we educate and parent our children, the opportunities and experiences we give them.

Biology, Evolution and the Origins of Intelligence

The fundamental starting point for any effort to understand the development of the human mind must be a recognition that we are biological creatures with an evolutionary history. This obvious and apparently simple truth has more far reaching implications than one might suppose, implications which are only now beginning to be explored (Bjorklund and Pellegrini, 2000; Geary and Bjorklund, 2000). Our biological inheritance includes not only a certain genetic endowment determining the shape of our minds at birth and contributing to their propensity to develop in certain ways, but also a physical body with the capacity to do some things but not others: to see colour, but not infra-red, for example; to walk, swim and climb but not to fly; to balance upright in some postures but not others, and so on. Through our genetic endowment, evolutionary history has shaped the course of development to fit us for certain environments, and for certain roles within those environments.

A genetic blueprint for the mind

To some extent, it is clear that minds grow in response to the genetic pro-gramme which defines our species. We are born already equipped with quite sophisticated mental apparatus to allow us to perceive and recognise the world (Chapter 2), to orient to people and learn language (Chapter 3), to learn to associate one thing with another, draw simple inferences, remember and solve problems (Chapters 5 and 6). The first stage of mental growth (before birth) is more or less entirely governed by this genetic inher-itance. Assuming no untoward event in the womb, no defect in the genetic code, the initial structure of the human mind grows without needing input from the world and without any effort on the part of the individual or anyone else. But why does the infant mind progress beyond this initial stage? And why does development take such a similar path in all normal children?

Some theorists believe that the subsequent development of the mind, at least in the few years after birth is *also* pre-determined by our biological and specifically genetic endowment: it involves the maturing of pre-pro-grammed mechanisms, just as puberty involves the maturing of a pre-pro-grammed physical development. For example, a number of theorists believe that babies are born with mental structures already geared up to *expect* and search for the grammatical structure of language, and to learn vocabulary mapping word meanings into this structure (Chomsky, 1980; Kuhl *et al.*, 1997; Pinker, 1997). These innate mechanisms act to ensure that we will acquire a language, and dictate exactly when and how we approach each step in doing so (Chapter 3). For such theorists, input from the environ-ment serves only to 'prime' mental mechanisms already set and waiting to receive it. One claim often made in justifying this view is that without such a genetic 'leg-up', learning language would simply be too hard for the infant mind to master.

A similar claim has been made about other kinds of knowledge, too. Various theorists have argued that if there were no genetic constraints on what knowledge we acquire and how we acquire it, the task of making sense of the world in a useful way would be too difficult (Keil, 1981, 1990; Geary, 1998; Gelman and Williams, 1998). Certain kinds of knowledge are important for our survival, and evolutionary processes are likely to have ensured that we are well equipped to orient to and acquire such knowledge (Geary, 1998). Learning in these areas is too important for survival to be left to chance, or to idiosyncratic processes within an individual (Gelman and Williams, 1998). These important knowledge domains include not only various forms of social knowledge (including language), but also knowledge about various aspects of the physical world, living creatures (our prey and our predators, for example), tool use and the like (Geary, 1998). Many theorists believe that the infant mind is innately structured to be particularly sensitive to gathering information in each of these key knowledge domains, and indeed, that the kind of knowledge likely to be gathered within each domain is genetically predetermined (Keil, 1990; Geary, 1998; Gelman and Williams, 1998). For example, there is evidence that infants are pre-set from birth to attend to the kinds of perceptual cues which will later allow them to differentiate between the movements of animate and inanimate objects, and to use this information in specific ways to develop an understanding of the concept of animacy (Poulin-Dubois, 1999; Slater, 1997; and see Chapter 2).

In areas where there is a powerful evolutionary function or purpose to the acquisition of knowledge, human babies may learn through the action of pre-set innate mechanisms somewhat like those found in other species. For example, a male stickleback will attack anything that looks even vaguely like the red chest of a potential rival (Timbergen, 1951). These tiny fish are innately predisposed to react in certain ways to certain stimuli. Mechanisms such as this could constrain what human infants attend to in key areas of knowledge, and what kinds of connection they most easily learn (Bjorklund and Pellegrini, 2000). Biases towards learning one sort of thing rather than another are common, across other species. For example, dogs can learn to respond to danger by *running away* far more easily than they can learn to eradicate the danger by less 'natural' responses (standing on three legs, say, or twisting round and round). And some stimuli are far more readily learned as signals of potential danger than others: far easier to associate a dark passage with danger than a cup of tea, for example. Species specific 'preparednesses to learn' some things more easily than others play a major, and functional part in shaping the development of behaviour in other species. There is every reason to suppose that they play an important part in the development of human learning, too.

The structure of the mind: general and domain specific processes

This recent emphasis on the innate origins of not only the initial structures into which learning is fitted, but also the ease with which certain types of thing can be learned is associated with a new view of the way the mind is structured.

Traditionally, we assumed that the key to intelligence was the possession of very powerful and very general tools for reasoning, such as logic. Such general tools work across all areas of knowledge in the same way, creating a single coherent structure for the mind (Piaget, 1968) so that reasoning in any one area would be very similar to reasoning in any other area. An analogy for this view would be a library, where there are books on many different subjects, but all are organised within a single system and processed by a single team of librarians, who treat each book in the same way whether it be on gardening or ancient history. This view of the way the mind is structured lends itself to the idea that there are global 'stages' in intellectual development, so that at a given age a child's thinking will have certain characteristics, no matter what the child is thinking about (Piaget, 1967, 1968).

The notion that there are special domains of knowledge which are of evolutionary importance and about which we are preset to learn in certain ways is associated with a very different view. Various theorists have suggested that the mind is in fact divided into a number of quite separate modules, each specifically devoted to acquiring and using one particular type of knowledge (about living things, say), and each equipped with processes designed specifically to handle that particular type of information in the best possible way (Fodor, 1983; Gardner, 1983; Pinker, 1997). The analogy would be to a library where books on one subject matter were stored quite separately from those on another subject, and were processed by quite different teams of librarians who had no contact with one another. Thus there might be one team who only handled books on biology, and another who only handled books on poetry, and so on, and each team would use different techniques reflecting the subject matter they manage. They might happen to evolve the same techniques for processing loans, but would do so entirely independently, because they do not communicate with one another. Some advocates of this 'modular' model of the mind suggest that every domain of knowledge is processed by a special module, so that there are modules for mathematics and musical skills as well as for knowledge obviously more vital to survival (Gardner, 1983).

The notion that there are certain core cognitive competencies or core domains of knowledge which we are genetically pre-programmed to attend to and to learn about in certain ways, and that this pre-programming shapes the content of what we learn in early childhood is now very widely accepted. Exactly how such processes operate in early infancy, and the extent to which genetic pre-programming controls early conceptual development is far more controversial. For example, almost every researcher would accept that there is a genetic predisposition to attend to and try to imitate language, and that this plays an important part in supporting the infant in learning to understand and produce language. But opinions differ as to exactly how much of the structure of what the child learns about language is already 'wired into' the brain at birth, as we saw in Chapter 3.

What is clear is that genetic pre-programming cannot shape more than the beginnings of knowledge, even in these core domains, because there is far too much variability in what children in different cultures learn. Most obviously, the specific features of the language to which the child is exposed determines what he or she learns about language: Greek children learn Greek, while English children learn English, and in the process, learn quite a different grammar (Kuhl *et al.*, 1997). More subtly, the knowledge children acquire about the physical world also varies in structure and form from one culture to another (Coley, 2000) reflecting the different experiences provided by different environments. The speed with which knowledge is acquired varies too, reflecting the demands of the different contexts in which children grow up. The human mind draws on many processes besides a genetic blueprint in achieving its final adult form.

Epigenesis

And in fact, it is a tenet of evolutionary biology that not only the mental structures but also the physical body that we see in any individual is the product not solely of genetic processes, but of *epigenesis* (Bjorklund and Pellegrini, 2000; Geary and Bjorklund, 2000; Johnson, 1998). All biological processes, whether they determine one's height or the way one understands the world, reflect the interaction between fixed innate processes and specific experience in the world.

Biological constraints on learning are far more fluid and flexible than might be supposed. Undoubtedly, there are specific types of thing which we are preset to learn almost as a reflex, such as the connection between *heat* and *pain*. One need not touch the hotplate on a cooker twice to learn that this will be damaging, though it may take a great many trials to realise that pressing a particular level in an experimental task will have bad consequences.

But our innate endowment for learning also includes certain extremely general and powerful mechanisms, such as those which determine that actions which achieve our goals will be repeated more often than those which do not (Siegler, 1996). In effect, such associative learning processes are nothing but the process of natural selection operating on our behaviour rather than on the evolution of our bodies. Natural selection, the basic mechanism of evolution, can shape not just what we learn but the very processes by which we learn it.

Intelligence and survival

Of course, the question as to why intelligence develops is not just a puzzle about cognitive development in the individual infant. There is a larger question: why did intelligence as we know it develop *at all*? What evolutionary purpose does it serve? And does identifying that purpose help us to understand what motivates the individual human mind to develop, or explain the role of our biological and genetic endowment in that process?

The most serious attempt to understand the evolution of intelligence is that of Piaget (1967, 1968). He argued that one of the defining features of any organism, from an amoeba upwards, is that it must strive to maintain its existing structure or cease to exist. To maintain one's structure one must be able to respond effectively to the environment, and counteract or avoid events which might destroy you. Some organisms have handled this problem by investing heavily in reproducing themselves, and settling for short individual lives. For example, some creatures live in pools which dry out in summer, and adapt to this by leaving eggs under the mud which will survive the dry spell and hatch out when the pool refills, though the parent dies as the water evaporates. A more sophisticated (and individually satisfying!) solution is to avoid the problem, for example by moving to another, better pool as the dry season approaches. But this more sophisticated solution can only work if the individual can, in some way, *anticipate* when it will be necessary to move, and *judge* between pools as to which is the better bet: and this requires the beginnings of intelligence.

Piaget has pointed out that in fact, the perceptual senses provide a basis for anticipating events. Touch allows you to anticipate very proximate events. This is often useful, but is not much help to a snail, say, who has wandered onto a railway track in the path of an oncoming train. Many events require a greater period of anticipation than touch can provide, if the organism is to react successfully and survive. Sight and hearing give us the ability to anticipate events much furthur away than touch, and so increase the organism's ability to maintain its structure. But there is little point in being able to see a pack of predators on the horizon or a juicy meal in the distance without the means of processing this information in such a way as to focus one's responses advantageously. There is an enormous evolutionary advantage in perceptual processes being integrally coordinated with the animal's goals and actions. Thus the senses themselves begin to create the basis for an intelligence, albeit a limited one. According to Piaget, intelligence of the kind human beings possess is the ultimate extension of the senses, an almost 'extra-sensory perception': it is a means of anticipating not just distant events which are already visible or audible (such as the train in the distance), but events which are yet to happen (such as the changing seasons or the harvest consequent on planting seeds) or may never happen (such as winning the lottery or being cornered by a mugger). The evolutionary advantage for a species with *that* ability seems completely obvious.

Piaget argued, therefore, that the evolution of intelligence in all organisms, be they mice, men or martians, is driven by the need to anticipate events in order to survive. This biological imperative determines the shape intelligence takes. Some mental structures are more adequate, more effective in predicting the world than others. More effective mental structures are more stable than less effective ones, because they are less prone to contradiction (and hence brutal eradication) by events. Thus there is a powerful, general biological pressure towards the evolution of progressively more stable mental structures which are effective in predicting what will happen next. Piaget argues that this pressure becomes an end in itself within the individual, so motivating the individual child to constantly improve and upgrade his or her mental structures until a stable adult intelligence is formed.

Piaget's view of the origins of intelligence in our evolutionary drive to survive is still the most powerful explanation of the biological basis of our drive to learn and develop. It is worth noting that this aspect of Piaget's theory about intelligence is still viable, even if he was wrong about the overall structure of the mind or the specific form which mental or developmental processes take within the child. His analyis of the evolutionary origins of the human mind applies just as well whether minds are modular or not, whether intelligence relics on logic or not, and whether the child must construct every aspect of mind for him- or herself, as opposed to drawing on genetic predispositions or social processes. There is still no better account of the evolutionary pressure towards the development of intelligence than that provided by Piaget.

Evolutionary pressure, ecology and the scope of intelligence

However, Piaget's account of why intelligence develops at all leaves us with a question. If all creatures face the same problem of maintaining their physical structure against the depradations of a not always benign environment, why is human intelligence so unique? Why have we alone evolved the complex and sophisticated structures which characterise our species?

One answer to this question lies in the nature of evolutionary forces. Nature's goal is not so much that the individual will survive indefinitely as that it will survive long enough to breed successfully (Darwin, 1859). There are many solutions to this problem in nature, some of which more or less entirely bypass the need for complex anticipation of events or rearrangements of the environment. For example, a pool dwelling creature that can reach sexual maturity in a matter of days, lay a million eggs of which approximately one hundred will hatch out and survive to reproduce themselves might be viewed as very much more successful, in evolutionary terms, than you or I, who must labour for twenty years or more to produce each one of our progeny (and with considerably more stress than the pool dweller knows). In effect, the particular *ecological niche* which a species occupies determines the extent to which there is an evolutionary advantage in developing complex intellectual structures (Bjorklund and Pelllegrini, 2000; Geary and Bjorklund, 2000).

Comparisons between human beings and other primates suggest that the ecological niche which our family of species occupies puts an enormous premium on the growth of social and technological skills. Like us, for example, chimpanzees are highly social and adept in tool use to an extent not seen in species other than primates. There is a family resemblance between their intelligence and ours, despite the enormous gulfs between us. The implication is that the particular structures of our minds have specific evolutionary advantages, in the ecological space which primates occupy.

Support for the idea that human intelligence was shaped by ecological forces comes from studies of human evolution. It is increasingly clear that *homo sapiens* was only one of a number of hominid species which began to walk upright, paint pictures, use language and other tools and generally show signs of an emerging complexity in intelligence. What happened to the others? Were our ancient ancestors somehow more successful than other groups of proto-human beings, gradually taking over and dominating through the process of natural selection? Did we murderously wipe out rival groups of hominids, as chimpanzees (Goodall, 1986) appear to do? Or did seperate streams of hominids intermingle and merge? The answers are (perhaps mercifully) unclear.

But what is clear from evolutionary research is that a common environment creates the same problem for any organism, and tends to shape a common solution. Perhaps this becomes clearest when one examines the development of individuals displaced from the environment which is normal for their species. Chimpanzee babies reared by human beings are far more like humans in their use of tools, and in their apparent abilities to mentally represent events and communicate than are chimps raised among their own species (Call and Tomasello, 1996). The key to this effect is that human caregivers actively try to engage the infant chimp in shared attention to some object or goal, in ways which chimp mothers do not (Call and Tomasello, 1996). Reciprocally, human babies reared outside normal human contexts (for example, so-called 'feral' children abandonned in infancy to their own devices, or subjected to extreme isolation by abusive or inadequate parents) do not develop the normal characteristics of human intelligence.

That changing the social context in which primate infants are raised has such striking effects on the development of intelligence underlines a key feature of the ecology of human (and other primate) survival. Like many other mammals, our solution to the problem of survival and reproductive success is primarily *collaborative* (Cosmides and Tooby, 1992), so that we depend on others for support and invest our own energies in social altruism for evolutionary gains of one sort or another. Social intelligence is highly functional in primate life, and a capacity to engage in social exchange is a key part of our genetic endowment. As we shall see below, it is also a key vehicle for development, creating effects far beyond those wired in at birth.

This research shows that human intelligence has evolved to be importantly prefigured and constrained by innate biological processes, designed by our evolutionary history. But these processes *assume* a certain environment. Human intelligence is *designed* to be both technologically adept, informed by experience, and to be shaped to, *and for,* social processes. Biology is important, but is not enough to explain the eventual shapes of our minds.

The Social Bases of Intelligence

Human beings are supremely social creatures. Right from birth babies orient to human beings as something different and special, something peculiarly attractive in the world (Poulin-Dubois, 1999; Trevarthen, 1993a). And all through life, an extraordinary amount of our time each day is spent interacting with others, watching others, talking to and about one another. Unsurprisingly, the development of reasoning turns out to be a social process to a far greater extent than was traditionally supposed.

Unlike other physcoligist, Wygotsky believed

Knowledge and skill as social constructions

It is easy to assume that, when a child learns about the physical world, he or she is learning objective facts from a fixed universe. But this is not so: you and I, for example, 'know' that the world is sort of spherical, whereas our remote ancestors believed it to be flat. But our 'knowledge' is as much hearsay as that of our ancestors: *someone told us.* Few of us have checked it out for ourselves, or would have the slightest idea how to do so. A very great deal of what we understand about the world is socially constructed and transmitted in this way: quite young children in our culture come to understand things which took the greatest minds of our species many hundreds of years to discover (Carey, 1985), either through being directly taught these ideas or through being deliberately exposed to the kinds of experience likely to make a given discovery salient. You can see this effect for yourself, in studying the psychological research into the development of intelligence reviewed in this book: ideas which seem *obvious* to us now (such as the notion that one can solve logical problems without necessarily using mental processes with a logical structure, see Chapter 4) took decades of research to discover. Every individual's apparently objective knowledge rests on discoveries made by others and incorporated into the way a given culture views the world.

Even at a very mundane level, the 'facts' we know about the world are influenced by social conventions. Take, for example, Piaget's famous 'conservation' task (Chapter 4): a child is shown two identical glasses, A and B, containing identical amounts of water. The water in glass A is then poured into a third, different shaped glass: a taller, thinner one, say. The child is asked to say whether the amount of water in the tall thin glass is the same as that in glass B. Below the age of about seven years, children say that it is not, because the amount looks different. According to Piaget, this error comes about because the young child cannot 'mentally undo' the act of pouring the water from one glass to another, and so cannot understand the relationship between the water in the thin glass and that in the original glass. He or she must therefore rely on how things look. By the age of eight, children give the same answer in this task as would an adult, namely that the water in the thin glass is the same as that in glass B, because the two quantities were originally identical before the pouring. Now, this is normally judged to be the correct answer: but in fact, it is *objectively* wrong! The emptied glass will still be damp inside, because some of the water has adhered to the glass instead of pouring into the new, thin glass. So if the amounts of water in the two original glasses were identical at the outset, there will now be *less* water in the thin glass, because some remains in glass A. But this is a difference which is *socially* agreed to be too small to matter (Light and Perret-Cleremont, 1989). To a far greater extent than we realise, learning to think like an adult is a matter of learning to share the way our own particular culture looks at things, the meanings and assumptions which define our shared understanding of the world, and of what is or is not a good solution to a problem.

The power of cultural expectations on the way we think and reason is powerfully illustrated by two studies from cross cultural research. In the first, shortly after the Second World War, soldiers joining the Ghurka regiments in Nepal were asked to complete IQ tests, 'as fast as possible'. They did so, and scored extremely badly: they had entirely sacrificed accuracy for speed. Asked to try again, and get as many right as possible this time, they laboured extremely slowly and painstakingly over the test, failing to complete it in a time allowing a meaningful interpretation of the results: they had now entirely sacrificed speed for accuracy. Their culture simply did not prepare them for the notion of a *balanced trade* between speed and accuracy, although this is so fundamental a concept in our own culture as to seem completely obvious. In the second study (Cole and Scribner, 1974), researchers were comparing the categorising skills of tribesmen from a remote African area with those of American college students. Asked to group together the things which go together, the American students made taxonomic groupings (all the tools in one category, all the vegetables in another, and so on). But the Africans made completely different groupings, for example putting a mattock with the root vegetables, and so on. To the researchers, the African's behaviour seemed bizarre and immature: surely adults ought to understand the greater sense in sorting like with like? They asked the Africans why they had sorted as they did, and were told that it was because this was how a 'wise man' would arrange things: the things you need for planting a field all in the same place, for example. Asked to sort the things as a 'foolish man' would do, they produced taxonomic categories just as the Americans had done! Cultural norms and expectations had dictated the perception of what is or is not a mature way of solving problems, for both the African tribesmen and the American researchers.

Quite a few of the cognitive skills which we generally assume to reflect the basic character of our biological intelligence are in fact cultural artefacts, 'inventions' which children must be taught through more or less formal processes of socialisation or tuition (Bjorklund and Pellegrini, 2000). The more obvious of these culturally constructed mental processes include those involved in literacy, which is a comparatively late and far from ubiquitous invention requiring years of tuition (Scribner and Cole, 1981), and the ability to understand logical necessity, which can only be induced unreliably and through considerable effort in minds which naturally function in an entirely different way (Johnson-Laird, 1993; Kahneman, Slovic and Tversky, 1982; Sloutsky and Morris, 1998). But many other aspects of the way we approach reasoning and problem solving may owe far more than we recognise to our culture, rather than to our biology. For example, even something so apparently circumstantial to intelligence as how long you persist in trying to make a given strategy work can have far reaching effects on the success of your problem solving or the probability that you will reach a new insight (Siegler, 2000; Thornton, 1999). Our tendency to persist with a given approach of course reflects our own individual history, whether being persistent has paid off in the past, for example. And it reflects our understanding of the particular situation: it makes more sense to persist with a strategy which one has grounds for suspecting will eventually be fruitful than with a strategy about which there is no reason to be hopeful. But persistence also has an important social dimension: persist *too long* and you are seen as 'obsessive'. Give up *too soon* and you are 'a quitter'. Social norms affect not just what cognitive skills we value and use, but the ways in which we apply them.

Learning from watching and collaborating

Young children are keen observers of other people, and wonderful mimics. It seems that we are born pre-programmed to mimic other people's facial expressions and gestures: newborn babies will do this (Kugiumutzakis, 1986, and see Chapter 2). The drive to learn from observing and imitating others may be a basic element of our genetic inheritance. And it would be hard to underestimate the importance of such learning: a great many of the everyday skills and assumptions we acquire in childhood are the direct product of imitating those around us.

But imitation and observation are not the only social processes affecting cognitive development. For example, children learn by interacting with one another, playing together or solving problems together. Even where two children are both fairly inexpert at some task, it seems that they can achieve more working on it together than either one can, working individually (Doise and Mugny, 1984). In part, the advantage of collaborating with another child is that each child may have something to contribute which the other would not have thought of, and the consequent pooling of ideas gives the children an advantage. But collaborating with someone else can stretch the child's understanding in other ways, too.

Piaget (1967) believed that children learn from collaborations where one child, perhaps an older sibling, has a different, and perhaps better understanding of a problem or strategy for dealing with it than the other. Interactions between the children would then often lead to a conflict of views, with each child's perceptions of the task and its solution challenging the other's. Such conflict would create a pressure on the child to develop a better understanding of the task and a stronger strategy (Doise and Hanselmann, 1991).

However, being exposed to a view which conflicts with your own is not as important in generating development as Piaget and his followers thought. The mere existence of differences in approach between two children is not enough to ensure that either will learn anything from an effort to cooperate (Glachlan and Light, 1982). The key factor determining how much children learn from collaborating with one another is, rather, whether or not they find a way to share the decision making.

If two children with different approaches to a problem cannot find a way of sharing the decisions in a task cooperatively, neither will learn much from trying to cooperate. Cooperation can fail for a variety of reasons: the children's assumptions and approaches may simply be too far apart to allow any real sharing of decisions, or the children's personalities may preclude real collaboration. Typically, where there is no joint decision making, one child dominates and does everything his or her way, and the other passively watches. The dominant child learns exactly what he or she would have learned alone. The passive child may feel too excluded to really pay much attention, and so may learn nothing at all. But that is not always the case: the passive child may learn quite a lot from the dominant child's problem solving, if he or she is able to follow what is happening, and work out why the other child's approach works (Doise, 1978). If the dominant child explains what he or she is doing, the passive child can learn quite a lot, provided, of course, that the dominant child is the one with the better initial approach! But in some situations, the dominant child solves the problem so fast, and explains so little that the watching child has no opportunity to learn (Doise, 1978). If your experience is anything like mine, you will have suffered just such a situation when someone tries to explain a particular computer function to you: the expert's fingers fly so fast, and the explanations are so paltry that one is normally left at least as confused as before, if not more so.

Just how do children learn from sharing decisions when they solve problems or play together? Each joint decision is, necessarily, influenced by both children's starting assumptions and approaches to the problem. If these views differ, the children are likely to come to compromises which neither would have thought of alone. These compromises in effect disrupt *both* children's approaches, and so expose them to feedback from the task which they would not have encountered alone, and hence the opportunity to make more new discoveries than they would have, by themselves. So enriching is the effect of such new feedback that even two children starting out with very poor strategies can discover a much better one through their collaboration (Glachlan and Light, 1982). A great deal of learning and discovery in childhood must derive from collaborative play through this sort of process.

Learning from apprenticeship

Of course, children do not only learn from playing together or sharing tasks with their contemporaries. They learn a very great deal from joining in and helping with some activity with adults or older children who are more expert than themselves (Figure 7.1), and who set out, more or less deliberately, to teach the child something, or to support the child's own efforts in some way (Rogoff, 1990).

Figure 7.1 Learning by joining in

Vygotsky (1978) argues that in fact, joining in and sharing some activity with a more experienced partner is one of the main ways in which children learn to understand the world and to acquire skills. It is not simply that the child can learn by watching the more experienced person: sharing the activity actually extends what the child is able to do. For example, a three-year-old can be very successful in baking cakes, say, when his or her mother is there sharing the activity, even though the child would be very much less successful if left to do it alone. In effect, the mother provides a structure for the child's activities, prompting the next step, guiding and supporting the child's effort so that there is no need for the child to have a complete plan, or to remember all the steps involved in baking cakes. In providing what Bruner and Wood have called a 'scaffold' for the child's behaviour, the parent stretches the child's skills, giving the child the opportunity to make new discoveries and learn new things, until he or she is eventually able to complete the activity alone.

The classic description of this type of symbiotic interaction between parent and child is Wertsch's (1979) decription of how young children learn to solve jigsaw puzzles by interacting with an adult. Very young children cannot complete even the simplest of puzzles, and may not automatically view such tasks as fun. At first, the adult has to suggest doing a jigsaw, and to foster the idea that this is a pleasurable activity to share. Typically, with a very young child, the adult then does most of the work of completing the puzzle, searching for pieces that fit, commenting on progress and what needs to be done next, placing the pieces in position, and encouraging the child to do very specific things such as putting *this* piece right *there*. Gradually, the child will understand more and more about solving jigsaw puzzles, and as his or her understanding grows, the adult reduces his or her input allowing the child to take over more responsibility for solving the problem. As the child begins to evolve plans, and to decide what pieces to search for and where to place them the adult's comments become less directive. For example, the adult might say: 'is that the right piece?' Or 'try twisting it round' rather than the more didactic 'here's the next piece' or 'turn it up the other way'. Eventually the adult offers still more global advice ('why don't you leave the sky till later?'), as the child begins to move toward jigsaw expertise.

It is worth commenting that a child in such a symbiotic interaction is learning much more than how to solve a jigsaw, or that such activities are fun. By commenting on how well the task is going, or on what needs doing next, the adult is also teaching the child how to plan, and how to be reflective about his or her own skills and actions. Learning to comment on one's own problem solving in this way first aloud, and later in one's head is, according to Vygotsky, a critical step towards being able to regulate and apply one's skills effectively. Not only this: the strategies that the adult teaches the child to adopt in the face of obstacles (give up and try something else, keep trying till you fix the problem, approach the same problem in a different way) may have a great generality, in determining how the child deploys his or her skills.

Adults don't need to learn to 'scaffold' their children's performance in the way described by Vygotsky and Wertsch: it comes naturally. So, for example, McNaughton and Leyland (1990) found that mothers sharing an activity with a three-year-old spontaneously modify how much support they give to their child to reflect how much difficulty the child is having with the task. The greater the child's difficulty, the more the mother intervenes to help out. But individual adults vary in how effective their support actually is. Some adults are far more sensitive to the child's needs than others (Pratt, Kerig, Cowan and Pape Cowan, 1988; Wood, Wood and Middleton, 1978).

Vygotsky (1978) found that the most effective scaffolding is when the child is stretched to do something new, provided that the new thing is manageable, not too big a stretch over the child's existing capabilities. In effect, the adult lures the child into what Vygotsky calls the 'zone of proximal development': in other words, the area which the child is next ready to master. It is obvious why stretching a child to enter precisely this zone yields the most development: too small a stretch, and there is to little to learn. Too big a stretch, and there is too much to manage.

Parents differ not only in their success in gauging the child's zone of proximal development, but also in the style of support they offer. Children learn the most when the adult partner strikes the right balance between nurturing the child's efforts and demanding good progress with the task (Pratt *et al.*, 1988). Parents who describe and demonstrate what needs doing clearly teach their children more than those who do not (Wood *et al.*, 1978). But the crucial factor in the child's success in learning from such interactions is that the adult is able to actually share decision making with the child, rather than simply being didactic or dictatorial (Radziszewska and Rogoff, 1991).

Where does the ability to scaffold our children's learning come from? Even quite young children can modify their explanations of things and their behaviour to accommodate the needs of a younger or less skilled child, to a degree. But children are not so adept at this as are adults. For example, Radziszewska and Rogoff (1991) tested how much nine-year-old children would learn about how to plan effective routes between stores on a map either from interacting with an adult or from interacting with another nine-year-old who had already been trained to complete the task efficiently. Children learned more from interacting with the adult, because the adults were far better at explaining their decisions and actions than were the nine-year-old mentors, and far better at sharing the decision making with the pupil. Thus the ability to scaffold a child's learning must itself develop, perhaps out of our increasing ability to understand the child's needs and limitations, however natural the tendency to accommodate to a novice in this way may be.

Culture and the pace of development

Many theories of cognitive development note that there are regularities in the ages at which children master certain things: language by about three years, for example, biological knowledge by the age of ten years (Chapter 5), and the principles of balance between eight and eighteen (Chapter 5). Of course, not every child masters a given aspect of cognitive development at the same age: there can be wide variation between children in when they produce their first sentence, or master arithmetic, and so on. Nevertheless, the *sequence* in which things are mastered is often remarkably constant across different children.

Some of the regularities we see in the sequence of development through childhood reflect fundamental aspects of how children learn about the world. For instance, a child could hardly learn to add numbers together if he or she had not understood the nature of numbers. Certain things must be learned or discovered as a basis for future development, and this fact inevitably determines that children will master ideas in a certain sequence. Many aspects of knowledge or skill are *cumulative*, with each progressive step resting and depending on the one below (Gagne, 1968).

Does the cumulative nature of knowledge and skill wholly explain the pace and sequence of development? It does not. First, the mere fact that knowledge is cumulative does not, in itself, explain why children take a given amount of time to master a particular idea. Why, for example, do children typically not discover when it is necessary to take into account the position of a weight on a fulcrum as well as the amount of weight per se, before the age of fourteen? There is no constraint intrinsic to the mind which dictates this, since eight-year-olds can be taught the appropriate rule quite easily (Siegler, 1976). Nor is it obvious that the knowledge to be mastered in understanding the principles of balance in this way is more difficult or more time consuming to discover than, say, the principles underlying the many computer games which children master with ease at a much younger age.

Nor can the cumulative nature of knowledge explain why the sequence in which certain types of skills are acquired, and the form those skills take, can vary from one culture to another. For example, whereas ten-year-old 'Western' children are typically rather disorganised, impulsive and easily distracted, their counterparts in other cultures (whether historically or geographically separated from ours) may be the chief childminder, a soldier or in charge of the family's economic welfare, performing complex tasks in a focused and responsible way.

As Rogoff, Gauvain and Ellis (1984) have pointed out, the patterns of development, the sequence and speed with which various skills and knowledge are acquired reflect not just the mental readiness of the individual child to accept and understand a new idea, but also, and very importantly, the expectations about development of the culture around that child, the opportunities it provides to the child for experience and discovery, the pressures it puts on the child to achieve certain goals, and the tolerance it has for certain types of behaviour. Adults control children's opportunities to learn about the world in very direct ways. For example, toys are 'age graded', with certain things being sold as suitable for children of two to four years, say, while others are suitable for children of six to eight years. School activities, too, are designed for particular age groups, with certain goals set for the five-year-old, and other, more ambitious goals set for the eight- or twelve-year-old. Even domestically, parents set younger and older children quite different tasks: for example, few parents would expect a four year old to boil a kettle and make the tea, but most would expect a twelve-year-old to be able to do that.

In part, the things we expect of children of different ages reflect their actual abilities. For example, most four-year-olds lack the physical strength and coordination to handle a kettle full of boiling water safely. Tailoring the tasks we set children to their abilities, and increasing the difficulty of the tasks we set them as they grow older and more competent is a natural part of the process of gradually socialising or 'scaffolding' the child into adult competence. We give children the opportunity to learn about those things which we believe them to be *ready* to master.

But not all of the changing expectations which adults have as to what is or is not appropriate to a child of a given age reflect the child's own abilities or needs, as is clear from a comparison between cultures, or between modern society and earlier times (Rogoff *et al.*, 1984). For example, Alexander the Great had conquered most of the Greek world at the head of his armies, at an age, which today, most societies would think it inappropriate to let a boy go to war at all, still less as a leader making strategic decisions. In 'Western' societies, girls of ten and eleven years are regarded as children, quite unready for marriage or the duties of running a home. But girls of that age regularly marry in other cultures, (Rogoff *et al.*, 1984). Even the age at which we expect children to master more cognitive or scholastic skills, in mathematics or literacy, say, varies from one culture to another: four-year-old children in some Eastern countries presently face pressures to learn and achieve in these areas which would be deemed outrageous (not to mention hopelessly optimistic) in our own society.

What is striking from cross cultural research on child development, then, is that there are great differences between societies (and indeed, between families within a society) in the extent to which adults expect children to be able to plan, to problem solve, to learn and to reason in complex, important tasks. More striking still is the fact that, by and large, *children live up to* whatever expectations their culture has of them. A nine-year-old African boy *can* be trusted with the family's main economic resource, where his European counterpart may well lose the front door key if trusted with it for an afternoon.

Of course, adults cannot control every aspect of the child's experience and opportunities to learn. Some aspects of human existence are universal, because they reflect the character of our bodies or the features of the natural world. For example, a stone thrown in the air will behave in exactly the same way in a wet back garden in England and on a tropical beach in India. Some of the universal characteristics of cognitive development reflect these regularities in the structure of the world, of what is out there to be understood. But even at this level, differences in children's social situations can make a difference to the opportunities they have to learn about the physical world: a child living in a flat in an inner city, with no garden, will have far less opportunity for throwing stones than rural children or those with gardens, for example.

The powerful effect of social expectations on children's cognitive development is underlined by a study of children who normally performed poorly and impulsively in solving mathematical problems (Hartley, 1986). Hartley asked these children to tackle the same type of problem, but this time, pretending to be the cleverest person in their class. Remarkably, the children performed very much better when pretending to be the clever schoolmate than when working on their own account! Obviously, the *ability* to work more carefully and to do better was in their repertoire all along, but not being used. Hartley asked these children why they did not always work so carefully. Their answers reveal that *they knew their place*. They were the ones who were 'bad' at maths in their class. Their normal poor performance was a reflection of living up to this socially defined role.

Minds and Bodies in Interaction with the World

Thus the drive toward intelligence comes from evolutionary pressures to adapt more effectively to the ecological niche in which we humans live. Our species is fundamentally social, solving the problems of survival through processes of mutual dependence and support. Social processes play a vast role in shaping what the child knows, how this knowledge is acquired, and the pace at which this development proceeds. But it would be wrong to conclude that the child is a passive passenger through development, simply led by others, or merely the product of a genetic blueprint for the unfolding of an innate intelligence. Development is also very importantly a function of the child's own mental processes and how these interact with the world.

As we have seen in earlier chapters, babies are born with an impressive array of mental tools for learning, solving problems, planning, making new discoveries and generally making sense of the world around them. Using these tools, they develop their own ways of doing things, rather than simply copying what others about them do. For example, babies move about on all fours rather than walking as the older members of their families do. Young children produce systematic 'mistakes' in speech, such as 'I wented', which they are not copying from others. Their problem solving, too, shows characteristic developmental patterns as children invent and use strategies suited to their own level of understanding of the situation (Carey, 1985; Inhelder and Piaget, 1958, 1964; Siegler, 1996). In sum, children are *actively* engaged in interacting with the world, in processing information and in building up their own understandings: understandings which progressively come to resemble those typical of an adult, but which may be very different, along the way. Some theorists have suggested that we should view the child as a 'scientist', engaged in the same pursuit of knowledge and understanding as science, and using the same tools of experiment and exploration to build up and test theories (Kuhn, Amsel and O'Loughlin, 1988).

The mental mechanisms which allow children to develop rules and strategies for solving problems, construct new and better ways of structuring and using knowledge, discover new ideas and so forth are very powerful. Some theorists have suggested that such mechanisms may be the primary vehicle of intellectual development, that developmental processes themselves are really problem solving processes (Siegler, 1996). This thesis does not deny the influence of genetic and evolutionary processes on development, nor the strong social influences on cognitive change. But such forces can only affect a mind if there is some way in which that mind can respond to them. There is no point, for instance, in my trying to explain the origins of intelligence to my dachsund: he has no mental apparatus to make sense of what I say. For the same reason, inviting him into our human ecological niche and rearing him as if he were a child, a member of a human family, will not make him behave more like a human being (the experiment has been tried by millions of doting dog owners). The mental mechanisms of the individual mind must play a critical role in shaping the development of intelligence and mediating the effects of other factors.

Why are children so motivated to make sense of the world around them? It seems likely that the survival advantages of intelligence which we have already noted, and the social pressures to develop make an important contribution to the child's drive to make sense of the world. But it also seems likely that mental processes have an intrinsic tendency to develop towards more complete and adequate levels of understanding and effective action. First, much intelligent action is *goal directed*. That is to say, much of the time we are trying to solve problems in order to achieve an attractive goal, rather than for the sheer pleasure of doing so. Obviously, *learning to do it better* or more efficiently would be an implicit aspect of this goal. But there is substantial evidence that learning, problem solving and developing a better understanding readily become attractive as ends in themselves (Thornton, 1995), so that children invent problems to solve or continue to look for better understanding after the basic task has been succesfully completed (Karmiloff-Smith, 1992).

Mental mechanisms for development

A tendency to work towards better understanding and more efficient strategies may be inherent in the basic way in which problem-solving and learning work. These processes focus on feedback from the world, which continuously identifies which aspects of our action and understanding are useful and which are not (Siegler, 1996). Through a process very like Darwin's mechanism of natural selection, successful ideas and actions will come to dominate, thus inevitably creating developmental progress.

But human learning processes do not stop at making simple associations between success and failure, and selecting behaviour or ideas on that 'blind' basis. Rather, our mental equipment includes powerful devices for reflecting on our own behaviour and cognitive processes and detecting patterns and structures in them (Karmiloff-Smith, 1992). Noticing such patterns and structures allows the child to begin to explicitly use these things in a deliberate way: in effect, to have a degree of awareness of how his or her mind works. Such 'meta-cognition' does not develop all at once. Rather, it is a slow, step-by-step recursive process, where one change in problem-solving behaviour allows a new meta-cognitive insight which allows the construction of a new understanding in the child's mind. This in turn then influences problem solving and contributes to a new discovery, which itself allows yet another new meta-cognitive insight, and so on (Karmiloff-Smith, 1992).

Quite why the self-reflective mental mechanisms which generate meta-cognitive processes developed in our evolutionary history is unclear. Such processes may be unique to the human mind (Karmiloff-Smith, 1992). But the effect of such mechanisms is to move our species beyond developmental processes focused primarily on achieving *behavioural success* to lay the foundations for a new kind of self-reflective, self-aware intelligence that is freed from its concrete and specific roots.

Whatever their origin, the mechanisms which generate meta-cognitive awareness are the source of our characteristically human intelligence (Karmiloff-Smith, 1992). Through the gradual accretion of knowledge about how our own mental systems work, we can construct ever-more abstract understandings of both the specific information we have about the world and of the range of tools available to our minds. Through this process we can come to perceive ever-more widespread analogies both within and across specific domains of knowledge, and hence, step by step, create for ourselves a very general form of intelligence which can bring its tools to bear across almost any domain.

Certain key insights seem to lay the foundation for this new and general meta-cognitive intelligence. Chief among these is probably the realisation that people have minds, that these minds work in certain ways and have certain limitations (Chapter 3). This discovery is associated with a very general upsurge in meta-cognitive understanding across many domains, for example in understanding memory processes and strategies. The growth of this awareness may explain the very remarkable changes which we see typically in children between the ages of six and eight years, across all cultures (Piaget, 1968).

Development in physical context

Powerful as the mental mechanisms of the mind are in generating both cognitive and meta-cognitive development, such mechanisms do not operate in isolation even within the individual problem solver working alone. Their operation is constrained, not just by their own nature and existing structure, but also by the physical properties of the world in which they operate.

Our human intelligence reflects the specific physical circumstances in which it develops. The human body has a certain shape, limbs with certain properties, an opposable thumb. And this body exists in a physical universe with certain properties, such as gravity, the fact that an object cannot be in two different places at once, that one solid object cannot pass through another nor time run backwards, and the like. These physical properties of the universe constrain the discoveries our mental mechanisms make, in complex and subtle ways.

Quite obviously, the physiological constraints of our bodies limit what we can do and what we can discover, and encourage us to make some kinds of discoveries and inventions rather than others. Our arms have a certain length and strength, and our efforts to reach out and grasp things must be shaped by this unavoidable fact. We cannot fly as birds do, nor walk on water as many insects can, and the plans we make for reaching distant objects must reflect these physical limitations. But not all the constraints which come from living in human bodies *limit* our activities (Gelman and Williams, 1998). In fact, the physical properties of our bodies in interaction with the world can be a rich source of new discoveries. For example (see Chapter 2), a baby need have no idea that crawling is a possible means of moving from A to B, nor even any idea that it is possible to move *oneself* from one location to another (which has always been accomplished by being carried by someone else, in the infant's experience so far) and yet can learn to crawl as a result of the properties of the human body (Adolph, Vereijken and Denney, 1998). The baby sees an attractive object, out of reach, and stretches a hand out toward it. The further the stretch, the more the child's centre of gravity shifts dangerously forward, to the point of complete instability: *the body* tips over. In lowering the outreached hand to prevent a complete crash to earth, the child has, from an objective point of view, taken a 'step' nearer to the desirable object. The hand first reached out is now fully occupied in counteracting gravity, so the child reaches forward again with the other . . . overbalances again, and is a another step closer to the goal, quite by serendipity. Through such processes, the physics of the body, in interaction with the physics of the world, open up a whole new class of activities and adventures to the infant: the fact of crawling *by accident,* and its attractive rewards can now gradually be 'discovered' and enacted deliberately.

Likewise, more subtle and sophisticated elements of knowledge can be imparted almost accidentally by the physical properties of the world. Young children's theories about the world (like the theories of adult scientists) are not necessarily very good theories. The best minds of our species, for example, have held some theories about the origins and structure of the universe or the shape and centrality of our planet in that enterprise which strike us now as laughably naive (perhaps it is a blessing that we shall not live to see the humour with which our own conceptions may be regarded, in the twenty-fifth century). But however partial or wrong human theories about the physical world are, whether held by young children or by erudite scientists, these theories are not *independent* of the properties of the world. They are always shaped by the facts of physics. Neither scientists nor young children adopt theories that fly in the face of the evident properties of the physical world (Sophian, 1997). This need not involve any conscious process on the individual's part (Siegler and Stern, 1998; Thornton, 1999). Structures inherent in the physical world determine the feedback we get from our actions and theories, and this feedback shapes our discoveries, whether we understand why or not, as we saw in Thornton's (1999) study of a child learning to build a counterbalanced bridge in Chapter 6.

An Integrated Model of Intellectual Development

As we have seen in this chapter, a wide variety of factors shape and influence the development of the human mind, from the biological endowment selected for us through evolution and the social instruction and pressures integral to our species's solution to the problems of survival, to the specific structure of the mental mechanisms we have evolved to mediate between such forces and the impact of the physical properties of our bodies and our world on what we are likely to discover. Until recently, developmental psychology consisted of a vast range of different theories each of which emphasised one or other of these factors as the key to the development of intelligence. But at the start of this new millennium we have, for the first time, the possibility of developing an understanding of how all these factors come together to create intelligence. Furthermore, this new approach is not peculiar to developmental psychology. Rather, it draws on principles which apply equally well in understanding how complex patterns and structures develop in the natural world, in physics, chemistry, the evolution of life as a whole. For the first time in human history we may be on the verge of a theory which can explain how animate, feeling, self-aware intelligence can develop from the raw and insensate elements of which we are composed (Lewis, 2000).

Dynamic systems theory

Dynamic systems theory is not really a single theory at all. Rather, it is what Darwin called a *dangerous idea*, in much the same way as his own concept of evolution through natural selection was a dangerous idea (Dennett, 1996; Kauffman, 1995; Lewis, 2000). Darwin's notion changed forever our understanding of human nature and its origins in a very fundamental way. Dynamic systems theory is set to have an equally revolutionary effect on how we understand the world and our intellectual development in it (Lewis, 2000).

According to this approach, the development of the mind is just one example of a very universal tendency for complex order and structure to emerge from repeated interactions between very simple elements, without there being any programme or agenda to create such order inherent in those elements. The new complex structure is not prefigured in the simple processes in any way, but rather, is an *emergent property* of those processes: it 'just happens'.

This 'self-organising' tendency in simple systems was first noticed in mathematics, where it was given the name 'chaos theory'. The same basic principles of self-organisation have been used across all the natural sciences, to explain the origins of structures as varied as the origins of the universe itself to the structure of complex chemicals or the genesis of a snowflake or the evolution of a snail. These same principles of nature can also apply in explaining human development (Lewis, 2000; Thelen and Smith, 1994).

What is a self-organising system like? In the context of human development, the *system* we are talking about is not the individual child per se, but all the bodily and mental processes which make up that child *in interaction* with all the properties of the physical and social world the child inhabits (Thelen and Smith, 1994). It is the interaction of *all* of these elements together which creates surprising new outcomes in the child's behaviour and understanding, as we have seen earlier in this chapter in the child learning to crawl without meaning to through the effects of gravity on a reaching arm; or in the child discovering how to build a counterbalance bridge through being compelled by the natural forces of physics to adjust her efforts to factors she does not anticipate or understand, as in the study described in Chapter 6.

Changes in self-organising systems can be truly novel and entirely unexpected (Thelen and Smith, 1994). They arise through a sort of feedback loop through which tiny changes in an ongoing process (such as the way muscles coordinate with one another in reaching out for a toy) gradually allow what was once a set of disconnected events to become a single functional unit (deliberate reaching, for example, as opposed to merely waving the arm about hopefully in the general direction of the toy). This new unit of behaviour (deliberate reaching) can be recruited to new functions (such as reaching for ever more distant objects and eventually overbalancing) in ways which *both* reinforce the new structure (the coordination of arm muscles) *and* allow new patterns and functions to emerge (such as crawling). New structures emerge because of the properties of the system *as a whole*, rather than because the baby has any intention to learn to reach or to crawl, or any genetic program to do so.

A critical feature of self-organising processes in human development is that they are functional (Lewis, 2000). That is to say, what holds a newly emergent structure together is the fact that it serves a purpose. As the system becomes ever more complex, goals themselves become organised into complex patterns, so that crawling changes from being an exciting end in itself (when first discovered) to a mere subcomponent in the pursuit of a much more ambitious goal (exploring a cupboard, perhaps). Patterns among goals hold patterns among other elements of the system together, allowing for the progressive development of more complexity.

According to this view, there is nothing fore-ordained in the patterns we see in child development (Thelen and Smith, 1994). A wide variety of different structures and patterns can develop, through the same simple self-organising processes. To the extent that there are clear regularities in development, common patterns across all children, these reflect common features of the system each child inhabits: so far, all children of our species have grown up in earth's gravity, for example, and virtually all have fairly similar physical bodies, and so on.

As this brief outline suggests, dynamic systems theory has an enormous potential for explaining the origins of intelligent and adaptive action in infancy, and the later emergence of complex new ideas. This potential has only just begun to be explored (Lewis, 2000). A key part of the power of this approach lies in the fact that it can be applied to every aspect of human behaviour and experience, including emotional development (Lewis and Douglas, 1998). But more than that, the principle used here to explain the origins of human intelligence draws on principles which also apply in physics, chemistry and biology at large. The power of this approach is that, for the first time, psychology can provide explanations of its subject matter rooted in principles common across the sciences (Lewis, 2000).

Is there a Limit to the Development of Human Intelligence?

One important feature of dynamical systems theory is that it implies that what human beings can know or discover is limited by the particular features of our evolved minds and bodies and the physical universe we inhabit. There are a number of factors which might constrain what we can know. For example, the physical universe might have only a certain number of secrets to reveal, and once these are known, no further progress in science might be possible (Horgan, 1996). Or, the sensory and conceptual structures we construct in interaction with the physical world might have properties which limit what we can explore or discover next (Fodor, 1983). The social structures we inhabit and rely upon may even make some ideas too dangerous to contemplate. Overall, the implication of such worries is that there are finite bounds to human intelligence, that there are important things about the universe that we are incapable of discovering.

The fear that human intelligence is limited, confined within certain boundaries defined by its current form, has haunted us for a long time. It was widely believed, at the end of the nineteenth century, that all the important discoveries in the physical sciences had already been made and therefore that science had nothing left to contribute. The ensuing century showed how absurdly wrong this idea was (Maddox, 1998). But the fact is that human beings persist in believing that the present structure of our minds is the key to knowledge and development. The idea that our minds are shaped by forces which are literally beyond our imagination offends us, because in this one area, we are all (and quite wrongly) 'control freaks'.

How far we can actually evolve beyond our current intelligence is an open question. We can no more answer it than a medieval monk could anticipate the invention of the hovercraft, or our technological society. But it is worth noting here that social systems and cultures are themselves complex structures whose origins and development may be emergent functions of self-organising systems every bit as much as the individual child's mind. As culture changes, so does the social environment, a key part of the system in which the child's mind develops. Social, rather than individual processes may hold the key to how far human minds can evolve.

In Summary

The evidence suggests that the development of intelligence is influenced by a wide variety of factors. Evolotion has shaped for us a biological form, a genetic endowment which specifies the basic characteristics of our brains and bodies. This endowment includes a powerful drive to be social, to orient to and learn from others. Social processes account for a great deal of the specific knowledge the child acquires, and for the mental tools he or she develops, from forms of reasoning to the adoption of particular cultural inventions such as literacy or mathematics. Our own mental processes are inherently disposed toward new discovery, in the search for more effective strategies, and through the effort to understand the nature of the structures we already possess. All of these factors interact in producing development, functioning as a single system. Drawing on principles from mathematics, physics and chemistry, we are beginning to understand how the rich complexity of human intelligence could be shaped by the interaction of these factors.

EXERCISES

1   How long we persist with a given strategy in trying to solve a problem reflects many different factors. Design an experiment to test the circumstances under which social factors have the most influence on persistence. Could this methodology be used with young children?
2   What are the methodological difficulties in identifying the evolutionary function of a given piece of behaviour?

SUGGESTED READING

For an introduction to evolutionary approaches to development:
Bjorklund, D. and Pellegrini, A. (2000) 'Child development and evolutionary psychology'. *Child Development 71*, pp. 1687–708.

For a study of social factors in cognitive development:
Rogoff, B. (1998) 'Cognition as a collaborative process'. In: D. Kuhn and R. Seigler (eds), W. Damon (series ed.), *Handbook of Child Psychology*, vol. 2: *Cognition, Perception and Language* (New York: Wiley).

For a view of how dynamical systems theory may give us an integrated account of development:
Lewis, M. (2000) 'The promise of dynamical systems approaches for an integrated account of human development'. *Child Development 71*, pp. 36–43.

Individual Differences

So far, each of the chapters in this book has focused on the general pattern of cognitive development through childhood. But, as we began to see in Chapter 7, development does not necessarily follow one single path, nor progress at the same speed, for children in different cultures (Rogoff, Gauvain and Ellis, 1984). Within a culture, there may be variations in the pattern of development between social groups or classes. And indeed, within a single family, each child is a unique individual, and may develop quite different skills, or grow at quite a different pace from his or her brother or sister. Even the age at which major milestones are passed, such as producing a first word or taking a first step, may be vastly different across different children. What accounts for these differences between individuals?

Genetic Differences and the IQ Debate

Just before the start of the twentieth century, Frances Galton observed that abilities seemed to run in families: thus one family might produce talented writers, thinkers or musicians in successive generations, while another family consistently produced individuals with little apparent ability in any area. Such observations led him to the thesis that there is a general *capability* for learning and reasoning, inherited from one's parents, which varies between individuals and which characterises each individual's overall level of cognitive ability. This inherited capability is what we commonly mean by 'intelligence' or IQ.

In a sense, each of us has a fair grasp on what Galton meant by intelligence: we would all, for example, view someone who was a fluent debater, or who was adept at solving abstract puzzles as more intelligent than someone who was poor at those things. In everyday life we constantly judge

how intelligent others are, and explain differences between people by referring to how clever they are. But just how useful is this conception of intelligence in explaining individual differences between people?

It is important to remember two things about intelligence as analysed by
Galton and the psychometric testers who followed him: first, that it is a
theory, and not a fact, that individual human minds can be characterised as
having a given level of general intelligence, a theory which we need to
examine carefully. Second, however self -evident it may seem to us that
there must be something in Galton's idea of general genetic capability
accounting for individual differences, our ancestors found the notion novel
and surprising, not all that long ago.

Psychometric concepts of intelligence

At one level, we know just what intelligence is. It is the capacity to solve
problems and interact with the world in adaptive ways, and has been the
subject matter of every chapter in this book so far. Intelligence is the
product of all one's knowledge, one's strategies and mental tools. Through
earlier chapters of this book, we have focused on the question of how these
abilities develop and change through childhood. We have focused, therefore, on the *processes* which underly intelligent behaviour.

But research into individual differences did not start out from an analysis
of the processes which generate intelligent behaviour. Rather, the aim was
to find ways of measuring differences in the *power* of these processes
between one person and another. The science of psychometrics aimed to
measure intelligence across individuals, not to explain how it works within
an individual. Thus this line of research focused on constructing tests
which would differentiate between one individual and another, and predict
how successfully an individual would complete tasks requiring intelligence
beyond the test situation.

The tendency for early psychometric research to pay very little attention
to the processes which underly intelligent behaviour created great problems
for this line of research, as we shall see through the course of this chapter.
One consequence was that there was very little rationale justifying the
choice of items to include in tests of intelligence. Different tests used very
different items, selected very much on intuitive grounds. For a research
field that assumed that intelligence is a very general function, and that the
same level of intelligence characterises all an individual's behaviour, this
did not seem to matter: general intelligence should function in the same
way across all the different tests. But the one conclusion that has firmly
emerged from psychometric research is that the items you use in testing
intelligence matter enormously. Different items can produce very different

results, as we shall see. This is scarcely surprising, given what we know about how the mind works and the processes through which reasoning is produced, as the earlier chapters of this book reveal. A review of psychometric research supports the view that psychology should start from understanding the mental processes which underly behaviour, even when the primary goal is to measure how much of some process is present in an individual.

Does general intelligence exist?

Overall, ability in one cognitive task does tend to correlate with ability in another area, as one would expect if there were a general component to intelligence, operative across all tasks (Anderson, 1992). But this correlation is not very strong, and the pattern of an individual's abilities can be patchy. For example, you may be very good at solving verbal puzzles, but fairly poor at solving visuo-spatial ones, or vice versa. Or you may be good at science subjects but terrible at learning languages, and so on. Such irregularites in ability in individuals who share the same opportunities to learn are familiar and common (Gardner, 1983). This variability suggests that levels of cognitive skills are not determined by a single factor: not simply the product of a general intelligence. And indeed, modern research into the processes which underly such skills suggests that very specific knowledge in a particular area is critical to how well one can reason that area, so that we would expect the intelligence of an individual's performance to vary from one context to another (Carey, 1985; Chi and Ceci, 1987).

Does this contextual variation in performance from one situation to another mean that there is no such thing as general intelligence contributing to differences between one individual and another? Not necessarily: we still have to explain why there is *some* correlation between an individual's abilities across all cognitive tasks, even if this correlation is not large.

Psychometric theorists tried to explain the patchiness of an individual's abilities by suggesting that general intelligence has more than one dimension: a verbal fluency component, for example, and a visuo-spatial reasoning component (Spearman, 1927; Thurstone, 1938). Others identified a multiplicity of dimensions to intelligence. For example, Guildford (1967, 1988) suggested that it has 180 separate components, and that an individual's mental abilities reflect his or her profile across all of these components. Other researchers have argued that, rather than reflecting an individual's profile across component subskills, variable performance on different types of task reflects the existence of a range of quite separate intelligences, each such 'module' being specifically evolved to deal with a particular area: mathematics, say, or music (Gardner, 1983; Howe 1989).

Whether or not there are multiple separate intelligences as Gardner and Howe suggest remains controversial. As we have seen in earlier chapters, there is some evidence that babies are born with a range of special modules for processing particular kinds of information: physical objects, human faces, language. There is even some evidence that babies are more widely pre-programmed (for example, to be sensitive to number), in ways which suggest that the mind might, indeed, start out with a number of specialist modules (Gelman and Williams, 1998). But it is also evident that to develop any skills, even basic perceptual ones, the child must interact with the world and learn, and that this draws on more general processes and creates a much more integrated, non-modular structure for the mind (Karmiloff-Smith, 1992). Implicit in much early psychometric work on intelligence was the notion that it is these very general processes for learning and reasoning which define an individual's mental power.

Testing mental power

The fact that specific skills such as mathematical or musical ability or even very mundane forms of problem solving reflect learning raises another important issue for tests of intelligence. In measuring such skills, one is not measuring 'pure' intelligence: at a minimum, one is also measuring the extent to which an individual has had the opportunity to learn and develop skills in some area. Scores on tests of mathematical or musical ability reflect experience as much as native wit.

Cattell (1963) responded to this problem by arguing that intelligence has two basic components: *fluid* intelligence, reflecting the general reasoning capacity of the individual, which can be measured in a way uncontaminated by cultural advantages or experiences, and *crystallised* intelligence, which reflects the knowledge and skill the individual has acquired, and is therefore very much influenced by cultural advantages and experiences. Typically, tests of fluid intelligence offer testees puzzles to solve like the one in Figure 8.1, which test the ability to detect visual patterns. The assumption is that such tests are relatively pure tests of processing power, uncontaminated by cultural experience. But whether or not this is really so is unclear. For example, even a test like this assumes that the individual knows how to trade off speed and accuracy in a test-appropriate way, and there is evidence that not all cultural backgrounds prepare the individual for this (see Chapter 7). Children from middle class Western backgrounds may be more familiar than those from other backgrounds with the basic notion of being tested, and the 'rules of the testing game', in ways that continue to affect their performance.

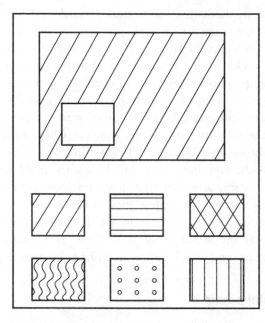

Figure 8.1 A test item of the type used in Raven's Progressive Matrices

What is it that a test of fluid intelligence should be aiming to measure? One theory comes from the work of Anderson (1992). He argued that there is a basic processing mechanism underlying intelligence, the efficacy of which differs between individuals as a function of inherited neurophysiological differences in the speed and efficiency with which information can be processed. The efficiency of this basic mechanism (which is, in effect, very like the concept of working memory we met in Chapter 4) affects all cognitive activity. Some individuals can process information faster than others, and can process more information before their working memory becomes overloaded. The faster you process information, and the more information you can process, the more complex the processing you can do, the more you can learn and the better you can reason. The basic speed and efficiency of the individual's processing system would affect his or her performance across almost all tasks, thus yielding a fairly generalised basis for intelligence.

Theories such as Anderson's may explain why there is a degree of correlation between an individual's success in one area of cognitive skills and another. However, Anderson argues that not all mental activity involves the basic processor, and that the efficiency of the basic processor is therefore not sufficient to explain all the individual differences we observe in the ease of mastering particular skills.

In some cases, we see far less variation between individuals than we would expect, if all mental performances drew on this basic 'working memory' processor. For example, even children with severe cognitive disabilities are adept at interpreting visual depth cues, even though one might assume that this is quite a complex process: it involves translating two dimensional images on the retina into three dimensional objects. Anderson suggests that the lack of individual differences in seeing depth comes from the fact that this basic perceptual process is handled by a special pre-set module in the brain which needs no intelligent processing to function, and does not draw on the power of basic working memory. And in fact, there is strong evidence that infants are born with quite a range of pre-set perceptual skills of this kind, as has been discussed in Chapter 2 (Slater, 1997).

In other cases, pure measures of the power of the basic processor cannot predict individual differences because the skills concerned draw on specific processes for reasoning in that particular domain. Anderson argues that there are specific processors for abilities such as verbal reasoning or spatial processing, mathematics, music, etc. Each individual has these specialised processors, but the speed and efficiency of each specific processor varies between one individual and another. Anderson argues that these specialised processors do not act alone. They are not truly separate modules of the mind, therefore. They draw on the central basic processor. Thus any given ability, in mathematics, say, will reflect the combined strengths or weaknesses of *both* the basic processor *and* the specialist processor, to yield the rich patterns of variation in ability we see between individuals.

Anderson's model of intelligence is innovative and in many ways coherent. It reflects a move away from research which simply tries to measure or define a hypothetical intelligence, and towards an approach more rooted in understanding the processes by which individuals actually process information. However, it is still within the historic tradition begun by Galton, in that it still assumes that the central element determining the intelligence of an individual's behaviour can be defined in terms of innate, stable properties of the power of his or her mental system per se. For Anderson, the best test of general intelligence is a pure measure of processing speed.

Individual variation in intelligence and genetics

The issue of whether of not intelligence is genetically specified is complex and emotive, not least because it has become entangled in questions about racial differences. But there is clear evidence that cognitive abilities *can* be selectively bred for, implying that there is indeed a genetic component in intelligence. For example, Tryon (1940) tested rats for their ability to find their way through mazes. He identified two groups of rats, 'maze bright' and 'maze dull', and bred the bright with the bright, and the dull with the dull. Over a few generations the offspring of the bright rats systematically outperformed the offspring of the dull rats in running mazes. This was so even where the offspring were swapped round so that the bright babies were fostered by the dull parents and vice versa, indicating that the effect was genetic, rather than to do with parenting.

And in fact, as we saw in Chapter 2, every aspect of a human being must have a genetic basis. We grow into baby human beings rather than kittens or ducklings through the unfolding of our genetic blueprint. Quite a lot of the variation between one human body and another is plainly inherited, so that tall dark haired parents are more likely to produce tall dark haired children rather than short blond ones. However, it cannot be the case that any cognitive ability is *entirely* inherited.

Even physical properties such as our height are affected by the environment in which we grow up and by our experiences. Poor nutrition can stunt the growth, and good nutrition enhance it. Childhood illnesses and infections can also reduce growth and affect one's adult height. The steady increases in the height of European and American populations over the centuries reflect the rise in living standards and reduction of disease rather than a genetic change in the population. The current generation of teenagers are the tallest ever, reflecting the vast explosion of preventive medicine and access to foodstuffs of the past twenty years. In the same way, intelligence is quite plainly affected by experience and environment. For example, children who have been severely malnourished show a marked decrease in intelligence. Those deprived of appropriate stimulation show clear decreases in the basic ability to learn.

Thus the issue for research is not whether or not intelligence is inherited as opposed to being formed by our experience and environment: both *must* be involved. The question is, therefore, how much each contributes. But this question is harder to answer than you might think (Petrill, Saudino, Cherny, Emde, Fulker, Hewitt and Plomin, 1998).

Identical twins develop from a single genetic code (since they develop from the same egg) and have much more similar levels of intelligence than do less genetically similar individuals, as one would expect, if there were a clear element of heritability in intelligence. Likewise, adopted children's intelligence correlates more highly with that of the biological parents than with that of their adoptive parents, pointing to a clear hereditary element in intelligence. But even in identical twins, the correlation in intelligence is far from perfect, showing that intelligence is not entirely inherited, but is affected by other things.

Can we calculate what proportion of intelligence is inherited, and what proportion is due to the environment or experience? No: or at least, not in any generally meaningful way. This is because the relative importance of each factor will vary, reflecting the situation. Imagine a science fiction world where every child somehow has exactly the same experiences. In such a world, the relative lack of variation in the environment means that differences between individuals will almost entirely reflect genetic factors, and intelligence will appear to be very highly heritable. Or imagine a world in which a set of cloned children are each reared in vastly different environments. Here, the lack of genetic variation will mean that differences between the individual children will entirely reflect environmental factors, and intelligence will appear to be due to environmental factors. Of course, neither of the extreme worlds imagined here actually exists (yet). But the problem this 'thought experiment' reveals applies to measures of the heritability of intelligence. How much individual variation in intelligence seems to reflect genes depends on how much variation there is in the environment and in the gene pool in which the measure is taken. No absolute measure is possible.

Does intelligence develop through childhood?

In one sense, of course, intelligence obviously develops through childhood, as we have seen throughout this book. A five-year-old child is capable of a range of intelligent behaviour far beyond the powers of a two-year-old, but far less than that of the average twelve-year-old. Those components of intelligent action which reflect learning and experience change powerfully as the child grows older. However, Anderson (1992) argues that the power of an individual's basic processing mechanism (its speed and efficiency) does not change through childhood. In effect, his thesis is that an individual's basic mental ability is a constant.

Testing Anderson's thesis is quite difficult, in that it is hard to find tests of processing speed and efficiency which will work as reliably for young infants as those for older individuals. Usually, intelligence in infancy is measured by comparing the individual child's progress on various developmental milestones to that of the average child. For example, the Bayley Scales of Infant Development (Bayley, 1969, 1993) looks at the child's motor skills (such as grasping and throwing objects), mental skills (such as searching for a hidden object, following instructions) and behaviours (such as goal directedness, social responsivity). Each child is given a development quotient (DQ), with a DQ of 100 representing average progress, DQ scores above 100 reflecting accelerated development, and those below 100 reflecting developmental delay behind the average. However, DQ scores do not correlate with the scores the child will later achieve on IQ tests

(Honzik, 1983). Since what DQ tests measure is very different from the abstract reasoning power measured by IQ tests, or from the pure processing power identified as the root of intelligence by Anderson, this is perhaps not surprising. More recent research has tried to make more direct estimates of basic processing power in infants, for example by measuring how fast six-month-old babies habituate to a novel stimulus, and how much they prefer novel stimuli over familiar ones (Thompson, Fagan and Fulkner, 1991). Such measures show a reasonable correlation (0.46, on average) with IQ in childhood.

Studies of older children's scores of intelligence tests seem to support the idea that levels of intelligence remain fairly constant through life. For example, Honzik, Macfarlane and Allen (1948) followed 250 children from the age of four to eighteen years, testing their intelligence at regular intervals. It is true that the shorter the interval between testing, the greater the similarity in the IQ score achieved: so, for example, scores achieved at age four show a correlation of only 0.42 with scores achieved at age eighteen, whereas scores achieved at age eight show a correlation of 0.88 with those achieved at age ten. But the low correlation between scores at age four and eigteen years is hard to interpret, since IQ tests are far less reliable for such young children than they are for even slightly older ones. And indeed, there is an impressive correlation (0.61) between IQ scores obtained at age six and those at age eighteen, suggesting a powerful stability in IQ through childhood.

However, Honzik et al.'s data present the average relationship between IQ scores across a group of children. Other studies have looked at what happens to IQ scores for an individual child, and these data paint a rather different picture. For example, McCall, Applebaum and Hogarty (1973) found that, between the ages of two and a half and seventeen years, more than half of the children studied showed changes in IQ over time, with the average change being over 28 IQ points, and twenty children out of 140 showed changes in IQ score of over 40 points! These data suggest that IQ may be quite stable for some children, but fluctuate strongly for others.

Of course, the finding that IQ fluctuates within an individual child over time need not necessarily challenge Anderson's view that the speed and efficiency of the basic procesor remains constant through childhood. The IQ tests used by Honzik et al. and by McCall et al. were traditional IQ tests, and not pure measures of processing speed per se. Scores on traditional IQ tests reflect many factors besides processing speed or efficiency, including motivation, confidence, and learning (Cattell's 'crystalised knowledge'). The fluctuations in IQ reported by McCall et al. may reflect more changes in the individual's *performance* than in his or her basic ability to learn. This conclusion is reinforced by Honzik et al.'s finding that the children in their study who showed the least stable IQ scores were from unstable home environments, whose life experiences would be less consistent than their peers, and who might well have experienced more fluctuations in factors likely to affect their cognitive performance (such as motivation or self-confidence) than their contemporaries from more stable environments.

Predicting future performance from measures of IQ

Originally, the concept of intelligence gained its popularity because it led to the construction of tests which allowed educationalists to identify children who were going to struggle with normal school work (Binet and Simon, 1916). Certainly, those who score very poorly on intelligence tests can be predicted to have very general problems, not just in education, but in many aspects of everyday life (Ross, Begab, Dondis, Giampiccolo and Myers, 1985). At the other end of the spectrum, extremely able individuals will score very highly on intelligence tests (Terman, 1954), and these high IQ scores will correlate with high levels of success across a wide range of measures. For example, Terman found that individuals scoring over 140 on IQ tests (gifted individuals) were systematically healthier, happier, better paid and more successful in their careers than those with average IQs.

These data seem to suggest that intelligence tests can be useful in predicting how well individuals will perform on various tasks, and through life. But this conclusion is more controversial than you might think. First, the two groups noted above are at the very extremes of the intelligence scale. It is scarcely surprising that individuals who are classed as learning disabled should generally show consistent and markedly lower performance across more or less every task than those identified as gifted. But in fact, even this apparently obvious conclusion must be handled with caution.

For example, Ross et al. (1985) followed up men who had been classified as retarded on the basis of IQ scores averaging 67, and had been placed in special education for the retarded. Although in midlife these individuals had lower incomes, poorer housing and poorer social relationships than their non-retarded peers or siblings, the differences were not so great as you might suppose. For example, 29 per cent of the retarded men held jobs in the retail trade, or were skilled workers, as compared to 32 per cent of their non-retarded siblings. Only 18 per cent of retarded individuals were in fairly unskilled jobs, as compared to 13 percent of their non-retarded siblings. The major effect of this mild level of retardation was to create a bias away from professional or managerial jobs toward semi-skilled or clerical ones relative to non-retarded peers. This is scarcely surprising, not least because the retarded group had been given special education premised on low expectations of their achievements, and so in effect denied the educational opportunities to acquire qualifications offered to their siblings.

Ross *et al.*'s results suggest that relatively low IQ need not be a bar to normal life, and that individuals with low IQs may blend with the normal population more easily than we expect. These data can, of course, be criticised: for example, as we have seen, IQ scores can fluctuate throughout childhood, and may reflect a child's performance on a given day, or his or her general life experiences rather than any consistent underlying ability. Some of those sent to special education may have been wrongly assigned low IQs. But the key point to note is that an IQ score is not sufficient to predict an individual's future achievement.

This point is also underlined by Terman's study of gifted children. All the children enrolled in his study had comparable, and very high IQs, averaging around 150. One group of these children went on to show consistently high IQ, and to be successful in most aspects of life. Another group showed a marked decline in their IQ scores, their academic achievements and their later success in life. Those who were stably successful came from stable homes with more intellectual stimulation and support than those who showed a decline. Twice as many of the latter group came from homes where there had been a divorce or other family disruption, and were twice as likely to be divorced themselves.

Thus neither very high, nor very low scores on IQ tests are *sufficient* to predict how successful or happy an individual's life will be. Of course, there is some correlation between an individual's present IQ score and his or her success in school. On average, the correlation is around 0.50 (Minton and Schneider, 1980). And IQ scores are also fairly good at predicting future performance in school (Crano, Kenny and Campbell, 1972). However, it is important to remember that these correlations reflect the *average* over a group of children. An individual child's achievements might be very different from what you would expect from his or her IQ, as Terman's study of gifted children and Ross *et al.*'s study of low IQ children show. Thus an IQ score alone should never be used to predict or shape an individual's future.

Intelligence as an explanation of individual differences

If IQ can't predict the performance of individual children, can it explain why individual differences in cognitive abilities exist? To answer this question, we must pause and think a little about what we mean by an explanation.

Let's take a simple example. My son and I each have a propelling pencil. Mine is an entirely functional thing, made by a mass manufacturer and bought for a few pounds. His (as befits a stylish teenager) is a thing of beauty, made by a specialist company, and probably cost enough to run a small house for a fortnight. If I tell you that his pencil works wonderfully, that the lead feeds down obediently to a twist of the cap and never jams or breaks, but that I spend hours wrestling with mine, unable to extrude a new lead or finding it stuck or broken, I'm sure you will not be in the least surprised. You'll probably think: *you get what you pay for*! Things with big price tags normally work better than things with small ones. And of course, this is a direct analogy with IQ scores: people with 'big ones' normally work better than people with 'small ones'. But is the price tag (or IQ score) a useful *explanation* of why the pencils (or brains) work differently?

Certainly, there is a *correlation* between what you pay for a propelling pencil and how well it works. But the correlation is not perfect: some expensive pencils are duds, and some cheap ones work just fine. It is not the *price per se* which causes the pencil to work well or badly. So the price may be a *marker* letting us predict (more or less) how well the pencil will work, but it does not *explain* why one pencil works better than the other. To understand that, you have to take the two pencils to pieces and examine how they work. The expensive one has been made more carefully, and each mechanism inside it fits very well with every other, and works efficiently as a result. The cheap pencil has been mass produced, and the mechanisms inside it don't quite fit together tightly enough, and so it often doesn't work very well. To *explain* how something works, you have to understand the process or mechanism which makes it work.

IQ scores, whether they be from traditional tests or from tests of basic processing efficiency of the kind Anderson describes, are like price tags on propelling pencils. They provide markers which allow us to predict (but less well than you might suppose, as we have seen) individual differences in cognitive abilities. But the psychometric concept of intelligence is not enough to explain why such differences exist. Even if IQ were a perfect measure of an individual's *potential* ability (which it clearly is not), an individual's *actual* achievements will depend very strongly on a wide range of factors. However fast your basic processor, you still need to learn the rules before you can play chess, for example. However good your innate specific processor for musical skills, you cannot develop such skills without exposure to music and the opportunity to learn and discover in that area. And if your early efforts are met with praise and success, you are likely to persist with a task and learn more than if someone criticises or tells you you're bad at something. Motivation and application can be as important as opportunity to learn or basic processing efficiency in determining individual differences in achievement. Indeed, motivation, experience and opportunity may yield greater explanatory power than processing speed in both predicting and accounting for achievement. As we all know intuitively, a potentially gifted child who does little or no work on a given topic will not outshine an industrious plodder.

Thus to *explain* individual differences in cognitive abilities, we need to look very directly at the detail of the processes by which individuals learn, make discoveries and approach reasoning or problem solving. Traditional IQ tests and concepts of intelligence do not do this. Some researchers (Howe, 1989) believe that the whole notion of IQ has distracted research from where it ought to be focused, namely directly on the processes yielding individual differences in particular levels of achievement. The psychometric concept of intelligence alone cannot possibly explain the rich variety of differences we see across individuals. Howe argues that psychology took a wrong turning: instead of inventing the idea of intelligence as a general property of the individual mind, we should all along have focused on understanding how intelligent behaviour is produced through the interaction of a diverse range of processes.

Modern psychometric measures of individual differences

No student of cognitive development can afford to be ignorant of psychometric research on intelligence. But the concept is one which needs to be treated with some caution. It may be much less useful than is commonly supposed. Indeed, recent efforts to measure individual differences in cognitive abilities have moved a long way away from the search for an inherited, stable capacity in the individual.

For example, Sternberg (1988) argues that knowing how fast an individual can succeed in mastering an arbitrary task is not a useful measure of intelligence at all. Success can reflect the individual's *past experience* so that, in a task familiar to one child and novel for the other, the child who succeeds most easily may be using far less intelligence (because he or she is repeating a well learned solution) than the child who struggles (who may be working for the first time through unknown territory). Equally, being able to master an arbitrary, abstract problem is not necessarily a good marker of how 'street smart' an individual is. Behaviour is not intelligent in the abstract, but in *context*. For example, we tend to admire the individual who can produce a complex analysis of a problem more than one who cannot. That is all very well. But if the problem to be solved is, say, putting a fire out, then an individual who fetches the extinguisher and douses the flames is behaving more adaptively and so more intelligently than one who stands by and gives a lecture on the nature of combustion, however erudite. Furthermore, traditional IQ tests may miss the point in asking only whether an individual can successfully solve a given problem, or how fast. Some ways of solving problems are better than others, as we have seen in Chapters 5 and 6. Some strategies are more richly informed, more sophisticated and will be more generally useful than others. These are the more intelligent strategies, even if they are slower, or even sometimes less successful (Siegler, 1996; see Chapter 5). Sternberg argues that a proper estimate of an individual's ability ought to look at what kind of *strategies* he or she uses to solve problems, as well as taking his or her past experience and ability to react appropriately to the context into account.

Sternberg's approach to measuring individual differences in cognitive abilities fits very much more closely with modern accounts of the processes which underly skilled cognitive performance than was the case for earlier psychometric measures. Nonetheless, one should be cautious in assuming that even tests as sophisticated as Sternberg proposes provide a *definitive* measure of the child's abilities, or a basis for predicting that individual's future.

Psychometrics and creativity

Of course, even within the psychometric tradition, IQ is not the only factor believed to lead to differences in reasoning and problem solving between one individual and another. Ability is also importantly a function of a variety of other processes, which determine the style or flavour of the way the individual approaches cognitive activities.

Scores on IQ tests have a limited power to predict which individuals will make outstanding novel discoveries or be innovators (Guildford, 1967). Few individuals with very low IQs are creative. But for those with IQs over about 125, IQ does not predict who will or will not be successfully creative. Guildford (1967) identified two main styles of reasoning which he argued account for the difference between individuals who are creative and those who are not: there are 'convergent' thinkers, who think in very conventional ways and are unlikely to come up with new or unusual ideas. And there are 'divergent' thinkers, whose thought patterns are less conventional and who are more creative as a consequence.

Psychometric measures of divergent thinking tend to rely on measuring how imaginative an individual is in inventing different uses for common objects such as a a brick (Guilford, 1967). The more uses the individual produces, the more divergent, that is creative he or she is said to be. However, this whole approach is subject to a number of serious criticisms. First, there is very little evidence to suggest that useful innovations are actually achieved through thinking of *more* alternatives, rather than *better* ones. For example, Darwin's seminal work on evolution was indisputably creative, but he can scarcely be imagined to have reached his conclusions by making a list of all the possible ways species might have arisen! Only where one solves a problem by guessing in a trial and error way would the ability to generate more possible solutions be likely to be relevant. And even then, it is only if one is able to recognise which solutions were better, or were moving in the right direction that a useful new discovery is likely. Recognising such things involves very different mental processes from merely listing more alternatives.

As with the concept of IQ, the concept of creativity per se does not offer an explanation of the process by which innovative ideas actually arise. Nor is there convincing evidence that scoring high on tests of creativity is associated with useful innovation.

Process Accounts of Individual Differences

Psychometric approaches have dominated research into the origins of individual differences in abilities largely because researchers who focus more directly on the mental processing which underlies cognitive performance have been more interested in understanding the basic nature of those processes across all individuals than in looking at how such processing varies between one individual and another. There is an astonishing lack of research directly focused on how the mental processes of individuals who learn quickly differ from those of individuals who learn slowly, and filling in this gap may become an important issue for developmental research in the next decade.

Every factor which contributes to the general nature of human mental processes as a whole can also contribute to the occurrence of individual differences in processing between one individual and another. Thus every influence on development noted in Chapter 7, from evolutionary factors to social and individual ones may be a source of variation between one child and another.

Evolution and individual differences

At first it seems absurd to suggest that the evolutionary forces which shaped our species as a whole could contribute to differences between individual children in the way they develop into intelligent beings. Surely such large scale forces should have the same effect on us all? Surely evolutionary effects are too fixed in our fundamental natures to influence the path development takes in an individual child? Such assumptions may be too simple (Bjorklund and Pellegrini, 2000).

Evolutionary forces shape the form a species takes, both its body type and its behaviour, to fit a particular evolutionary niche. The behaviours and body types selected are those which function best in the environment in which we live (Darwin, 1859). Where the niche a species occupies is fairly stable, there are evolutionary advantages to developing very fixed patterns of skill, and in 'wiring in' critical skills into the genetic endowment of each individual. But too rigid a genetic system leaves a species unable to react effectively to changes in the environment, and makes it vulnerable to extinction. Thus there is a certain premium, in nature, on the capacity for variability within a species. One type of individual within a species (chubby ones, for example) may be far better suited to surviving cooler climates than another (skinny ones). It is an advantage to the species to have both, on a planet where the climate does change both over long periods of time and over very short periods of time (if some local pressure forces individuals to move from a tropical zone to a temperate one, for example).

Within an individual lifespan, too, there are evolutionary advantages to being able to adapt to changes in the environment which often occur. For example, food supplies can vary enormously as a function of droughts or floods, the action of volcanoes, the rivalry for scarce supplies between competing groups, and so on. A species which did not adapt to such fluctuations would waste considerable resources producing babies who will merely die in times of famine. Such waste would undermine the fitness of the species. The evidence is that human beings have always moderated their reproductive behaviour in response to changing environmental conditions of this sort.

Most interestingly from the point of view of understanding individual child development is the observation that individual human beings also moderate their reproductive strategies to reflect the relative security of their social situations. Thus individuals who grow up in stable backgrounds and stable families adopt strategies involving more secure emotional attachments, higher levels of investment in choosing the right mate (and so deferring marrying and reproducing to allow for this search), in maintaining a monogamous relationship (and so divorcing and remarrying less often) and in childrearing (having fewer children and investing more effort in parenting them) than individuals who grow up in unstable families and social situations. War, poverty and divorce radically change how we approach the main biological task of our lives: reproductive success (Bjorklund and Pellegrini, 2000).

If evolutionary considerations such as reproductive success can affect our strategies in solving problems in one psychological area (marriage, attachment and emotional development), then there is every reason to suppose that similar factors can affect all the cognitive strategies we adopt. There is little point, for example, in investing enormous time and effort in developing complex abstract conceptual skills (such as mathematics) in an environment where there is a constant threat to survival which mathematics cannot solve. Very unstable and unpredictable environments put a premium on being flexible, adopting new behaviours quickly rather than persisting with strategies which may no longer meet the needs of the situation.

Thus evolutionary pressures toward adaptive survival may influence the specific character of cognitive development in many ways, selecting for confident, affectionate individuals who persist in difficult tasks and value abstract concepts in one context, and more insecure, alienated individuals whose behaviour is more inconsistent and more oriented to basic functions in another (Bjorklund and Pellegrini, 2000; Geary and Bjorklund, 2000). These evolutionary influences on the basic strategies of our lives can work to produce differences between one individual and another at the level of cultures, or subcultures (such as richer or poorer social classes) within a culture, or even at the level of individual families with differing resources.

Social factors in individual differences

Social processes make an enormous contribution to the development of intelligence, as we have seen in Chapter 7. Children learn from watching and interacting with others (Luria, 1976; Radziszewska and Rogoff, 1991; Rogoff, Gauvain and Ellis, 1984; Wertsch, 1979; Vygotsky, 1978). They are implicitly led to develop new skills both through the subtle processes with which adults support and shape the child's performance, through direct tuition and formal schooling. The way the child comes to represent the world is a clear reflection of the science and philosophy of the culture within which he or she grows up, so that individual children need not re-invent the great discoveries of our species: you and I understand the nature of oxygen and respiration, say, in the way our culture defines that knowledge, which is entirely different from the way air and breathing were understood a thousand years ago (Carey, 1985). It follows from all this that differences in the way children are parented and taught (Pratt, Kerig, Cowan and Pape-Cowan, 1988; Radzisewska and Rogoff, 1991) or educated (Scribner and Cole, 1981), differences in the culture to which they are exposed (Luria, 1977; Cole and Scribner, 1974: Scribner and Cole, 1981), differences in what the culture around the individual *demands and expects* (Rogoff, 1998), will create differences in cognitive functioning between one individual and another. There is a profound sense in which many aspects of variation between one individual and another are artefacts of the social environment in which he or she happens to grow up.

The impact of such social processes on individual differences in abilities is hard to overestimate. It is visible in the vast differences in reasoning and responsibility between eight-year-olds in complex urban cultures and those in subsistence economies offering an entirely different educational and social experience (Cole and Scribner, 1974; Luria, 1977; Scribner and Cole, 1981; Rogoff, 1990). It is visible in the systematic differences between only children and those with siblings, and between first borns and those who are born second or late in a larger family: parental practice changes with experience, so that a second or third child will be treated more casually and instructed more effectively than firstborns or only children, and may well be subjected to far lower levels of parental anxiety and pressures to achieve. Very much of what we know, how we reason, the form and structure of our intellectual lives is determined by the culture and family in which we grow up. Cognitive processes, cognitive style, the very value we place on abstract reasoning is very much socially constructed. It would be impossible to explain individual differences in cognitive functioning without taking the social context of development into account.

Social processes can even offer us new insights into such apparently extraordinary phenomena as are presented by acts of great scientific or artistic creativity. Conventionally, when we see a Darwin or an Einstein, we assume that we are looking at a rare creature possessed of some special talent obscure and mysterious to the rest of our species. But looking at such extreme acts of creativity in their social context can suggest a very different picture. Darwin was not the only man to identify the principle of natural selection, and so unlock the key to understanding evolution, in the middle of the nineteenth century: Wallace, working alone in Australia, reached the same conclusions at more or less the same time. And indeed, this implicit rivalry may have been a factor in precipitating the better connected Darwin into publishing his 'dangerous' and (then) unpopular idea (Dennett, 1996). Likewise, the camera was invented more or less simultaneously by two men working entirely independently in England and in France. Movements in painting and music show the same character, with apparently startling innovations being discovered separately, *but at the same time* by different artists. The implication of such parallel discoveries is that the keys to creative breakthrough lie not in the mind of the individual, but in the collective understanding of a culture. Gradual changes in the way a given culture reasons, and in the information it has, may lay the foundations for such revolutionary change in how we view the world. What appear as *individual* acts of genius may really be very collective and social things. Perhaps Darwin and Wallace were merely the *right kind of men*, open to information and ideas from their shared culture, well placed to make the observations which might explore the implications of those ideas, to mediate the transition to a radical new idea whose foundations were already culturally laid.

Cognitive processing and individual differences

To say that Darwin was the right man in the right place to precipitate what has been one of the most fundamental, upsetting and exciting changes in human understanding of all time in no way belittles his achievement, nor disavows the contribution individual processes make to the development of intelligence and conceptual understanding. As a keen sailor and scientist myself I am sadly aware that, offered the chance of several years on 'Beagle', I would have returned with a perfect suntan, a rooted dislike for the captain and an unreadable manuscript on the management of canvas (and skirts) in sundry wind pressures.

Temperamental features of the individual child or adult, from the things which interest them to the care or impulsiveness with which they approach problem solving, their persistence in worrying at a idea or trying to apply a given strategy, even the level of stress they find optimal, all contribute to the way reasoning and problem solving develop in and differ between one person and another. These factors produce effects over and above the more obviously cognitive features of individual minds, such as what particular knowledge they have of a given problem or expertise in that area, what strategies they know for solving it or how efficient their basic mental processes such as working memory may be, important as these factors are as sources of individual difference in reasoning (Carey, 1985; Chi and Ceci, 1987), as we have seen in Chapter 5. There is no advantage, for instance, in knowing exactly how to solve a problem if one lacks the interest or motivation to apply that knowledge. Persisting too long or not long enough in trying to solve a problem in a given way can mean failure where a more appropriate judgement of when to try something new will lead to new discovery and success (Siegler, 1996; Thornton, 1999).

Temperamental or stylistic differences in how individual children approach problem solving can have a surprisingly large impact on the speed with which a child learns, or the character of what is learned. For example, Siegler and Jenkins (1989) have shown that children differ in how sensitive they are to feedback from the environment. As we saw in Chapter 6, children typically have more than one strategy which they might use in any situation (Siegler and Jenkins, 1989). Which strategy they choose to use at any one time is a matter of the experience they have had with that strategy in the past: the more successful it has been, the more likely they are to use it. But until the difference in the relative success of two strategies passes some critical threshhold, the child will continue to use both strategies more or less interchangeably. It is only once one strategy has become markedly more successful than another that the child will begin to systematically use that strategy and reject the other. However, exactly where the critical threshhold for difference between two strategies lies varies from one child to another. For example, Siegler and Jenkins have shown that, where one child will not begin to trust a new strategy until it has proven itself to be, say, twice as effective as older and more familiar strategies, another child might start to prefer the new strategy when it is only 25 per cent more likely to succeed. In effect, the first of these children is far more cautious and conservative in learning and making new discoveries than the second, and will change their approach to problem solving or reasoning more slowly. Often this will mean that the more cautious child learns and develops more slowly. But occasionally, such a child will have an advantage, because he or she will avoid leaping prematurely to the conclusion that a strategy which happens to be good in particular circumstances is necessarily generally better, when it is not. However, even this advantage may be rare: the more readily adaptive child will soon detect such errors and correct them. Overall, the more rapidly a child differentiates between one approach and another, the more he or she will learn about a task.

The effect of individual differences in persistence and in readiness to try new things on children's discovery is well illustrated in the bridge building task described in Chapter 6 (Thornton, 1999). In this task, children must build a bridge across a 'river' using blocks, each of which is too short to span the river alone. The solution is to use the principles of balance to span the distance. Five-year-olds have great difficulty with this task. Thornton (1999) reported a case study of one child who did successfully discover the way to solve the problem (see Table 6.1), through making a series of changes to her subgoals and strategies until new discoveries emerged. Other children in this experiment moved some way along the same general path this child had followed, but they failed to find the solution that she found. In some cases, this was because the child perseverated far too long with an unsuccessful strategy: continuing to try to 'glue' one block to another somehow (no effective glue was available) rather than moving on to try something else, for example. In other cases, the children failed because they did not keep trying a potentially good solution long enough to make the relevant discoveries.

Stylistic differences in the child's approach to cognitive tasks may have some basis in inherited characteristics of the child's temperament (Kochanska, Coy, Tjebkes and Husarek, 1998). For example, babies differ from birth in how irritable or how readily soothed by cuddling they are, how upset by loud noises, and so on. There may be innate differences in infants' tendency to seek out new stimuli, with one infant needing more stimulation to avoid a noxious boredom than another, or one infant unpleasantly stressed by a level of stimulation which merely excites another.

However, stylistic differences in problem solving between one child and another can also be learned very directly from experience, or influenced by social pressures. For example, the precise detail of the strategy a child uses in addressing some problem interacts with the precise detail of the task in hand to create a set of feedback. Not all feedback is equally useful in directing the child to make new discoveries (Thornton, 1999): some is fruitful in leading to new ideas, and some is not (see Chapter 6). A child who *happens* to use a strategy which generates fruitful feedback, and who is therefore successful in making discoveries in that task is not just learning about the task. Such a child is learning that he or she is *good* at solving that kind of problem. There is clear evidence that this kind of experience makes us more confident and more successful problem solvers, while the opposite experience, namely failing in a task can teach us that we are bad at solving those problems, and can make our efforts more inadequate, and still less successful (Hartley, 1986; Seligman, 1975). Equally, children who solve a problem through trying out many different strategies will learn to vary their approach more readily, where children who are successful through persistence will learn to persist with a single strategy, and so on. The experience of solving problems teaches the child not just how to solve that particular type of problem, but how to go about structuring the process of problem solving per se, and so can influence the development of a particular cognitive style.

A footnote on intelligence and creativity as cognitive processes

It is important to notice that the psychometric distinction between intelligence and creativity in understanding individual differences may be fundamentally misguided, when viewed from the perspective of the processes which produce them (Boden, 1990). Outstanding acts of innovation in science or the arts are, by definition, rare and special events. But novel discovery and the processes which allow it are the everyday matter of the cognitive mechanisms which generate both problem solving and development (Boden, 1990).

Intellectual development through childhood involves an almost continuous process of new learning, new understanding and new discovery, creating revolutions in conceptual understanding in the child (Kuhn, Amsel and O'Loughlin, 1988). Every normal child shows an astonishing capacity of this kind, as the ordinary basis of developmental growth. The differences between children in the speed and range new discoveries made reflect a variety of factors, from the specific detail of the strategy used to the child's willingness to try something new rather than the operation of some special 'creative' function. Creativity is a byproduct of ordinary intelligent processing, as we saw in Chapter 7 (Boden, 1990; Siegler, 1996; Sophian, 1997; Thornton, 1999).

Developing Differently

Throughout this book we have been concerned with normal development: with the patterns and regularities which characterise all children as they grow up and develop an adult mind. Within this normal process of development there is a vast scope for variety and difference between one child and another, with *this* child being musical, for example, and *that* child being tone deaf but very good at languages. But there are also patterns of development which are quite outside this normal range: children whose development is very delayed, or that takes a path very different from the norm.

Abnormalities of development come in all shapes and sizes. As we have seen, the normal process of development depends on a vast range of factors, genetic, physiological, social, environmental and individual. We are all the product of such a fantastically complex process that it is surprising that development does not 'go wrong' more often than it does. A failure in any factor can potentially derail development.

Diagnosing developmental abnormalities

As we have seen in this chapter, there is a great deal of variety between individuals in the speed with which they learn and develop, the patterns of ability they display, and the levels of achievement they finally attain. All this variety is perfectly normal: we accept a fairly broad degree of variation in how normal individuals learn, think and reason. Abnormal development, then, is identified as a very *marked* deviation from the normal range of developmental progress, a marked failure of the child to behave as expected.

Exactly where the border between a 'normal' pattern of development and an 'abnormal' one lies is a little hazy. Some children are so very severely different from the average that there is no question but that their development is abnormal. But for milder problems, it can be rather unclear where the line should be drawn between a normal but very slow developer, say, and a child with a real difficulty in some area that is worth diagnosing and treating as such.

Nor is it the case that all developmental abnormalities reflect abnormalities in the child per se. For example, imagine that you are a teacher. In your class of five-year-olds, there is a very disruptive little boy. He can't be quiet or sit still; he can't make friends or get along with the other children; he's fairly destructive and aggressive. His command of language is very much behind that of his peers, and his progress on schoolwork is more or less non-existent. What is the matter with him? What is the solution? A pattern such as this might have very many causes. Perhaps there is something wrong with the child, some underlying failure in the developmental process. But it is entirely possible that the child himself is normal, but has come from a home which is very unsupportive, and which sets him on a damaged developmental trajectory from birth. Figure 8.2 provides a vivid illustration of the life pattern that such a background may well lead to. The child's poor parenting sets him off on a disastrous school career, in which his poor behaviour is likely to be interpreted as low ability, whatever his actual potential might have been. His disruptive behaviour may be diagnosed as a conduct disorder, or a disorder of attention and impulse control. Once this reputation has been acquired, the child will be treated differently, very often in ways that will lock him into his abnormality. This is particularly sad, in that developmental problems stemming from such social causes as poor parenting and poor tuition are the easiest to remedy, with the right input.

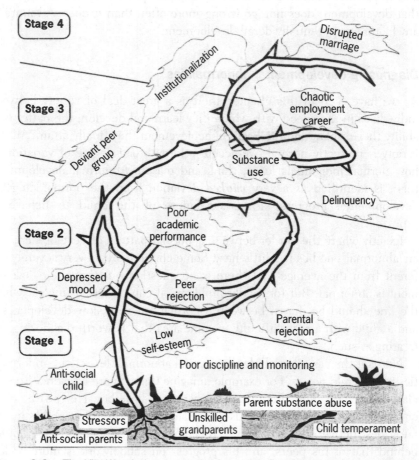

Figure 8.2 The Vile Weed: the unrestrained growth of problems across the lifespan
Source: Patterson *et al.* (1992).

Diagnosing developmental abnormalities, particularly in milder cases, can be fraught with difficulty as the example in the last paragraph shows. Not least of the difficulties is that putting a label on a child carries a cost. Sometimes, identifying a specific sort of deficit (in learning to read, say) is very helpful to the child: it directs teachers to provide that child with the extra support he or she needs to master the skill in question. Having such a specific difficulty acknowledged and supported can be a great relief to the child, taking away a sense of hopelessness and failure. But as we have seen in Chapter 7, labels can also be damaging. Social reputations ('Paul can't learn maths') can become self-fulfilling prophecies (Hartley, 1986), trapping a child in under-achievement or poor behaviour.

Delayed development

Some abnormalities of development involve very marked delay in a child's progress toward the normal milestones of childhood: learning to talk very late, for example, or having unusual difficulties with spatial skills or maths. The child may be as much as several years behind his or her peers. Such delays worry parents and professionals. But if the basic pattern of development is pretty much the same as for other children, the slower child will often eventually catch up. Such delayed development is likely to be labelled as a 'learning disability' or a 'learning disorder' (the two terms are generally used interchangeably).

Why do such delays occur? The possibility that the problem lies in the child's environment, rather than in the child per se must never be overlooked, as we have seen. Indeed, a fair percentage of such delays may reflect the poor opportunities and lack of encouragement the child has had. But in many cases, there does seem to be some specific difficulty holding the individual back: an unusual degree of difficulty in differentiating the orientation of shapes, say, which makes learning to read more difficult, or some specific problem differentiating sounds, which makes learning to talk much harder.

Exactly why some children have more difficulty than average in mastering certain skills is not well understood. Some children lag behind their peers in virtually all aspects of development. For these children, the probable cause is low general intelligence: slow processing speed, for example, or a general inefficiency in processing or remembering information. But other children seem to show a developmental delay in one specific area: being very slow at learning to express themselves verbally, for instance, though generally very able; or being slow to learn to read or manage numbers, despite a normal or high general intelligence. Some research suggests that learning disabilities of this selective kind may reflect very specific minor neurological deficits. This idea, however, is controversial.

For example, the most familiar form of learning disability is dyslexia, where the child has considerably more difficulty in learning to read and write than one would expect from his or her general abilities. Some studies using brain imaging techniques suggest that the areas of the cortex activated by reading are different in dyslexic and normal children (Frith and Frith, 1996). There is also some evidence that dyslexia is associated with poor lateralisation of the brain, so that the dyslexic child has general problems with spatial orientation, is generally ill-coordinated and does not develop a clear left or right handedness (Wolff, Michel, Ovrut and Drake, 1990). But the data are harder to interpret than you might suppose. The different patterns of activity seen in brain imaging studies may be the result, rather than the cause of the different ways dyslexic and normal readers are processing information. And the majority of children who are labelled as dyslexic show no evidence of any neurological difference from good readers (Scarborough, 1990). Does that mean that there is no neurological basis for dyslexia, or does it mean that many children are wrongly diagnosed as dyslexic? McGuinness (1987) argues that there is really no evidence that children labelled as dyslexic are developmentally abnormal in any qualitative sense at all: the errors they make, and the problems they have in learning to read are typical of the normal child, except that these difficulties persist much longer in the dyslexic child. In other words, the process of development is the same; it is only the speed of progress which is different.

What are we to make of very marked delays in developmental progress? In some cases, very severe developmental delays may suggest that there is some serious underlying problem. For example, a child who failed to begin to learn to talk by age five, or who could not walk or crawl by twenty-four months, or who failed to make eye contact or respond to games such as 'Peek-a-boo!' in the first year of life would be a cause for concern, and might have one of the persistent developmental problems we shall meet in the next section. Severe delays in such basic human skills might well be markers predicting a qualitative difference in the path the child's progress will follow.

But even quite severe developmental delays may have no real significance for the child's final achievements at all. This is particularly true for developmental delays in mastering skills which are cultural artefacts, rather than basic to our human nature, such as reading, writing, maths and logic. For example, had they been at school today, Winston Churchill, Albert Einstein and Woodrow Wilson would almost certainly have been labelled as learning disabled: all had much less than successful school careers. There is a great deal of scope for variation in the speed with which skills are mastered, within the range of normal development.

McGuinness points out that we are used to, and tolerant of, the rich variety of individual differences in some areas of development: we aren't upset if our baby grows hair years after his peers, nor anxious that our first-born took his first steps eight months before his brother, but spoke his first sentence ten months later. Implicitly, we understand that all biological functions show a natural spread in the speed and timing of their development. But when it comes to schoolwork, we think differently.

School progress is different from other developmental change in two ways: it is taught, and it is taught to a pre-determined set of targets and norms. Children who don't keep up with these norms tend to be labelled as having a learning disability, and to be seen to be developing atypically. But this says more about our culture than it does about the child. Norms always reflect what the average child can do. All skills and abilities vary through the population, in what is called a 'normal' distribution (Figure 8.3). The

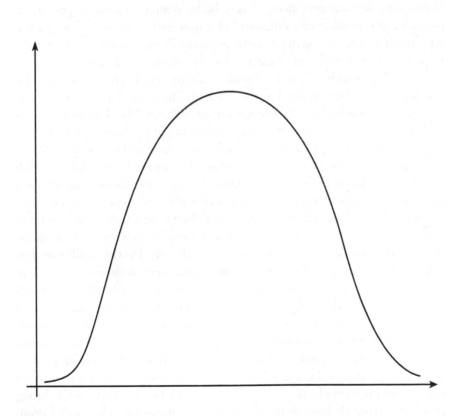

Figure 8.3 A normal distribution

majority of children are bunched around the mean in such a distribution. The further away from the mean in either direction, the fewer the number of children, though all are still in the 'normal' range. We ought, therefore, to *expect* that some perfectly normal children will be much faster, and some much slower than the average in learning any skill, including reading. Cultural expectations in relation to schooling overlook this fact: we behave as if *everyone* should be able to match the mean. Thus 'learning disabilities' may be as much in the eye of the beholder as in the child per se. Applying such a label to the child may seem a little unfair in this context! But so long as the label is used constructively to provide the child with extra help, rather than to stigmatise and lock the child in low progress, such 'diagnoses' may be useful. Such mild degrees of difference in development can usually be caught up, with the right help.

Different development

Sometimes development does go very badly wrong, leading to persistent, pervasive and qualitatively different behaviour and progress by comparison with normal children. Such problems normally do have some sort of physio-logical base, though the exact nature of the problem is not always clear.

Some children show a level of general ability that is entirely outside the normal range of human intelligence. Such children may fail to learn to talk, or to master the basic skills needed for an ordinary life. This level of dis-ability is always associated with some underlying physiological problem.

How is the basic physiology of intelligence damaged for such children? In some cases, the problem is inherited. For example, in children with 'fragile X' syndrome there is an inherited flaw on a particular gene on the X chromosome, which results in a distinctive physical appearance and very general cognitive, social and emotional deficits. In other cases, chromo-some damage seems to arise spontaneously, perhaps as a result of the decay of the older mother's ova, as in Downs syndrome. Downs syndrome pro-duces very distinctive facial peculiarities and very widespread cognitive deficits. It is associated with damage to chromosome 21, which is much more common in the children of older mothers. Spontaneous damage may occur to other chromosomes too – for example, to chromosome 15, which produces 'Prader-Willi' syndrome, involving mental retardation and strange, obsessive eating. Physiological damage which affects the development of intelligence can also be caused by a variety of toxins. The most common such poison is alcohol. Babies born to mothers who drank too much during pregnancy typically have distinctive faces and marked developmental prob-lems. Viruses too, such as rubella, or even mumps and measles can affect the development of the fetus in ways that damage the brain and distort development. And toxins, viruses and injuries at or after birth can have a similar effect. Oxygen deprivation at birth causes very profound developmental damage, for example, as does meningitis in infancy. Over 1000 separate physiological causes of damage to the developing brain have been identified.

Such physiological defects are associated with very severe abnormalities in development, which cannot be greatly alleviated. Of course, even among those with organic damage, there is a range of ability levels: not all Downs syndrome children are equally disabled, for example. Some are completely helpless; a very few are able to live more normal lives, hold down jobs. We do not understand why that is so, since all show the same chromosomal damage. And in fact, we do not understand why it is that certain genetic or chromosomal flaws have the effects they do (Simonoff, Bolton and Rutter, 1996). We do not know exactly what it is that is disrupted, in the brains of these children, to limit their development in these ways.

Not all patterns of abnormal development seem to be primarily a dysfunction of *ability* per se. For example, some children show an extraordinary level of energy and destructiveness, and an extraordinary inability to sit still and concentrate on anything. Figure 8.4 shows a case study description of one such child. This is attention-deficit/hyperactivity disorder, or ADHD. ADHD is exhausting and depressing to deal with as a parent or teacher. It interferes with the child's ability to learn and to make friends: the child can't concentrate and learn, and is too noxious to be attractive to other children. The result is fairly widespread damage to the child's social and cognitive development. The causes of ADHD are not known. There seems to be no genetic or organic cause. Quite possibly, the problem is metabolic. The ADHD child may have an atypical level of arousal, either too high, so that the child reacts to ordinary life as if he or she were high on, for example, caffeine all the time, or too low, so that the child becomes hyperactive to escape a noxious underarousal. Drugs which affect the metabolism and alter the child's levels of arousal may have some effect in addressing this problem, though the issue is very controversial.

The ADHD child is a very extreme case of the limited powers of concentration and the huge and poorly controlled energy of the normal infant. All children become more able to concentrate as they grow older, and more able to control their energy, and the same is true for ADHD children, many of whom gradually calm into a more normal pattern of development as they reach middle and late childhood.

In autism, too, the primary deficit is not intellectual. Many autistic children do have severe intellectual problems, but about 20 per cent have normal intelligence. The autistic child has a specific deficit in relating to

Seven-year-old Dusty awoke at 5.00 one recent morning in his Chicago home. Every muscle in his 50lb body flew in furious motion as he headed downstairs for breakfast. After pulling a box of cereal from the cupboard, Dusty started grabbing cereal with his hands and kicking the box, scattering the cereal across the room. Next he began peeling the decorative paper covering off the TV table. Then he started stomping the spilled cereal to bits. After dismantling the plastic dustpan he had gotten to clean up the cereal, he moved onto his next project: grabbing three rolls of toilet paper from the bathroom and unravelling them around the house.

Figure 8.4 'Dusty': a child with ADHD
Source: Wallis (1994).

other people: he or she will not make eye contact as normal babies do, will not play baby games such as 'peek-a-boo', won't smile or use other non-verbal gestures, will learn to speak very late or not at all. Autistic children prefer objects to people, and develop unusual and obsessive interests and rituals. It is as if the innate preparedness to orient to other people and be social which characterises the normal child (see Chapter 2) has somehow been left out of these children. The result is an extreme aloneness, an extreme unawareness of others. It used to be thought that these children could not even recognise others, and could not form attachments, but more recent research shows that this is not so (Mash and Wolfe, 1999): autistic children do respond differently to their own parents, for example. They use the parent for security, which suggests that they do feel an attachment. As we saw in Chapter 3, more recent research suggests that these children fail to discover that other people have minds, and are unable to understand other people's feelings, thoughts or intentions (Baron-Cohen, Tager-Flusberg and Cohen, 1993).

Autism is the syndrome associated with the 'idiot-savant', the apparently very abnormal individual who shows an extraordinary talent in one area. Figure 8.5 shows a drawing made by Nadia, aged three: it is quite different and *startlingly* better than the drawings a normal three-year-old could make. We have no idea how such special talents arise. Only 5 per cent of autistic children show any such talent. Even so! That *any* three-year-old could make such a precocious drawing demands an explanation we cannot yet give. In many cases, the autistic individual is locked for life in social isolation and low achievement. But about 20 per cent of autistics gradually become more normal as they grow older. There are instances of autistic children going on to be university researchers, who manage very well so long as no one expects them to have subtle interactions with other people. And, in fact, mild degrees of autism may be very much more common than

Figure 8.5 Nadia's drawing of a horse, age 3
Source: Selfe (1977).

we suppose. Mild autism in high IQ individuals is likely to be diagnosed as
Asperger's syndrome. Here, the individual is relatively normal, but surprisingly low on empathy, social intuition and compassion.

Lessons from abnormal development

Delayed development across a broad range of areas tells us relatively little
about the process of normal development other than that it is variable
across individuals. But *specific* delays in development and qualitatively *different* patterns of development offer the possibility of discovering more
about how normal processes work.

For example, specific problems in learning in an otherwise intelligent
child may suggest that certain skills are *particular,* isolated from other
mental processes. This has implications for our understanding of the basic
structure of the developing mind. Exploring the origins and effects of these
specific deficits would enhance our understanding of the extent to which
the mind is compartmentalised or modular, and the way one system meshes
with another in normal development

Equally, the *disruption* of one function may well impact on other aspects
of development. For example, the extreme social ineptness of the autistic
clearly interrupts intellectual development in some ways. Why? How?
Understanding this would illuminate the role that a social orientation or an

understanding of other minds plays in normal development. And autism is associated with an extreme form of concentration, which allows surprising talents to develop in a few of its victims. Unpicking exactly how that happens may reveal things about how normal learning works.

And in the case of severe retardation, how is it that the very same chromosomal damage can have such very different effects in different individuals? Any physiological damage to the brain knocks out some systems, but such damage occurs in the context of an overall underlying inherited endowment. Chromosomal damage in a fetus otherwise destined for high ability may have radically different effects from the very same damage in a fetus otherwise destined for average or less than average ability. Unravelling how this is so may clarify our understanding of the neurology of developing ability.

In Summary

For nearly a century, the thesis that individual differences in cognitive ability reflect inherited traits such as general intelligence or special processes for creativity (such as divergent thinking) has dominated research. But as we have seen, efforts to measure these traits have not produced tools which can predict a child's future achievements, nor explain just why it is that one child is more successful than another. More direct analyses of the processes involved in problem solving have provided us with a far better basis for understanding, not only of how and why individuals differ, but also what might be done about it.

Differences in what is adaptive in different physical and social environments, differences in opportunities to learn, in encouragement, support and sensitivity in teaching and in the expectations of the culture in which the child grows up account for a great deal of the differences we see between children. None of these factors necessarily reflects much about the individual child per se, though attractive, biddable children are more likely to be advantaged through social processes than aggressive or rejecting ones. But individual children also differ in impulsiveness, in their sensitivity to feedback, the extent to which they will persist with a strategy as opposed to moving on and trying something new. Such differences are the product of complex processes from inherited personality traits through to the expectations and strategies the child has learned from experience in past cognitive activities.

Overall, the history of research suggests that we shall understand the origins of differences between individuals far better by directly examining the differences between one person and another in how they actually approach cognitive tasks, rather than by looking for what correlates with greater or lesser success as traditional psychometric approaches did. Modern psychometric work, such as that of Sternberg, is beginning to incorporate this more process-oriented approach.

EXERCISES

1   How would you go about identifying which of a group of dolphins was the most intelligent?

2   One little studied area is the fact that, in very many situations, different individuals will have different opinions: for example, on how you make pancakes or what is the matter with the toaster. Next time you observe two people having such a difference of opinion, note down what information each has about the situation, what information each is willing to accept from the other (and on what basis), and what kinds of reason each produces to persuade the other to their point of view. How far is the difference of opinion driven by differences in what each knows, and how far by differences in the way each thinks about the problem? How much of it is driven by personality rather than pure problem solving considerations?

SUGGESTED READING

For an introduction to Sternberg's work on measuring individual differences in cognitive functioning:
Sternberg, R. (1988) 'Intellectual development: psychometric and information processing approaches'. In: M. Bornstein and M. Lamb (eds), *Developmental Psychology: An Advanced Textbook* (Hillsdale, NJ: Erlbaum).

For a discussion of the mental processes underlying creativity:
Boden, M. (1990) *The Creative Mind: Myths and Mechanisms* (London: Weidenfeld and Nicolson).

For a taste of just how complex it can be to try to disentangle environmental and genetic influences on intelligence:
Petrill, S., Saudino, K., Cherny, S., Emde, R., Fulker, D., Hewit, J. and Plomin, R. (1998) 'Exploring the genetic and environmental etiology of high general cognitive ability in fourteen- to thirty-six-month-old twins'. *Child Development 69*, pp. 8–74.

For a review of abnormal development:
Mash, E. and Wolfe, D. (1999) *Abnormal Development* (Belmont, VA: Wadsworth).

Conclusions and Overview

Human intelligence is an extraordinary thing, unique to our species, so far as we have yet discovered. It arises, time and again, in a biological organism which starts out as a single cell, albeit one carrying a complex genetic blueprint. The mystery of how that is possible is what motivates the study of childhood cognitive development. And that mystery has both deepened and been clarified, through the course of the past forty years of research, as is clear from a consideration of how the themes and questions which characterise research have changed in that time, and are now set to change again.

Piaget and the Study of Development

It is a tribute to the remarkable contribution made by Piaget that it is still impossible to understand the themes and issues in developmental research without knowing something of Piaget's theory, nearly half a century after that theory was first put forward. In a profound sense, Piaget *invented* developmental psychology. Before his extraordinary work, understanding how intelligence develops was generally conceptualised as quite a simple matter. There was the child's basic intellectual power (IQ) which determined the individual's ability to learn. And there was the lengthy process of learning through relatively simple associative processes. Piaget changed not just the answers which research gave to the problem of how intellect arises, but the very questions which researchers ask.

Perhaps Piaget's most powerful contribution comes from pointing out that intelligence involves conceptual understanding, and that explaining how such a thing can arise in a biological entity which starts out with no understanding of anything at all, as the fertilised ovum does, is a substantial problem. With no initial understanding of anything, how can the infant make sense of information from the world or learn anything about it?

Piaget's theory of how such an extraordinary feat is possible completely rev-
olutionised research on children's minds. It presented a view of the child
not as a passive learner of associations, but as an active agent *constructing*
the very processes on which intellect rests from the raw materials of simple
reflexes. It characterised development not as the steady accretion of more
facts, but as a progression through qualitatively different stages of thought,
reflecting the character of the mental structures the child had so far
achieved. And Piaget identified two fundamental principles as critical to
the development of mind: first, that the infant must build mental structures out of the limited range of actions available, so that intelligence is initially tightly embedded in very concrete ways of interacting with the world.
And second, that the true growth of intelligence must involve the progressive freeing of thought from such concrete bases, so that it becomes more
fluid, more general and more deliberate.

Piaget was wrong about many things: for example, infants are not born
quite as helpless and ill equipped to understand the world as he supposed,
as we saw in Chapter 2. Furthermore, human reasoning does not rest on
abstract, general, logical mental processes as he supposed, so that childhood cognitive development can hardly be a matter of evolving such
processes as his theory claims, as we saw in Chapters 4 and 5. And individual minds do not develop in such isolation as Piaget supposed.
Nonetheless, the broader claims of his theory are still powerful influences
on the way we understand cognitive development.

Taking Biology Seriously

If there is a single theme which characterises the way our understanding of
cognitive development has changed in the past forty years, it lies in the
extent to which the biological nature of human intelligence has become a
dominant perspective in research.

Although Piaget was arguably the first influential theorist to take biology
seriously in explaining the growth of the mind, he was surprisingly reluctant
to put any emphasis on our specifically *human* biology. Piaget was not a
psychologist. His concern was to explain the growth of intelligence in biological organisms, rather than in human beings per se. His focus, therefore,
was on how general biological mechanisms common to all animals, such as
adaptation, might lead to intellectual functioning.

Subsequent research has taken a broader view of biological influences
on development, noting that many species have strong genetic predispositions to learn certain things or behave in certain ways, and that there are
powerful advantages to such preparedness. Intelligence might arise over

and over in individual minds, as Piaget supposed. But even when it does so, such development starts out in an evolutionary context, and in a genetically determined organism. Human intelligence evolved in our *species*, rather than being the separate invention of individual members of that species. That being so, genetic predispositions to learn certain things and to view the world in certain ways seem more likely than not.

One of the striking breakthroughs in research over the past twenty years is the discovery of the extent to which the human neonate is pre-programmed to see and interact with the world. Far from being born with only a few simple reflexes, we start life with complex perceptual abilities and with minds already set to identify certain classes of information as *important*, and to pay special attention to them. Much of this information is social: we are born predisposed to treat other human beings as something special and different from the rest of the universe, to pay attention to them, find them attractive, imitate them and interact with them. And we are born predisposed to attend specifically to human language, already primed with the ability to hear every possible speech sound and to hone in on those which characterise the language spoken around us. Understanding the difference between animate and inanimate objects is important, and babies are born well equipped to learn this distinction. But understanding the physical world is important too. Babies are also born ready to perceive structure and form in the inanimate objects which make up their world, to learn about the properties of those objects and the physical constraints which determine those properties.

A very new approach to exploring the biological origins of human intelligence is provided by evolutionary psychology, which looks at the structure of human behaviour within the ecological niche our species occupies. This approach has enormous potential in identifying genetic contributions to development: for example, in explaining the degree to which a given predisposition is likely to be firmly genetically fixed as opposed to being free to be more variable, as a function of the evolutionary advantage of either strategy for nature. Evolutionary psychology may provide new impetus in explaining the patterns of innate mental structure in the human mind.

One ongoing debate in relation to innate mental structures relates to the extent to which the unfolding of development in core areas of knowledge (such as mastery of language or biological knowledge, and so on) is controlled or constrained by biological programmes which mature at a given pace, and in a given way. Exactly how much of what a child learns in mastering language, for instance, is already prefigured in the child's mind? Some theorists, such as Pinker (1997) believe that it would be extremely difficult, if not impossible, for a baby to learn language if there were no innate 'roadmap' as it were, of the character and shape of grammar. For such theorists, the development of language is, to a greater or lesser degree, a matter of the child looking out for features of speech which he or she is already genetically programmed to expect, and acquiring language by slotting the specifics of the mother tongue into this ready-made frame. Other theorists disagree, believing that language can be learned by gradually constructing longer and more complex units of speech and learning to generalise these (Lieven, Pine and Baldwin, 1997; Tomasello, 1998). Such theorists believe that we do not really learn grammar as such at all, nor use grammatical rules in generating speech, even in adult life. Rather, grammar is an abstraction we project onto language: it is in the eye of the (highly educated) beholder, rather than a dynamic element in the processes which directly produce language.

This controversy as to the genetic basis of language learning resonates with a much more general question for understanding how any mental function develops: to what extent are the things we learn to do ever prefigured, either innately in our genetic endowment or conceptually in the existing structures of our minds? For example, are the new discoveries we make as we develop necessarily dependent on our existing understanding? Piaget and many others would argue that they are, in that one can only learn about what one can make sense of. From this point of view, a child's existing mental structures must necessarily constrain what he or she can learn next. But if this is the case, how is it ever possible for the child to develop a radically new idea, as happens over and over again in the course of development?

One answer to the problem of where radical new ideas come from picks up on Piaget's idea that our actions are an important vehicle for developmental change. Quite clearly, the shape our actions takes is the product not just of our genetic pre-programming, not just of the present conceptual structures of our minds, but also of the interaction between these things and the physical and social world in which they exist. A child may not understand much about gravity, but the physics of our universe ensure that his or her actions will be shaped by gravity, whether the child is learning to crawl or trying to discover how to balance wooden blocks. Feedback from the world can shape our actions in ways we do not expect or understand, but which provide the basis for radical new discoveries.

Perhaps the most exciting recent development in research is the application of dynamic systems theory to understanding how development can occur in this way, without there being any biological programme shaping the direction or form of that development, and without the child starting with any sort of mental structure which prefigures what will come next. Dynamic systems theory stems from work in the sciences as a whole. Originating in chaos mathematics, the same basic principles have been applied in physics, chemistry, biology and now in psychology to explain how complex structures form themselves out of the repeated actions of far simpler elements. Over and over again in nature, it seems, simple systems work in self-organising ways to create more complex systems in surprising ways. This complexity is not planned for: it just happens, generating the strange beauty of a snowflake, the extraordinary patterns of the universe, or the equally extraordinary phenomenon of human intelligence. According to this perspective, the processes which form the human mind are not unique to us at all. They are only one example of a basic principle of the physical world, which applies to inanimate and animate systems alike.

The idea that the human mind develops through universal processes which are equally applicable to inanimate and animate systems is as dangerously exciting as Darwin's theory of evolution. On the one hand, it provides a powerful means of explaining just how intelligence could arise both through evolutionary time and in the individual child in what is, after all, a collection of inanimate atoms. On the other hand, the notion that human minds are the product of such simple and universal principles will seem to some to *reduce* the value of our minds, just as being told that we are related to chimpanzees once outraged, and seemed to many to belittle our culture.

Of course, imagining that the mind could in any way be belittled because it emerges from simple, universal self-organising processes is a mistake. To think that way is to confuse the *product* with the process which produces it. Products and processes can be very different. For example, there is an old wooden box-like object on the dresser in my dining room, full of clockwork elements and springs connected to a pendulum. For a hundred years, this unlikely device has measured out the elusive passage of time, striking the quarter hours as it goes. There is nothing in the mechanism of the clock itself which in any way resembles time. In the same way, our minds have transcendental properties entirely different from the processes which produce them. The fact that we are biological entities, and that biology itself is just a special case of physics in no way diminishes the value or experience of consciousness.

The Structure of the Mind

A second theme which characterises how our understanding of development has changed over recent decades lies in how we understand the structure of the mind. Progressively, research has moved away from asking *what* children of different ages can or cannot do, and towards studying more directly *how* any particular performance is produced. This focus on mental processes has been salutary. Almost every action, however small, turns out to be far more complex than we ever supposed. It is only when you begin to examine in detail what a baby must do, for example, to reach out and grasp a toy that you realise exactly how much knowledge and structure even such simple acts entail.

Focusing on the processes which underlie conceptual understanding and action has radically changed our theories about how the mind is structured. Piaget (and everyone else) thought that intelligence rested on very general skills, which would be used in reasoning across all domains so that the mind would, at any one time during development, have a general character reflecting the stage of development these processes had reached. But this is not the case. In fact, the tools we use in reasoning are very tightly tied to the specific detail of the knowledge we have about some particular topic. How much detailed, specific knowledge we have in a given domain determines not only what conclusions we can draw in that domain, but the very nature of the inference processes by which we draw them, our ability to learn and recall material, to plan and solve problems.

Rich knowledge about a given topic creates powerful tools and expertise in reasoning *about that topic*. But with another topic, about which we know far less, the quality and form of our reasoning will be entirely different. This is as true for an adult as it is for a child: it is *knowledge* and not *age* which determines the calibre of reasoning. And rich knowledge is far more relevant to reasoning than factors such as the speed or efficiency of basic mental processes such as working memory.

Thus intelligence develops patchily, topic by topic, as we acquire richer knowledge across a variety of domains. The fact that children are acquiring knowledge across a broad range of topics at the same time may mean that similar tools for drawing inferences, say, *happen* to develop in two separate areas at more or less the same time. But they are still separate tools, in separate domains. In effect, the young child can be viewed as a universal novice, and development as a matter of progressively acquiring expertise across many domains.

The Social Bases of Knowledge

Knowledge is not objective: it is always a theory, always capable of reinterpretation or new discovery. And it is, in important ways, socially and culturally defined. The things we think of as facts about the physical world are really the collective conclusions that our culture has come to about the way things are, and the 'facts' that the child learns reflect these cultural conclusions. For example, the average eight-year-old in our culture has an understanding of the structure of the solar system which was quite beyond the best minds of ancient civilisations (Carey, 1985). It is not to be supposed that modern eight-year-olds are wiser than ancient philosophers. Rather, they have acquired the ideas of their culture.

To a far greater extent than Piaget realised, children learn about the world through interacting with others, being directly taught things, encouraged to think in certain ways and do certain things. A great deal of what they know is socially given, rather than discovered by the individual child. Social processes foster the development of specific knowledge and cognitive strategies, but also provide the child with new mental tools, such as literacy, logic or mathematics. Such things do not develop naturally in the individual mind. They must be induced through formal education. Thus some of the abstract skills which Piaget saw as the natural end point of individual development are in fact cultural artefacts.

Cognition and meta-cognition

Yet Piaget was right to say that there is an important developmental change from skills which are tightly embedded in specific concrete contexts to ones which have a more abstract, general quality.

Within any particular conceptual area, the young child's earliest experience is tied to very specific aspects of the particular problems so far encountered. For example, if every exercise in addition so far encountered has laid the numbers to be added out in a vertical list, then vertical listing will be a key feature of adding for the child. Gradually, as different versions of the same basic problem are encountered, the features which are critical to the task (such as the function of addition per se) can be abstracted from those which are peripheral (such as whether the numbers to be added are listed vertically or horizontally, or written down at all). This more abstract conception allows the child to see connections across a broader range of situations, and so to use skills more abstractly and generally.

Increasingly abstract representations allow the child to draw analogies not only within a domain, but across domains too, so that reasoning developed in relation to one type of problem can be applied to a new, entirely different area. This power of analogy provides the beginnings of a more general intelligence, characteristic of adult life.

But children do not reflect only on the specific content of the domains about which they reason. Piaget was right in saying that reflection on one's own mental processes provides a powerful source of development, even if his account of what such reflection involved or produced was not correct. The very young child has little awareness of his or her own mental processes or how they work, what their limitations may be, or how best to control them. Indeed, before the age of about five years, children seem to have very little recognition of the fact that they, or anyone else, has a mind at all. This astonishing insight develops slowly as the child builds up a theory of what the human mind is like. Exactly how important developing a theory of mind is to cognitive development is still a matter of speculation. Is the start of such an idea a necessary precursor to noticing how your memory works, for example, and being able therefore to deliberately select when and where to use a given strategy to support its frailties? Or does an emerging meta-cognitive understanding about one's skills at large (language, say) trigger the child to notice that he or she has a mind? Or do both these effects work together to reinforce one another? For that matter, does meta-cognitive awareness develop from the individual child's own spontaneous reflections, or is it stimulated by social processes: invocations to 'make up your mind', for instance, or pressures to think about skills as part of formal schooling, from the earliest steps in literacy upwards.

Whatever its origins, an awareness of the mind and some of its contents and properties creates new possibilities for controlling and directing reasoning. This self-reflective awareness is characteristic of human intelligence. It is what we mean when we think of our minds, and it seems to be unique to our species.

Methodology and Theoretical Advance

Psychology is an empirical discipline. That is to say, unlike philosophers, we are interested in constraining our speculations about human intelligence and its development with evidence to support or refute our ideas. The history of the past twenty years in developmental psychology has been driven by advances in the methodologies we have used in studying children's behaviour.

For example, the development of 'habituation' techniques for use with newborn babies has opened up a whole new insight into what the infant brings into the world. Before the advent of this methodology, there was no way to tell what a young baby could really see or understand. Equally, the development of methods for very detailed recording of what children say and do, has provided us with rich new data about the nature of development. Before the use of such methods, it was thought that one level of reasoning superseded another in an orderly progression as a child mastered a task. Methods for microgenetic analysis of children's problem solving have shown that this is not so: old and new strategies co-exist alongside one another, so that development involves a gradual change in the preferred approach rather than the supersession of one strategy by another. Over and over, in every field of research, more detailed data have changed our perception of how intelligence develops. It would be difficult to overestimate the vital role which better data has played in shaping our new understanding of the origins of the human mind. For this reason those who study cognitive development must focus not only on the theories that we have, but on the methodologies through which those theories have arisen and the ways in which those methodologies might be improved to allow us to advance still further.

Present theories of intellectual development draw on data which were simply not available to Piaget. One wonders what he would have made of it, had he had the methodological tools in use today. As it is, one can only stand in awe of his achievement. For, despite all the radical change in how we now see the detail of the process of intellectual development, the broad outlines of our understanding, and the philosophical questions shaping our agenda for research are still recognisably Piagetian.

SUGGESTED READING

For an excellent collection of essays about recent advances in understanding cognitive development:

Kuhn, D. and Siegler, R. (eds), W. Damon (series ed.) (1997) *Handbook of Child Psychology*, vol. 2: *Cognition, Perception and Language* (New York: John Wiley).

For a collection of essays on where cognitive developmental research will go in the 21st century:

Child Development 71, issue 1.

References

Ackles, P. and Cook, K. (1998) 'Stimulus probability and event-related potentials of the brain in 6-month-old human infants'. *International Journal of Psychophysiology 29*, pp. 115–43.

Adolph, K., Vereijken, B. and Denny, M. (1998) 'Learning to crawl'. *Child Development 69*, pp. 1299–312.

Alibali, M. (1999) 'How children change their minds: strategy change can be gradual or abrupt'. *Developmental Psychology 35*, pp. 127–45.

Anderson, M. (1992) *Intelligence and Cognitive Development* (Oxford: Blackwell).

Anisfeld, M. (1984) *Language Development from Birth to Three* (Hillsdale, NJ: Lawrence Erlbaum).

Aslin, R., Pisoni, D. and Jusczyk, P. (1983) 'Auditory development and speech perception in infancy'. In: M. Haith and J. Campos (eds), *Handbook of Child Psychology*, vol. 2: *Infancy and Developmental Psychology* (New York: Wiley).

Astington, J. (1993) *The Child's Discovery of Mind* (Cambridge, MA: Harvard University Press).

Baddeley, A. (1976) *The Psychology of Memory* (New York: Harper Row).

Baillargeon, R. (1986) 'Representing the existence and the location of a hidden object: object permanence in 6- to 8-month-old infants'. *Cognition 23*, pp. 21–41.

Baillargeon, R., Spelke, E. and Wasserman, S. (1985) 'Object permanence in 5-month-old infants'. *Cognition 20*, pp. 191–208.

Baillargeon, R., Graber, M., DeVos, J. and Black, J. (1990) 'Why do infants fail to search for hidden objects?' *Cognition 36*, pp. 255–84.

Balacheff, N. (1988) 'Aspects of proof in pupils' practise of school mathematics'. In: D. Primm (ed.), *Mathematics, Teachers and Children* (London: Hodder and Stoughton).

Baker-Ward, L., Ornstein, P. and Holden, D. (1984) *Influences on Human Development: A Longitudinal Perspective* (Boston, MA: Kluwer Nijhoff).

Baron-Cohen, S., Tager-Flusberg, H. and Cohen, D. (1993) *Understanding Other Minds: Perspectives from Autism* (Oxford: Oxford University Press).

Bartlett, F. (1932) *Remembering* (Cambridge: Cambridge University Press).

Bartsch, K. and Wellman, H. (1995) *Children Talk about the Mind* (New York: Oxford University Press).

Bates, E., O'Connell, B. and Shore, C. (1987) 'Language and communication in infancy'. In: J. Osofsky (ed.), *Handbook of Infant Development* (New York: Wiley).

Bateson, M. (1979) 'The epigenesis of conversational interaction: a personal account of research development'. In: M. Bullowa (ed.), *Before Speech: The Beginning of Human Communication* (Cambridge: Cambridge University Press).

Bayley, N. (1969) *Bayley Scales of Infant Development* (New York: Psychological Corporation).

Bayley, N. (1993) *Bayley Scales of Infant Development: Birth to Two Years* (San Antonio, TX: Psychological Corporation).

Bee, H. (1989) *The Developing Child* (New York: Harper Row).

Benes, M. (1994) 'Development of the corticolimbic system'. In: G. Dawson and K. Fischer (eds), *Human Behaviour and the Developing Brain* (New York: Guildford Press).

Berko, J. (1958) 'The child's learning of English morphology'. *Word 14*, pp. 150–77.

Bertenthal, B. (1993) 'Infant's perception of biochemical motions: intrinsic image and knowledge-based constraints'. In: C. Granrud (ed.), *Visual Perception and Cognition in Infancy* (Hillsdale, NJ: Lawrence Erlbaum).

Binet, A. and Simon, T. (1916) *The Development of Intelligence in Children* (Baltimore, MD: William and Wilkins).

Bjorklund, D., Miller, P., Coyle, T. and Slawinski, J. (1997) 'Instructing children to use memory strategies: evidence for utilization deficiencies in memory training studies'. *Developmental Review 17*, pp. 411–41.

Bjorklund, D. and Pellegrini, A. (2000) 'Child development and evolutionary psychology'. *Child Development 71*, pp. 1687–1708.

Bjorklund, D. and Zeman, B. (1982) 'Children's organisation and meta memory awareness in their recall of familiar information'. *Child Development 53*, pp. 799–810.

Boden, M. (1990) *The Creative Mind: Myths and Mechanisms* (London: Weidenfeld and Nicolson).

Bomba, P. (1984) 'The development of orientation categories between 2 and 4 months of age'. *Journal of Experimental Child Psychology 37*, pp. 609–36.

Block, R. and Harper, D. (1991) 'Overconfidence in estimation: testing the anchoring-and-adjustment hypothesis'. *Organizational Behaviour and Human Decision Processes 49*, pp. 188–207.

Braine, M. (1971) 'The acquisition of language in the infant and child'. In: C. Reed (ed.), *The Learning of Language* (New York: Appleton-Century-Crofts).

Bremner, J. G.(1997) 'From perception to cognition'. In: G. Bremner, A. Slater and G. Butterworth (1997) *Infant Development: Recent Advances* (Hillsdale, NJ: Psychology Press, Erlbaum).

Brown, A. (1975) 'The development of memory: knowing, knowing about knowing, and knowing how to know'. In: H. Reese (ed.), *Advances in Child Development and Behaviour*, vol. 10 (New York: Academic Press).

Brown, A. (1990) 'Domain-specific principles affect learning and transfer in children'. *Cognitive Science 14*, pp. 107–33.

Brown, A. and Campione, J. (1972) 'Recognition memory for perceptually similar pictures in preschool children'. *Journal of Experimental Child Psychology 95*, pp. 55–62.

Brown, A. and DeLoache, J. (1978) 'Skills, plans and self regulation'. In: R. Siegler (ed.), *Children's Thinking: What Develops?* (Hillsdale, NJ: Erlbaum).

Brown, A. and Scott, M. (1971) 'Recognition memory for pictures in preschool children'. *Journal of Experimental Child Psychology 11*, pp. 401–12.

Brown, A., Bransford, J., Ferrara, R. and Campione, J. (1983) 'Learning, remembering and understanding'. In: J. Flavell and E. Markman (eds), *The Handbook of Child Psychology*, vol. 3 (New York: Wiley).

Brown, R. (1973) *A First Language: The Early Stages* (Cambridge, MA: Harvard University Press).

Bruner, J. (1975a) 'From communication to language: a psychological perspective'. *Cognition 3*, pp. 255–87.

Bruner, J. (1975b) *Beyond the Information Given: Studies in the Psychology of Knowing* (New York: W. W. Norton).

Bruner, J. and Kenney, H. (1965) 'Representation and mathematical learning'. *Monographs of the Society for Research in Child Development 30*, pp. 50–9.

Bryant, P. (1974) *Perception and Understanding in Young Children* (London: Methuen).

Bryant, P. and Trabasso, T. (1971) 'Transitive inferences and memory in young children'. *Nature 232*, pp. 456–8.

Bushnell, E. (1985) 'The decline of visually guided reaching in infancy'. *Infant Behaviour and Development 8*, pp. 139–55.

Bushnell, I. (1982) 'Discrimination of faces by young infants'. *Journal of Experimental Child Psychology 33*, pp. 298–309.

Bushnell, I., Sai, F. and Mullin, J. (1989) 'Neonatal recognition of the mother's face'. *British Journal of Developmental Psychology 7*, pp. 3–15.

Butterworth, G. (1991) 'The ontegeny and phylogeny of joint visual attention'. In: A. Whiten (ed.), *Natural Theories of Mind: Evolution, Development and Simulation of Everyday Mindreading* (Oxford: Blackwell).

Byrne, R. and Whiten, A. (1988) 'Toward the next generation in data quality: a new survey of primate tactical deception'. *Behavioural and Brain Science 11*, pp. 267–83.

Byrne, R. and Whiten, A. (1991) 'Computation and mindreading in primate tactical deception'. In: A. Whiten (ed.), *Natural Theories of Mind: Evolution, Development and Simulation of Everyday Mindreading* (Oxford: Blackwell).

Call, J. and Tomasello, M. (1996) 'The effects of humans on the cognitive development of apes'. In: A. Russon, K. Bard and S. Parker, *Reaching into Thought: The Minds of the Great Apes* (New York: Cambridge University Press).

Camaioni, L. (1992) 'Mind knowledge in infancy: the emergence of intentional communication'. *Early Development and Parenting 1*, pp. 15–28.

Carey, S. (1985) *Conceptual Change in Childhood* (Cambridge, MA and London: MIT Press).

Case, R. (1984) 'The process of stage transition: a neo-Piagetian view'. In: R. Sternberg (ed.), *Mechanisms of Cognitive Development* (New York: Freeman).

Case, R. (1985) *Intellectual Development: Birth to Adulthood* (New York: Academic Press).

Cattell, R. (1963) 'The theory of fluid and crystallised intelligence: a critical experiment'. *Journal of Educational Psychology 54*, pp. 1–22.

Ceci, S. and Liker, J. (1986) 'A day at the races: a study of IQ, cognitive complexity and expertise'. *Journal of Experimental Psychology: General 115*, pp. 255–66.

Chance, J. and Goldstein, A. (1984) 'Face recognition memory: implications for children's eye witness testimony'. *Journal of Social Issues 40*, pp. 6–85.

Chazan, D. (1993) 'High school geometry students' justification for their views of empirical evidence and mathematical proof'. *Educational Studies in Mathematics 24*, pp. 359–87.

Chi, M. (1978) 'Knowledge structures and memory development'. In: R. Siegler (ed.), *Children's Thinking: What Develops?* (Hillsdale, NJ: Erlbaum).

Chi, M. and Ceci, S. (1987) 'Content knowledge: its role, representation and restructuring in memory development'. *Advances in Child Development and Behaviour 20*, pp. 91–142.

Chi, M., Feltovich, P. and Glaser, R. (1981) 'Categorization and representation in physics problems by experts and novices'. *Cognitive Science 5*, pp. 121–52.

Chi, M., Glaser, R. and Rees, E. (1982) 'Expertise in problem solving'. In: R. Sternberg (ed.), *Advances in the Psychology of Human Intelligence 1*, pp. 7–75.

Chomsky, N. (1975) *Reflections on Language* (New York: Pantheon Books).

Chomsky, N. (1980) 'On cognitive structures and their development: a reply to Piaget'. In: M. Piattelli-Palmarini (ed.), *Language and Learning: The Debate Between Jean Piaget and Noam Chomsky* (Cambridge, MA: Harvard University Press).

Chugani, H., Phelps, M. and Mazziotta, J. (1987) 'Positron emission tomography study of human brain functional development'. *Annals of Neurology 22*, pp. 487–97.

Clark, E. (1973) 'What's in a word? On the child's acquisition of semantics in his first language'. In: E. Moore (ed.), *Cognitive Development and the Acquisition of Language* (New York: Academic Press).

Cole, M. and Scribner, S. (1974) *Culture and Thought: A Psychological Introduction* (New York: Wiley).

Coley, J. (2000) 'On the importance of comparative research: the case of folk-biology'. *Child Development 71*, pp. 82–90.

Cosmides, L. and Tooby, J. (1992) 'Cognitive adaptations for social exchange'. In: J. Barkow, L. Cosmides and J. Tooby (eds), *The Adapted Mind: Evolutionary Psychology and the Generation of Culture* (New York: Oxford University Press).

Cowan, W. M. (1979) 'The development of the brain'. *Scientific American 241*, pp. 106–17.

Cowan, N., Nugent, L., Elliot, E., Ponomarev, I. and Scott Saults, J. (1999) 'The role of attention in the development of short-term memory: age differences in verbal span apprehension'. *Child Development 70*, pp. 1082–97.

Crano, W., Kenny, J. and Campbell, D. (1972) 'Does intelligence cause achievement? A cross-lagged panel analysis'. *Journal of Educational Psychology 63*, pp. 258–75.

Crisafi, M. and Brown, A. (1986) 'Analogical transfer in very young children: combining two separately learned solutions to reach a goal'. *Child Development 57*, pp. 953–68.

Csibra, G., Tucker, L. and Johnson, M. (1998) 'Neural correlates of saccade planning in infants: A high-density ERP study'. *International Journal of Psychophysiology 29*, pp. 201–15.

Darwin, C. (1859) *On the Origin of the Species by Means of Natural Selection* (London: John Murray).

De Groot, A. (1965) *Thought and Choice in Chess* (The Hague: Mouton).

DeLoache, J., Cassidy, D. and Brown, A. (1985) 'Precursors of mnemonic strategies in very young children's memory'. *Child Development 56*, pp. 125–37.

DeLoache, J., Miller, K. and Pierroutsakos, S. (1998) 'Reasoning and problem solving'. In: D. Kuhn and R. Siegler (eds), W. Damon (series ed.), *The Handbook of Child Psychology*, vol. 2: *Cognition, Perception and Language* (New York: Wiley).

Dempster, F. (1985) 'Short-term memory development in childhood and adolescence'. In: C. Brainerd and M. Pressley (eds), *Basic Processes in Memory Development: Progress in Cognitive Development Research* (New York: Springer-Verlag).

Dennett, D. (1996) *Darwin's Dangerous Idea: Evolution and the Meanings of Life* (New York: Touchstone/Simon and Schuster).

Doise, W. (1978) *Groups and Individuals* (Cambridge: Cambridge University Press).

Doise, W. and Hanselmann, C. (1991) 'Conflict and social marking in the acquisition of operational thinking'. *Learning and Instruction 1*, pp. 119–27.

Doise, W. and Mugny, G. (1984) *The Development of Social Intellect* (Oxford: Pergamon Press).

Donaldson, M. (1978) *Children's Minds* (London: Fontana).

Dunn, J. and Munn, P. (1985) 'Becoming a family member: family conflict and the development of social understanding in the second year'. *Child Development* 56, pp. 480–92.

Dunn, J., Brown, J. and Beardsall, L. (1991) 'Family talk about feeling states and children's later understanding of others' emotions'. *Developmental Psychology* 27, pp. 448–55.

Dunn, J., Brown, J., Slomkowski, C., Tesla, C. and Youngblade, L. (1991) 'Young children's understanding of other people's feelings and beliefs: Individual differences and their antecedents'. *Child Development* 62, pp. 1352–66.

Ericsson, K. and Simon, H. (1993) *Protocol Analysis: Verbal Reports as Data* (Cambridge, MA: MIT Press).

Evans, J. St. (1989) *Bias in Human Reasoning: Causes and Consequences* (Hove: Erlbaum).

Evans, J. St. and Pollard, P. (1990) 'Belief bias and problem complexity in deductive reasoning'. In: J. Caverni, J. Fabre and M. Gonzales (eds), *Cognitive Biases* (Amsterdam: North Holland).

Evans, J. St. B., Barstow, J. and Pollard, P. (1983) 'On the conflict between logic and belief in syllogistic reasoning'. *Memory and Cognition* 11, pp. 295–306.

Evans, J. St., Newstead, S. and Byrne, R. (1993) *Human Reasoning: The Psychology of Deduction* (Hove: Erlbaum).

Fabricius, W. (1988) 'The development of forward search in preschoolers'. *Child Development* 59, pp. 1473–88.

Fabricius, W. and Wellman, H. (1983) 'Children's understanding of retrieval cue utilisation'. *Developmental Psychology* 19, pp. 15–21.

Fagan, J. (1984) 'Infant memory: history, current trends and relations to cognitive psychology'. In: M. Moscovitch (ed.), *Infant Memory: Its Relation to Normal and Pathological Memory in Humans and Animals* (Hillsdale, NJ: Erlbaum).

Field, T., Woodson, R., Greenberg, R. and Cohen, C. (1982) 'Discrimination and imitation of facial expressions by neonates'. *Science* 218, pp. 179–81.

Fischbein, E. (1975) *The Intuitive Sources of Probabilistic Thinking in Children* (Boston, MA: Riedel).

Flavell, J. (1985) *Cognitive Development* (Englewood-Cliffs, NJ: Prentice-Hall).

Flavell, J. and Miller, P. (1998) 'Social cognition'. In: D. Kuhn and R. Siegler (eds), W. Damon (series ed.), *Handbook of Child Psychology* vol. 2: *Cognition, Perception and Language* (New York: Wiley).

Flavell, J. and Wellman, H. (1977) 'Metamemory'. In: R. Kail and J. Hagen (eds), *Perspectives on the Development of Memory and Cognition* (Hillsdale, NJ: Erlbaum).

Flavell, J., Green, F. and Flavell, E. (1995) 'Young children's knowledge about thinking'. *Monographs of the Society for Research in Child Development* 60, pp. 1–243.

Fodor, J. (1983) *The Modularity of Mind* (Cambridge, MA: MIT Press).

Frith, C. and Frith, U. (1996) 'A biological marker for dyslexia'. *Nature* 382, pp. 19–20.

Frye, D. and Moore, C (eds), (1991) *Children's Theories of Mind: Mental States and Social Understanding* (Hove: Erlbaum).

Gagne, R. (1968) 'Contributions of learning to human development'. *Psychological Review* 75, pp. 177–91.

Gardner, B. and Gardner, R. (1980) 'Two comparative psychologists look at language acquisition'. In: K. Nelson (ed.), *Children's Language*, vol. 2 (New York: Basic Books).

Gardner, H. (1983) *Frames of Mind: The Theory of Multiple Intelligences* (London: Heinemann).

Geary, D. (1998) *Male and Female: The Evolution of Human Sex Differences* (Washington, DC: American Psychological Association).

Geary, D. and Bjorklund, D. (2000) 'Evolutionary developmental psychology'. *Child Development* 71, pp. 57–65.

Gelman, R. (1980) 'Cognitive development'. *Annual Review of Psychology* 29, pp. 297–332.

Gelman, R. (1982) 'Assessing one-to-one correspondence: Still another paper about conservation'. *British Journal of Developmental Psychology* 73, pp. 209–20.

Gelman, R. and Brenneman, K. (1994) 'First principles can support both universal and culture-specific learning about number and music'. In: L. A. Hirschfeld and S. A. Gelman (eds), *Mapping the Mind: Domain Specificity in Cognition and Culture* (New York: Cambridge University Press).

Gelman, S. and Markman, E. (1986) 'Categories and induction in young children'. *Cognition* 23, pp. 183–209.

Gelman, S. and Markman, E. (1987) 'Young children's inductions from natural kinds: the role of categories and appearances'. *Child Development* 58, pp. 1532–41.

Gelman, R. and Meck, E. (1992) 'Early principles aid initial but not later conceptions of number'. In: J. Bideaud, C. Meljac and J. Fischer (eds), *Pathways to Number* (Hillsdale, NJ: Erlbaum).

Gelman, R. and Williams, E. (1998) 'Enabling constraints for cognitive development and learning: domain specificity and epigenesis'. In: D. Kuhn and R. Siegler (eds), W. Damon (series ed.), *Handbook of Child Psychology*, vol. 2: *Cognition, Perception and Language* (New York: Wiley).

Gentner, D. (1982) 'Why nouns are learned before verbs: linguistic relativity versus natural partitioning'. In: S. Kuczaj, II (ed.), *Language Development*, vol. 2: *Language, Thought and Culture* (Hillsdale, NJ: Erlbaum).

Gentner, D. (1983) 'Structure mapping: a theoretical framework for analogy'. *Cognitive Science* 7, pp. 155–70.

Gholson, B., Dattel, A., Morgan, D. and Eymard, L. (1989) 'Problem solving, recall and mapping relations in isomorphic transfer and non-isomorphic transfer among preschoolers and elementary school children'. *Child Development* 60, pp. 1172–87.

Gibson, J. (1979) *The Ecological Approach to Visual Perception* (New York: Appleton Century Crofts).

Glachlan, M. and Light, P. (1982) 'Peer interaction and learning: can two wrongs make a right?' In: G. Butterworth and P. Light (eds), *Social Cognition* (Brighton: Harvester).

Gleitman, L. (1990) 'The structural sources of verb meanings'. *Language Acquisition 1*, pp. 3–55.

Gnepp., J. and Hess, D. (1986) 'Children's understanding of verbal and facial display rules'. *Developmental Psychology* 22, pp. 103–8.

Goldfield, E. (1994) 'Dynamical systems in development: action systems'. In: L. Smith and E. Thelen (eds), *A Dynamical Systems Approach to Development: Applications* (Cambridge, MA: MIT Press).

Goldin-Meadow, S. and Feldman, H. (1979) 'The development of language-like communication without a language model'. *Science 197*, pp. 401–3.

Goodall, J. (1986) *The Chimpanzees of Gombi: Patterns of Development* (Cambridge, MA: The Belknap Press).

Goswami, U. (1992) *Analogical Reasoning in Children* (Hillsdale, NJ: Lawrence Erlbaum Associates).

Goswami, U. (1995) 'Transitive relational mappings in 3- and 4-year olds: the analogy of Goldilocks and the three bears'. *Child Development 66*, pp. 877–92.

Goswami, U. and Brown, A. (1989) 'Melting chocolate and melting snowmen: analogical reasoning and causal relations'. *Cognition 35*, pp. 69–95.

Greeno, J., Riley, M. and Gelman, R. (1984) 'Conceptual competence and children's counting'. *Cognitive Psychology 16*, pp. 94–143.

Guildford, J. (1967) *The Nature of Human Intelligence* (New York: McGraw Hill).

Guildford, J. (1988) 'Some changes in the structure-of-the-intellect model'. *Educational and Psychological Measurement 40*, pp. 1–4.

Hadwin, J. and Perner, J. (1991) 'Pleased and surprised: children's cognitive theory of emotion'. *British Journal of Developmental Psychology 9*, pp. 215–34.

Halford, G. (1993) *Children's Understanding: The Development of Mental Models* (Hillsdale, NJ: Lawrence Erlbaum).

Harris, P. (1991) 'The work of the imagination'. In: A. Whiten (ed.), *Natural Theories of Mind: Evolution, Development and Simulation of Everyday Mindreading* (Oxford: Basil Blackwell).

Hartley, R. (1986) 'Imagine you're clever'. *Journal of Child Psychology and Psychiatry and Allied Disciplines 27*, pp. 383–98.

Hawkins, J., Pea, R., Glick, J. and Scribner, S. (1984) ' "Merds that laugh don't like mushrooms": evidence for deductive reasoning by preschoolers'. *Developmental Psychology 20*, pp. 584–95.

Hebb, D. (1949) *The Organization of Behaviour* (New York: Wiley).

Hirsh-Pasek, K., Gleitman, H., Gleitman, L, Golinkoff, R. and Naigles, L. (1988) 'Syntactic bootstrapping: evidence from comprehension'. Boston Language Conference.

Holyoak, K., Junn, E. and Billman, D. (1984) 'Development of analogical problem solving skill'. *Child Development 55*, pp. 332–40.

Honzik, M. (1983) 'Measuring mental abilities in infancy: the value and limitations'. In: M. Lewis (ed.), *Origins of Intelligence: Infancy and Early Childhood* (New York: Plenum).

Honzik, M., Macfarlane, J. and Allen, L. (1948) 'The stability of mental test performance between two and eighteen years'. *Journal of Experimental Education 17*, pp. 309–24.

Hood, B. (2001) 'Combined electrophysiological and behavioural measurement in developmental cognitive neuroscience: some cautionary notes – comment'. *Infancy 2*, pp. 213–17.

Hopkins, B. and Butterworth, G. (1997) 'Dynamical systems approaches to the development of action'. In: G. Bremner, A. Slater, and G. Butterworth (eds), *Infant Development: Recent Advances* (Hillsdale, NJ: Psychology Press, Erlbaum).

Horgan, J. (1996) *The End of Science* (London: Abacus).

Howe, M. (1989) 'Separate skills or general intelligence: the autonomy of human abilities'. *British Journal of Educational Psychology* 59, pp. 351–60.

Huttenlocher, P. (1994) 'Synaptogenesis, synapse elimination, and neural plasticity in human cerebral cortex'. In: C. Nelson (ed.), *Threats to Optimal Development: The Minnesota Symposia on Child Psychology* 27, pp. 35–54.

Inhelder, B. and Piaget, J. (1958) *The Growth of Logical Thinking from Childhood to Adolescence* (New York: Basic Books).

Inhelder, B. and Piaget, J. (1964) *The Early Growth of Logic in the Child* (London: Routledge).

Istomina, Z. (1975) 'The development of voluntary memory in preschool age children'. *Soviet Psychology 13*, pp. 5–64.

Jacobs, J. and Potenza, M. (1991) 'The use of judgment heuristics to make social and object decisions: a developmental perspective'. *Child Development 62*, pp. 16–178.

Jacobson, J., Boersma, D., Fields, R. and Olson, K. (1983) 'Paralinguistic features of adult speech to infants and small children'. *Child Development 54*, pp. 436–42.

Johnson, M. (1998) 'The neural basis of cognitive development'. In: D. Kuhn and R. Siegler (eds), W. Damon (series ed.), *Handbook of Child Psychology*, vol. 2: *Cognition, Perception and Language* (New York: Wiley).

Johnson, M. and Morton, J. (1991) *Biology and Cognitive Development: The Case for Face Recognition* (Oxford: Blackwell).

Johnson, M. and Foley, M. (1984) 'Differentiating fact from fantasy: the reliability of children's memory'. *Journal of Social Issues 40*, pp. 33–50.

Johnson, S. and Nanez, J. (1995) 'Young infant's perception of object unity in two-dimensional displays'. *Infant Behaviour and Development 18*, pp. 133–43.

Johnson, M., Dziurawiec, S., Ellis, H. and Morton, J. (1991) 'Newborn's preferential tracking of face-like stimuli and its subsequent decline'. *Cognition 40*, pp. 1–19.

Johnson-Laird, P. (1983) *Mental Models* (Cambridge, MA: Harvard University Press).

Johnson-Laird, P. (1993) *Human and Machine Thinking* (Hillsdale, NJ: Erlbaum).

Johnson-Laird, P. and Byrne, R. (1991) *Deduction* (Hove: Erlbaum).

Johnson-Laird, P. and Shafir, E. (1993) *Reasoning and Decision Making* (Amsterdam: Elsevier).

Johnson-Laird, P., Oakhill, J. and Bull, D. (1986) 'Children's syllogistic reasoning'. *Quarterly Journal of Experimental Psychology 38*, pp. 35–58.

Joseph, R. (2000) 'Fetal brain behaviour and cognitive development'. *Developmental Review 20*, pp. 81–98.

Jusczyk, P., Hirsh-Pasek, K., Kemler-Nelson, D., Kennedy, L. Woodward, A. and Piowoz, J. (1988) Perception of accoustic correlates of major phrasal units by young infants. Unpublished MS, quoted in A. Karmiloff-Smith (1992) *Modularity of Mind* (Cambridge, MA: MIT Press).

Kahneman, D. and Tversky, A. (1973) 'On the psychology of prediction'. *Psychological Review 80*, pp. 237–51.

Kahneman, D., Slovic, P. and Tversky, A. (eds) (1982) *Judgment under Uncertainty: Heuristics and Biases* (Cambridge: Cambridge University Press).

Kail, R. (1990) *The Development of Memory in Children*, 3rd edn (San Francisco, CA: Freeman).

Karmiloff-Smith, A. (1979) 'Macro- and micro-developmental changes in language acquisition and problem solving'. *Cognitive Science 3*, pp. 81–118.

Karmiloff-Smith, A. (1992) *Beyond Modularity: A Developmental Perspective on Cognitive Science* (Cambridge, MA: MIT Press).

Karmiloff-Smith, A. (1994) *Baby It's You* (London: Ebury Press).

Kauffman, S. (1995) *At Home in the Universe: The Search for the Laws of Self Organisation and Complexity* (New York: Oxford University Press).

Keil, F. (1981) 'Constraints on knowledge and cognitive development'. *Psychological Review 88*, pp. 197–227.

Keil, F. (1990) 'Constraints on constraints: surveying the epigenetic landscape'. *Cognitive Science 14*, pp. 135–68.

Kellman, P. and Banks, S. (1998) 'Infant visual perception'. In: D. Kuhn and R. Siegler (eds), W. Damon (series ed.), *The Handbook of Child Psychology*, vol. 2: *Cognition, Perception and Language* (New York: Wiley).

Kellman, P., Spelke, E. and Short, K. (1986) 'Infant perception of object unity from translatory motion in depth and vertical translation'. *Child Development 57*, pp. 72–86.

Kisilevsky, B., Fearon, I. and Muir, D. (1998) 'Fetuses differentiate vibroacoustic stimuli'. *Infant Behaviour and Development 21*, pp. 25–45.

Kitajima, Y., Kumoi, M. and Koike, T. (1998) *Japanese Journal of Physiological Psychology and Psychophysiology 16*, pp. 93–100.

Klahr, D. (1984) 'Transition processes in quantitative development'. In: R. Sternberg (ed.), *Mechanisms of Cognitive Development* (New York: Freeman).

Klahr, D. and MacWhinney, B. (1998) 'Information processing'. In: D. Kuhn and R. Siegler (eds), W. Damon (series ed.), *Handbook of Child Psychology*, vol. 2: *Cognition, Perception and Language* (New York: Wiley).

Klahr, D. and Robinson, M. (1981) 'Formal assessment of problem solving and planning processes in preschool children'. *Cognitive Psychology 13*, pp. 113–48.

Klahr, D. and Wallace, J. (1976) *Cognitive Development: An Information Processing View* (Hillsdale, NJ: Lawrence Erlbaum).

Kochanska, G., Coy, K., Tjebkes, T. and Husarek, S. (1998) 'Individual differences in emotionality in infancy'. *Child Development 69*, pp. 375–90.

Koffa, K. (1935) *Principles of Gestalt Psychology* (New York: Harcourt Brace).

Komatsu, L. and Galotti, K. (1986) 'Children's reasoning about social, physical and logical regularities: a look at two worlds'. *Child Development 57*, pp. 413–20.

Kreutzer, M., Leonard, C. and Flavell, J. (1975) 'An interview study of children's knowledge about memory'. *Monographs for the Society for Research in Child Development 40*.

Krouse, H. (1986) 'The use of decision frames by elementary school children'. *Perceptual and Motor Skills 63*, pp. 1107–12.

Kugiumutzakis, G. (1986) 'The origin, development and function of early infant imitation'. Doctoral thesis, quoted in Slater and Butterworth (1997).

Kugiumutzakis, G. (1993) 'Intersubjective vocal imitation in early other-infant interaction'. In: J. Nadel and L. Camioni (eds), *New Perspectives in Early Communicative Development* (London and New York: Routledge).

Kuhl, P., Andruski, J., Chistovich, I., Chistovich, L., Kozhevnikova, E., Ryskina, V., Stolyarova, E., Sundberg, U. and Lacerda, F. (1997) 'Cross-language analysis of phonetic units in language addressed to infants'. *Science 277*, pp. 684–6.

Kuhn, D. (1995) 'Microgenetic study of change: what has it told us?' *Psychological Science 6*, pp. 133–9.

Kuhn, D. (2000) 'Does memory development belong on an endangered species list?' *Child Development 71*, pp. 21–5.

Kuhn, D., Amsel, E. and O'Loughlin, M. (1988) *The Development of Scientific Thinking Skills* (San Diego, CA: Academic Press).

Kuhn, T. (1962) *The Structure of Scientific Revolutions* (Chicago: University of Chicago Press).

Kunzinger, E. (1985) 'A short-term longitudinal study of memorial development during early grade school'. *Developmental Psychology 21*, pp. 642–6.

Larkin, J. (1983) 'The role of problem representation in physics'. In: D. Gentner and A. Stevens (eds), *Mental Models* (Hillsdale, NJ: Erlbaum).

Lee, L., and Wheeler, D. (1989) 'The arithmetic connection'. *Educational Studies in Mathematics 20*, pp. 41–54.

Legerstee, M. (1992) 'A review of the animate–inanimate distinction in infancy: implications for models of social and cognitive knowing'. *Early Development and Parenting 1*, pp. 59–67.

Legerstee, M., Anderson, D. and Schaffer, A. (1998) 'Five- and eight-month-old infants recognise their faces and voices as familiar and social stimuli'. *Child Development 69*, pp. 37–50.

Legrenzi, P., Girotto, V. and Johnson-Laird, P. (1993) 'Focussing in reasoning and decision making'. In: P. Johnson-Laird and E. Shafir (eds), *Reasoning and Decision Making* (Cambridge, MA: Blackwell).

Lemaire, P. and Siegler, R. (1995) 'Four aspects of strategic change: contributions to children's learning of multiplication'. *Journal of Experimental Psychology: General 124*, pp. 83–97.

Lempers, J., Flavell, E. and Flavell, J. (1977) 'The development in very young children of tacit knowledge concerning visual perception'. *Genetic Psychology Monographs 95*, pp. 3–53.

Leslie, A. (1987) 'Pretence and representation: the origins of "theory of mind"'. *Psychological Review 94*, pp. 412–26.

Leslie, A. (1994) 'ToMM, ToBy and agency: Core architecture and domain specificity'. In: L. Hirschfield and S. Gelman (eds), *Mapping the Mind: Domain Specificity in Cognition and Culture* (Cambridge: Cambridge University Press).

Lewis, M. (2000) 'The promise of dynamic systems approaches for an integrated account of human development'. *Child Development 71*, pp. 36–43.

Lewis, M. and Douglas, L. (1998) 'A dynamic systems approach to cognition-emotion in development'. In: M. Mascolo and S. Griffin (eds), *What Develops in Emotional Development?* (New York: Plenum).

Liben, L. (1977) 'Memory in the context of cognitive development: the Piagetian approach'. In: R. Kail and J. Hagen (eds), *Perspectives on the Development of Memory and Cognition* (Hillsdale, NJ: Erlbaum).

Lieven, E., Pine, J. and Baldwin, G. (1997) 'Positional learning and early grammatical development'. *Journal of Child Language 24*, pp. 187–219.

Light, P. and Gilmour, A. (1983) 'Conservation of conversation? Contextual facilitation of inappropriate conservation judgments'. *Journal of Experimental Child Psychology 36*, pp. 356–63.

Light, P. and Perret-Clermont, A. (1989) 'Social context effects in learning and testing'. In: A. Gellattly, D. Rogers and J. Sloboda (eds), *Cognition and Social Worlds* (Oxford:Clarendon Press).

Light, P., Buckingham, N. and Robbins, A. (1979) 'The conservation task as an interactional setting'. *British Journal of Educational Psychology* 49, pp. 304–10.

Lindberg, M. (1980) 'Is knowledge base development a necessary and sufficient condition for memory development?' *Journal of Experimental Child Psychology* 30, pp. 401–10.

Luria, A. (1976) *Cognitive Development, its Cultural and Social Foundations* (Cambridge, MA: Harvard University Press).

Luria, A. (1977) *The Social History of Cognition* (Cambridge, MA: Harvard University Press).

MacLeod, A., Williams, M. and Berkian, D. (1991) 'Worry is reasonable: the role of explanations in pessimism about future personal events'. *Journal of Abnormal Psychology* 100, pp. 478–86.

Macnamara, J. (1972) 'Cognitive basis of language learning in infants'. *Psychological Review* 9, pp. 1–13.

McCall, R., Applebaum, M. and Hogarty, P. (1973) 'Developmental changes in mental test performance. *Monographs for the Society for Research in Child Development* 38, pp. 1–83.

McGarrigle, J. and Donaldson, M. (1975) 'Conservation accidents'. *Cognition* 3, pp. 341–50.

McGarrigle, J., Grieve, R. and Hughes, M. (1978). 'Interpreting inclusion: a contribution to the study of the child's cognitive and linguistic development'. *Journal of Experimental Child Psychology* 26, pp. 528–50.

McGuinness, D. (1987) *When Children Don't Learn: Understanding the Biology and Physiology of Learning Disabilities* (New York: Basic Books).

McNaughton, S. and Leyland, J. (1990) 'The shift in focus of maternal tutoring across different difficulty levels on a problem solving task'. *British Journal of Developmental Psychology* 8, pp. 147–55.

McNeill, D. (1970) *The Acquisition of Language* (New York: Harper Row).

Maddox, J. (1998) *What Remains to be Discovered* (London: Macmillan).

Mandler, J. (1988) 'How to build a baby: on the development of an accessible representational system'. *Cognitive Development* 3, pp. 113–36.

Manning, A. (1972) *An Introduction to Animal Behaviour* (London: Edward Arnold).

Maratsos, M. (1983) 'Some issues in the study of the acquisition of grammar'. In: P. Mussen (ed.), *Handbook of Child Psychology*, vol. 3 (New York: Wiley).

Martin, W. and Harel, G. (1989) 'Proof frames of pre-service elementary teachers'. *Journal for Research in Mathematics Education* 20, pp. 41–51.

Mash, E. and Wolfe, D. (1999) *Abnormal Child Psychology* (Belmont: Wadsworth).

Mastropieri, D. and Turkewitz, G. (1999) 'Prenatal experience and neonatal responsiveness to vocal expressions of emotion'. *Developmental Psychobiology* 35, pp. 204–14.

Mehler, J., Lambertz, G., Jusczyk, P. and Amiel-Tison, C. (1986) 'Discrimination de la langue maternelle par le nouveau-ne'. *Comptes Rendes Academie Des Sciences* 303, serie II: pp. 637–40.

Mehler, J. and Dupoux, E. (1994) *What Infants Know* (Oxford: Blackwell).

Meltzoff, A. N. (1981) 'Imitation, intermodal co-ordination and representation'. In G. E. Butterworth (ed.), *Infancy and Epistemology: An Evaluation of Piaget's Theory* (London: Harvester Wheatsheaf), pp. 85–114.

Meltzoff, A. (1994) 'Representation of persons: a bridge between infant's understanding of people and things'. International Conference on Infant Studies, Paris.

Meltzoff, A. and Moore, M. (1983) 'Newborn infants imitate adult facial gestures'. *Child Development 54*, pp. 702–9.

Miller, G. (1956) 'The magical number seven plus or minus two: some limits on our capacity for processing information'. *Psychological Review 63*, pp. 81–97.

Miller, S., Seier, W. and Nassau, G. (1995) 'Children's understanding of logically necessary truths'. Paper presented at the biennial meeting of the Society for Research in Child Development, Indianapolis.

Minton, H. and Schneider, F. (1980) *Differential Psychology* (Pacific Grove: Brooks/Cole).

Moore, C. (1996) 'Evolution and the modularity of mind reading'. *Cognitive Development 11*, pp. 605–21.

Moore, C. and Frye, D. (1986) 'The effect of experimenter's intention on the child's understanding of conservation'. *Cognition 22*, pp. 283–98.

Morris, A. and Sloutsky, V. (1998) 'Understanding logical necessity: developmental antecedents and cognitive consequences'. *Child Development 69*, pp. 721–41.

Moshman, D. (1990) 'The development of metalogical understanding'. In: W. Overton (ed.), *Reasoning, Necessity and Logic: Developmental Perspectives* (Hillsdale, NJ: Erlbaum).

Munakata, Y. (1998) 'Infant perseveration and implications for object permanence theories: A PDP model of the AB task'. *Developmental Science 1*, pp. 161–84.

Nelson, C., Thomas, K., de Haan, M. and Wewerka, S. (1998) 'Delayed recognition memory in infants and adults as revealed by event-related potentials'. *International Journal of Psychophysiology 29*, pp. 145–65.

Nelson, K. (1973) 'Structure and strategy in learning to talk'. *Monographs of the Society for Research in Child Development 38*, pp. 1–136.

Nelson, K. (1981) 'Individual differences in language development: implications for development of language'. *Developmental Psychology 17*, pp. 170–87.

Nelson, K. (1986) 'Event knowledge and cognitive development'. In: K. Nelson (ed.), *Event Knowledge: Structure and Function in Development* (Hillsdale, NJ: Erlbaum).

Nelson, K. (1996) *Language in Cognitive Development: The Emergence of the Mediated Mind* (New York: Cambridge University Press).

Nelson, K. and Kosslyn, S. (1976) 'Recognition of previously labelled or unlabelled pictures by 5-year-olds and adults'. *Journal of Experimental Child Psychology 21*, pp. 40–5

Newcombe, N., Rogoff, B. and Kagan, J. (1977) 'Developmental changes in recognition memory for pictures of objects and scenes'. *Developmental Psychology 13*, pp. 337–41.

Oakhill, J. and Johnson-Laird, P. (1985) 'The effect of belief on the spontaneous production of syllogistic conclusions'. *Quarterly Journal of Experimental Psychology 37A*, pp. 553–70.

Oakhill, J., Johnson-Laird, P. and Garnham, A. (1989) 'Believability and syllogistic reasoning'. *Cognition 31*, pp. 117–40.

Ornstein, P., Naus, M. and Liberty, C. (1975) 'Rehearsal and organisational processes in children's memory'. *Child Development 46*, pp. 818–30.

Ornstein, P., Medlin, R., Stone, B. and Naus M. (1985) 'Retrieving for rehearsal:

an analysis of active rehearsal in children's memory'. *Developmental Psychology* *21*, pp. 633–41.

Osherson, D. and Markman, E. (1975) 'Language and the ability to evaluate contradictions and tautologies'. *Cognition* 3, pp. 213–26.

Pascual-Leone, J. (1970) 'A mathematical model for the transition rule in Piaget's developmental stages'. *Acta Psychologica* 32, pp. 301–45.

Patterson, G., Reid, J. and Dihion, T. (1992) *Antisocial Boys* (Eugene, OR: Castilia).

Pavlov, I. (1927) *Conditional Reflexes* (London: Oxford University Press).

Perlmutter, M. (1986) 'A life-span view of memory'. In: P. Baltes, D. Featherman and R. Lerner (eds), *Lifespan Development and Behaviour*, vol. 7 (Hillsdale, NJ: Erlbaum).

Perner, J. (1991) *Understanding the Representational Mind* (Cambridge, MA: MIT Press).

Perner, J., Leekham, S. and Wimmer, H. (1987) 'Three-year-olds' difficulty with false belief: the case for a conceptual deficit'. *British Journal of Developmental Psychology* 5, pp. 125–37.

Perris, E., Myers, N. and Clifton, R. (1990) 'Long term memory for a single infancy experience'. *Child Development 61*, pp. 1796–807.

Petrill, S., Saudino, K., Cherny, S., Emde, R., Fulker, D., Hewit, J. and Plomin, R. (1998) 'Exploring the genetic and environmental etiology of high general cognitive ability in fourteen- to thirty-six-month-old twins'. *Child Development* 69, pp. 8–74.

Piaget, J. (1953) *The Origins of Intelligence in the Child* (London: Routledge and Kegan Paul).

Piaget, J. (1954) *The Construction of Reality in the Child* (New York: Basic Books).

Piaget, J. (1955) *The Origins of Intelligence in Children* (International University Press).

Piaget, J. (1967) *Biologie et Connaisance* (Paris: Gallimard).

Piaget, J. (1968) *Genetic Epistemology* (New York: Columbia University Press).

Piaget, J. and Inhelder, B. (1973) *Memory and Intelligence* (New York: Basic Books).

Pillemer, D. and White, S. (1989) 'Childhood events recalled by children and adults'. In: H. Reese (ed.), *Advances in Child Development and Behaviour 21*, (New York: Academic Press).

Pinker, S. (1984) *Language Learnability and Language Development* (Cambridge, MA: Harvard University Press).

Pinker, S.(1987) 'The bootstrapping problem in language acquisition'. In: B. MacWhinney (ed.), *Mechanisms of Language Acquisition* (Hillsdale, NJ: Erlbaum).

Pinker, S. (1997) *How the Mind Works* (New York: W.W. Norton).

Potts, G. (1974) 'Storing and retrieving information about ordered relationships'. *Journal of Experimental Psychology 103*, pp. 431–9.

Poulin-Dubois, D. (1999) 'Infant's distinction between animate and inanimate objects: the origins of naïve psychology'. In: P. Rochat and T. Striano (eds), *Early Social Cognition: Understanding Others in the First Months of Life* (New Jersey: Lawrence Erlbaum).

Povinelli, D. and Eddy, T. (1996) 'What young chimpanzees know about seeing'. *Monographs for the Society for Research in Child Development 61*, pp. 1–152.

Pratt, M., Kerig, P., Cowan, P. and Pape-Cowan, C. (1988) 'Mothers and fathers teaching three year olds: Authoritative parenting and adult scaffolding in young children's learning'. *Developmental Psychology* 24, pp. 832–9.

Premack, D. (1986) *Gavagai! Or the Future History of the Animal Language Controversy* (Cambridge, MA: MIT Press).

Premack, D. (1990) 'The infant's theory of self-propelled objects'. *Cognition* 36, pp. 1–16.

Pressley, M. (1995) 'What is intellectual development about in the 1990s? Odd information processing'. In: F. Weinert and W. Schneider (eds), *Memory Performance and Competencies: Issues in Growth and Development* (Hillsdale, NJ: Erlbaum).

Rabinowicz, T. (1980) 'The differentiate maturation of the human cerebral cortex'. In: F. Falkener and J. Tanner (eds), *Human Growth*, vol. 3: *Neurobiology and Nutrition* (New York: Plenum Press).

Radziszewska, B. and Rogoff, B. (1991) 'Guided participation in planning imaginary errands with skilled adult or peer partners'. *Developmental Psychology* 27, pp. 381–9.

Rakic, P. (1995) 'Corticogenesis in human and nonhuman primates'. In: M. Gazzaniga (ed.), *The Cognitive Neurosciences* (Cambridge, MA: MIT Press).

Reddy, V., Hay, D., Murray, L. and Trevarthen, C. (1997) 'Communication in infancy: mutual regulation of affect and attention'. In: G. Bremner, A. Slater and G. Butterworth (eds), *Infant Development: Recent Advances* (Hillsdale, NJ: Psychology Press, Erlbaum).

Richards, J. and Cronise, K. (2000) 'Extended visual fixation in the early preschool years: look duration, heart rate changes, and attentional inertia'. *Child Development* 71, pp. 602–20.

Rochat, P. and Striano, T. (1999) 'Social-cognitive development in the first year'. In: P. Rochat and T. Striano, *Early Social Cognition: Understanding Others in the First Months of Life* (Hillsdale, NJ: Lawrence Erlbaum).

Rogoff, B. (1990) *Apprenticeship in Thinking: Cognitive Development in Social Context* (New York: Oxford University Press).

Rogoff, B. (1998) 'Cognition as a collaborative process'. In: D. Kuhn and R. Siegler (eds), *Handbook of Child Psychology*, vol. 2: *Cognition, Language and Perception* (New York: Wiley).

Rogoff, B., Gauvain, M. and Ellis, S. (1984) 'Development viewed in its cultural context'. In: M. Barrister and M. Lamb (eds), *Developmental Psychology: An Advanced Textbook* (Hillsdale, NJ: Erlbaum).

Ronnqvist, L., and von Hofsten, C. (1994) 'Neonatal finger and arm movements as determined by a social and an object context'. *Early Development and Parenting* 3, pp. 81–93.

Rosch, E. (1978) 'Principles of categorization'. In: E. Rosch and B. Lloyd, *Cognition and Categorization* (Hillsdale, NJ: Erlbaum).

Ross, L. (1981) 'The "intuitive scientist" formulation and its developmental implications'. In: J. Flavell and L. Ros (eds), *Social Cognitive Development: Frontiers and Possible Futures* (Cambridge: Cambridge University Press).

Ross, R., Begab, M., Dondis, E., Giampiccolo, J. and Meyers, C. (1985) *Lives of the Mentally Retarded: A Forty-Year Follow-Up Study* (Stanford, CA: Stanford University Press).

Rovee-Collier, C. (1984) 'The ontegeny of learning and memory in human infancy'. In: R. Kail and N. Spear (eds), *Comparative Perspectives on the Development of Memory* (Hillsdale, NJ: Erlbaum).

Rovee-Collier, C. (1987) 'Learning and memory'. In: J. Osofsky (ed.), *Handbook of Infant Development* (New York: Wiley).

Ruffman, T. (1999) 'Children's understanding of logical inconsistency'. *Child Development 70*, pp. 872–86.

Russell, J., Mauther, N., Sharpe, S. and Tidswell, T (1991) 'The "windows task" as a measure of strategic deception in preschoolers and autistic subjects'. *British Journal of Developmental Psychology 90*, pp. 331–50.

Saxe, G. (1988) 'The mathematics of street vendors'. *Child Development 59*, pp. 1415–25.

Scarborough, H. (1990) 'Very early language deficits in dyslexic children'. *Child Development 61*, pp. 1728–43.

Schaal, B., Marlier, L. and Soussignan, R. (2000) 'Human foetuses learn odours from their pregnant mothers' diet'. *Chemical Senses 25*, pp. 729–37.

Schafer, V., Shucard, D., Shucard, J. and Gerken, L. (1998) 'An electrophysiological study of infants' sensitivity to the sound patterns of English'. *Journal of Speech, Language and Hearing Research 41*, pp. 874–86.

Schaffer, H. (1984) *The Child's Entry into a Social World* (London: Academic Press).

Schauble, L. (1996) 'The development of scientific reasoning in knowledge rich contexts'. *Developmental Psychology 32*, pp. 102–19.

Schneider, W. and Bjorklund, D. (1998) 'Memory'. In: D. Kuhn and R. Siegler, (eds), W. Damon (series ed.), *Handbook of Child Psychology*, vol. 2: *Cognition, Language and Perception* (New York: Wiley).

Schneider, W. and Pressley, M. (1989) *Memory Development Between 2 and 20* (Berlin: Springer-Verlag).

Schneiderman, L. and Kaplan, R. (1992) 'Fear of dying of HIV infection vs hepatitis B infection'. *American Journal of Public Health 82*, pp. 584–6.

Scribner, S. and Cole, M. (1981) *The Psychology of Literacy* (Cambridge, MA: Cambridge University Press).

Selfe., L. (1977) *Normal and Anomalous Representational Abilities in Children* (London: Academic Press).

Seligman, M. (1975) *Helplessness: On Depression, Development and Death* (San Francisco, CA: Freeman).

Shaffer, D. (1995) *Developmental Psychology: Childhood and Adolescence* (California: Brooks/Cole).

Sheingold, K. and Tenney, Y. (1982) 'Memory for a salient childhood event'. In: U. Neisser (ed.), *Memory Observed: Remembering in Natural Contexts* (San Francisco, CA: Freeman).

Shepard, R. (1967) 'Recognition memory for words, sentences and pictures'. *Journal of Verbal Learning and Verbal Behaviour 6*, pp. 156–63.

Shrager, J. and Siegler, R. (1998) 'SCADS: a model of children's strategy choices and strategy discoveries'. *Psychological Science 9*, pp. 405–10.

Shultz, T. (1980) 'Development of the concept of intention'. In: W. Collins (ed.), *Minnesota Symposia on Child Psychology*, vol. 13: *Development of Cognition, Affect and Social Relations* (Hillsdale, NJ: Erlbaum).

Siegal, M. and Peterson, C. (1994) 'Children's theory of mind and the conversational territory of cognitive development'. In: C. Lewis and P. Mitchell (eds), *Children's Early Understanding of Mind: Origins and Development* (Hillsdale, NJ: Erlbaum).

Siegler, R. (1976) 'Three aspects of cognitive development'. *Cognitive Psychology 8*, pp. 481–520.

Siegler, R. (1981) 'Developmental sequences within and between concepts'. *Monographs for the Society for Research in Child Development 46*, pp. 1–84.

Siegler, R. (1994) 'Cognitive variability: a key to understanding cognitive development'. *Current Directions in Psychological Science 3*, pp. 1–5.

Siegler, R. (1996) *Emerging Minds: The Process of Change in Children's Thinking* (New York: Oxford University Press).

Siegler, R. (1997) 'Beyond competence – towards development'. *Cognitive Development 12*, pp. 323–32.

Siegler, R. (2000) 'The rebirth of children's learning'. *Child Development 71*, pp. 26–36.

Siegler, R. and Chen, Z. (1998) 'Developmental diferences in rule learning: a microgenetic analysis'. *Cognitive Psychology 36*, pp. 273–310.

Siegler, R. and Crowley, K. (1991) 'The microgenetic method: a direct means for studying cognitive development'. *American Psychologist 46*, pp. 606–20.

Siegler, S. and Jenkins, E. (1989) *How Children Discover New Strategies* (Hillsdale, NJ: Erlbaum).

Siegler, R. and Shipley, C. (1995) 'Variation, selection and cognitive change'. In: T. Simon and G. Halford (eds), *Developing Cognitive Competence: New Approaches to Process Modelling* (Hillsdale, NJ: Erlbaum).

Siegler, R. and Shrager, J. (1984) 'Strategy choices in addition and subtraction: how do children know what to do?' In: C. Sophian (ed.), *Origins of Cognitive Skills* (Hillsdale, NJ: Erlbaum).

Siegler, R. and Stern, E. (1998) 'A microgenetic analysis of conscious and unconscious strategy discoveries'. *Journal of Experimental Child Psychology: General 127*, pp. 377–97.

Simon, T. and Klahr, D. (1995) 'A computational theory of children's learning about number conservation'. In: T. Simon and G. Halford (eds), *Developing Cognitive Competence: New Approaches to Process Modelling* (Hillsdale, NJ: Erlbaum).

Simonoff, E., Bolton, P. and Rutter, M. (1996) 'Mental retardation: Genetic findings, clinical implications and research agenda'. *Journal of Child Psychology and Psychiatry 37*, pp. 259–80.

Skinner, B. (1974) *About Behaviourism* (London: Jonathan Cape).

Skinner, B. (1957) *Verbal Behaviour* (New York: Appleton Century Crofts).

Slater, A. (1997) 'Visual organisation in early infancy'. In: G. Bremner, A. Slater, and G. Butterworth (eds), *Infant Development: Recent Advances* (Hillsdale, NJ: Psychology Press, Erlbaum).

Slater, A. and Butterworth, G. (1997) 'Perception of social stimuli: face perception and imitation'. In: G. Bremner, A. Slater and G. Butterworth (eds), *Infant Development: Recent Advances* (Hillsdale, NJ: Psychology Press, Erlbaum).

Slater, A. and Morison, V. (1985) 'Shape constancy and slant perception at birth'. *Perception 14*, pp. 337–44.

Slater, A., Johnson, S., Kellman, P. and Spelke, E. (1994) 'The role of three-dimensional depth cues in infants' perception of partly occluded objects'. *Early Development and Parenting 3*, pp. 187–91.

Slater, A., Mattock, A. and Brown, E. (1990) 'Size constancy at birth: newborn infants' responses to retinal and real size'. *Journal of Experimental Psychology 49*, pp. 314–22.

Slater, A., Mattock, A., Brown, E., Burnham, D. and Young, A. (1991) 'Visual processing of stimulus compounds in newborn babies'. *Perception 20*, pp. 29–33.

Slobin, D. (1979) *Psycholinguistics* (Glenview, IL: Scott, Foresman).

Smith, L. (1989) 'In defence of perceptual similarity'. Paper presented to the Biennial meeting of SRCD, Kansas City.

Smith, L. (1993) *Necessary Knowledge: Piagetian Perspectives on Constructivism* (Hove: Erlbaum).

Soken, N. and Pick, A. (1999) 'Infant's perception of dynamic affective expressions: do infants distinguish specific expressions?' *Child Development 70*, pp. 1275–82.

Somerville, S., Wellman, H. and Cultice, J. (1983) 'Young children's deliberate reminding'. *Journal of Genetic Psychology 143*, pp. 87–96.

Sophian, C. (1997) 'Beyond competence: the significance of performance for conceptual development'. *Cognitive Development 12*, pp. 281–303.

Sorce, J., Emde, R., Campos, J. and Klinnert, M. (1985) 'Maternal emotional signalling: its effects on the visual cliff behaviour of one year olds'. *Developmental Psychology 21*, pp. 195–200.

Spear, N. (1984) 'Ecologically determined dispositions control the ontogeny of learning and memory'. In: R. Kail and N. Spear (eds), *Contemporary Perspectives on the Development of Memory* (Hillsdale, NJ: Erlbaum).

Spearman, C. (1927) *The Abilities of Man* (New York: Macmillan).

Spelke, E., Breinlinger, K., Macomber, J. and Jacobsen, K. (1992) 'Origins of knowledge'. *Psychological Review 99*, pp. 605–32.

Stern, D. (1985) *The Interpersonal World of the Infant: View from Psychoanalysis and Developmental Psychology* (New York: Basic Books).

Sternberg, R. (1977a) 'Component processes in analogical reasoning'. *Psychological Review 31*, pp. 356–78.

Sternberg, R. (1977b) *Intelligence, Information Processing and Analogical Reasoning: A Componential Analysis of Intelligence* (Hillsdale, NJ: Lawrence Erlbaum Associates).

Sternberg, R. (1988) 'Intellectual development: Psychometric and information processing approaches'. In: M. Bornstein and M. Lamb (ed.), *Developmental Psychology: An Advanced Textbook* (Hillsdale, NJ: Erlbaum).

Terman, L. (1954) 'The discovery and encouragement of exceptional talent'. *American Psychologist 9*, pp. 221–38.

Thatcher, R. (1992) 'Cyclical cortical reorganisation during early childhood'. *Brain and Cognition 20*, pp. 24–50.

Thelen, E. and Smith, L. (1994) *A Dynamic Systems Approach to the Development of Cognition and Action* (Cambridge, MA: MIT Press).

Thompson, L., Fagan, J. and Fulker, D. (1991) 'Longitudinal prediction of specific cognitive abilities from infant novelty preference'. *Child Development 62*, pp. 530–8.

Thornton, S. (1995) *Children Solving Problems* (Cambridge, MA: Harvard University Press).

Thornton, S. (1996) 'Developmental change in the use of relevant recall as a basis for judgments'. *British Journal of Psychology 87*, pp. 417–29.

Thornton, S. (1999) 'Creating the conditions for cognitive change: the interaction between task structures and specific strategies'. *Child Development 70*, pp. 588–603.

Thurstone, L. (1938) *Primary Mental Abilities* (Chicago: University of Chicago Press).

Timbergen, N. (1951) *The Study of Instinct* (New York: Oxford University Press).

Tollefsrud-Anderson, L., Campbell, R., Starkey, P. and Cooper, R. (1992) 'Number conservation: distinguishing quantifier from operator solutions'. In: J. Bideaud, C. Meljac and J. Fischer (eds), *Pathways to Number* (Hillsdale, NJ: Erlbaum).

Tomasello, M. (1992) *First Verbs: A Case Study of Early Grammatical Development* (Cambridge: Cambridge University Press).

Tomasello, M. (1995) 'Joint attention as social cognition'. In: C. Moore and P. Dunham (eds), *Joint Attention: Its Origin and Role in Development* (Hillsdale, NJ: Erlbaum).

Tomasello, M. (1998) 'The return of constructions'. *Journal of Child Language* 25, pp. 431–42.

Tomasello, M. (1999) 'Social cognition before the revolution'. In: P. Rochat and T. Striano (eds), *Early Social Cognition: Understanding Others in the First Months of Life* (Hillsdale, NJ: Lawrence Erlbaum).

Tomasello, M. and Barton, M. (1994) 'Learning words in non-ostensive contexts'. *Developmental Psychology* 30, pp. 639–50.

Trabasso, T. (1975) 'Representation, memory and reasoning: how do we make transitive inferences?' In: A. Pick (ed.), *Minnesota Symposia on Child Psychology* 9, pp. 135–72.

Trabasso, T., Isen, A., Dolecki, P., McLanahan, A., Riley, C. and Tucker, T. (1978) 'How do children solve class inclusion problems?' In: R. Siegler (ed.), *Children's Thinking: What Develops?* (Hillsdale, NJ: Erlbaum).

Trevarthen, C. (1993a) 'The functions of emotions in early infant communication and development'. In: Nadel and L. Camioni (eds), *New Perspectives in Early Communicative Development* (London and New York: Routledge).

Trevarthen, C. (1993b) 'The self born in intersubjectivity: the psychology of an infant communicating'. In: U. Neisser (ed.), *The Perceived Self: Ecological and Interpersonal Sources of Self-knowledge* (New York: Cambridge University Press).

Tryon, R. (1940) 'Genetic differences in maze learning in rats'. *Yearbook of the National Society for Studies in Education* 39, pp. 111–19.

Tversky, A. and Kahneman, D. (1973) 'Availability: a heuristic for judging frequency and probability'. *Cognitive Psychology* 5, pp. 207–32.

Vygotsky, L. (1962) *Thought and Language* (Cambridge, MA: Harvard University Press).

Vygotsky, L. (1978) *Mind in Society: The Development of Higher Psychological Processes* (Cambridge, MA: Harvard University Press).

Walton, G., Bower, N. and Bower, T. (1992) 'Recognition of familiar faces by newborns'. *Infant Behaviour and Development* 15, pp. 265–9

Wellman, H. (1993) 'Early understanding of mind: the normal case'. In: S. Baron-Cohen, H. Tager-Flusberg and D. Cohen (eds), *Understanding Other Minds: Perspectives from Autism* (Oxford: Oxford University Press).

Wellman, H. and Gelman, S. (1997) 'Knowledge acquisition in foundational domains'. In: D. Kuhn and R. Siegler (eds), *Handbook of Child Psychology*, vol. 2: *Cognition, Perception and Language*, 5th edn (New York: Wiley).

Wellman, H., Collins, J. and Glieberman, J. (1981) 'Understanding the combination of memory variables: developing conceptions of memory limitations'. *Child Development* 52, pp. 1313–17.

Werker, J. and Tees, R. (1984) 'Cross-language speech perception: evidence for perceptual reorganisation during the first year of life'. *Infant Behaviour and Development* 7, pp. 49–63.

Werthheimer, M. (1945) *Productive Thinking* (New York: Harper).

Wertsch, J. (1979) 'From social interaction to higher psychological processes: a clarification and application of Vygotsky's theory'. *Human Development* 22, pp. 1–22.

Whorf, B. (1952) 'Language, mind and reality'. *A Review of General Semantics 9*, pp. 167–88.

Willatts, P. (1984) 'Stages in the development of intentional search by young infants'. *Developmental Psychology 20*, pp. 389–96.

Willatts, P. (1989) 'Development of problem solving in infancy'. In: A. Slater and J. Bremner (eds), *Infant Development* (London: Erlbaum).

Willatts, P. (1997) 'Beyond the couch potato infant: how infants use their knowledge to regulate action, solve problems and achieve goals'. In: G. Bremner, A. Slater and G. Butterworth (eds), *Infant Development: Recent Advances* (Hillsdale, NJ: Psychology Press, Erlbaum).

Willatts, P. (1999) 'Development of means–ends behaviour in young infants: pulling a support to retrieve a distant object'. *Developmental Psychology 35*, pp. 651–67.

Willatts, P. and Rosie, K. (1996) 'Development of means–ends analysis in young children'.

Wimmer, H. and Perner, J. (1983) 'Beliefs about beliefs: Representation and constraining function of wrong beliefs in young children's understanding of deception'. *Cognition 13*, pp. 103–28.

Wiser, M. and Carey, S. (1983) 'When heat and temperature were one'. In: D. Gentner and A. Stevens (eds), *Mental Models* (Hillsdale, NJ: Erlbaum).

Wolff, P., Michel, G., Ovrut, M. and Drake, C. (1990) 'Rate and timing precision of motor coordination in developmental dyslexia'. *Developmental Psychology 26*, pp. 349–59.

Wood, D., Bruner, J. and Ross, G. (1976) 'The role of tutoring in problem solving'. *Journal of Child Psychology and Psychiatry 17*, pp. 89–100.

Wood, D., Wood, H. and Middleton, D. (1978) 'An experimental evaluation of four face to face teaching strategies'. *International Journal of Behavioural Development 1*, pp. 131–47.

Wynn, K. (1992) 'Children's acquisition of number words and the counting system'. *Cognitive Psychology, 20*, pp. 220–51.

Yuill, N. (1984) 'Young children's coordination of motive and outcome in judgments of satisfaction and morality'. *British Journal of Developmental Psychology 2*, pp. 73–81.

Index